8—
24

MW01009281

XX V

Tonight at Six

Tonight at 6

A Daily Show
Masquerading as
Local TV News

Michael Olesker

Apprentice House
Baltimore, MD

Library of Congress Cataloging-in-Publication Data

Olesker, Michael.
Tonight at six : a daily show masquerading as local TV news /
Michael Olesker.
p.   cm.
ISBN-13: 978-1-934074-17-6
1. Television broadcasting of news--United States. I. Title.
PN4888.T4O44 2007
070.1'95--dc22
2007033953

Printed in the United States of America
First Edition

Special thanks to Shannon Morgan and Elissa Weissman
who reviewed the manuscript and page proofs at various stages of
this project. Thanks, too, to Ashley Tieperman for help with copyediting.

Jacket design: Gavie Heller
WJZ publicity photos: Jerry Turner and Al Sanders

Published by Apprentice House
The Future of Publishing...Today!

Apprentice House
Communication Department
Loyola College in Maryland
4501 N. Charles Street
Baltimore, MD 21210
410.617.5265 • 410.617.5040 (fax)
www.ApprenticeHouse.com

For Jerry Turner and Al Sanders,
who always dreamed TV news
could be better.

Table of Contents

Introduction

One summer day when he needed to send a television signal across the American racial divide, George W. Bush arrived on the 200 block of East Baltimore's blighted North Chester Street, trailed by political professionals and media types stepping lightly past rotted row houses, vagrant wads of trash, and a long history of political abandonment.

Of that visit, it was safe to say at least two things:

There had not been so many white people on North Chester Street in several decades.

And, it was a presidential campaign visit perfectly choreographed for television news, and utterly devoid of meaning for those interested in real news.

At this time, July of 1999, Bush was running for the Republican nomination for president as a "compassionate conservative." All visits to inner city neighborhoods were intended to show he was not one of those Republicans around whose efforts the GOP had previously managed to lose forty years' worth of black voters.

But, if he was not Strom Thurmond or Jesse Helms, this seemed like the right time to ask: Was he his father's son, ready to foist another Willie Horton on the country if the fight got tough? Was there a new Republican sensitivity toward places such as North Chester Street? In what ways did his visit count as more than an empty gesture?

These questions first got me into an ugly shouting argument with the people surrounding Bush, and then into an uncomfortable face-to-face chat with the candidate himself. They also got me thinking about this book: about the different ways news is perceived by broadcasters and by newspapers, and is thus presented to viewers and readers.

That day on North Chester Street, just before Bush's arrival, I asked one of his aides, "When will we have time to ask him some questions?"

"You won't," I was told.

"That's *bleep-bleep*," I said, not precisely editing myself for the occasion.

"He's just gonna talk to the kids. The cameras will set up inside The Door."

The cameras were television cameras, and the arrangement was perfectly suitable for them. It gave television the look of a story, if not an actual story. The Door was a faith-based community outreach program on Chester Street created by the Rev. Joe Ehrmann, who had played for the Baltimore Colts football team before finding God. The Door touched hundreds of children, some of whom had been abandoned by parents, and all of whom had been abandoned by those politicians who had no use for cities, or for black people, or for impoverished children who needed government assistance because there was no one helping at home.

"What do you mean?" I asked. "He's not talking to reporters?"

The aide glanced around, as though looking for a bouncer to assist me away.

"Just the kids," he said again, as though talking to a particularly dim one.

"Wait a minute," I said. "This guy's flying all the way into Baltimore, and he won't talk to anybody?"

The handler shrugged.

"We'll see about that," I said, feeling completely stupid because I already saw what was coming.

As a columnist for the *Baltimore Sun* and a nightly commentator for the CBS affiliate in Baltimore, WJZ-TV's *Eyewitness News*, I had learned a few unfortunate things about the needs of politicians and the needs of television. Politicians of both major parties figured they needed television (and not necessarily newspapers), and television news figured it needed pictures (and not necessarily news). This was their little minuet, which worked splendidly for them, if not for the American electorate. It was also the reason nobody from local television was pressing even slightly for any interviews on North Chester Street.

As we awaited Bush's arrival, I walked up and down the block. There were eight abandoned row houses, all converted to shooting galleries for junkies. Two were missing front doors and windows. The floors inside were covered by soiled mattresses and broken bottles and cans. Flies buzzed above bloody needles that lay next to a child's stroller and diapers.

It was a neighborhood crippled by drugs and guns, in a city with three hundred homicides a year, with a presidential contender arriving now whose record as governor of Texas included enacting one law allowing concealed handguns on the street, another protecting gun interests from lawsuits, and another against gun locks for firearms. Maybe there was justification for such laws, and maybe Bush could articulate it in the face of much evidence suggesting otherwise.

But he didn't want to talk about it with anybody on North Chester Street.

When Bush arrived and began moving through the heart of a small crowd, I went back to his handlers to ask again about talking to him.

"Why are you wasting our time if he doesn't want to talk?" I said.

They turned away. Bush, surrounded by Secret Service and television photographers, walked to some row house front steps. A neighborhood lady sat there with a couple of her children.

"Are you a good reader?" Bush asked a little boy named Aaron Parks. Aaron shook his head no. He was four years old.

"Well, let me give you a hint," Bush said. "Become a good reader."

That was as deep as it got. The television stations would capture Bush talking to a little boy about reading, but the city's schools had textbooks dating back to the Ford administration, and the computer revolution sweeping the whole country had not yet arrived in Baltimore's public schools, and here was the sound-bite fullness of an education position from a presidential contender: Become a good reader.

A few minutes later, Bush walked into The Door, a converted church building. About a hundred kids squatting on the floor cheered his arrival. Bush glanced around, making certain all the TV cameras were set up.

"This is *bleep-bleep*," I said again to one of Bush's handlers.

"You want to keep it down?" he replied.

"You're letting kids question him, but not reporters?" I said, feeling my composure start to leave. "What kind of *bleep-bleep* is that?"

Now I heard another voice, and felt a hand tapping gently on my shoulder.

"What's the problem, ol' buddy?" George W. Bush asked, smiling broadly.

"You're not talking to reporters?" I asked.

"What's the problem?" he asked again. The smile never left his face.

"The problem is, you're running for president and your people say we can't question you."

"I'm gonna talk to the kids, ol' buddy," Bush said, still smiling. "Maybe that'll help."

"Well, no, it doesn't actually," I said.

But Bush turned and walked to the center of the room, and people applauded. Then he introduced himself and pointed toward a little girl with her hand in the air for the first probing political question.

"What is your wife's name?" the little girl asked.

"My wife's name is Laura," said Bush.

"What are your hobbies?" a second child asked.

He said he liked to read.

"Why are you running for president?" asked another.

"Because I love America," Bush declared.

Swell.

He did ten minutes with the kids, and then he jumped into a limousine and he left town. On the local television news that night, there were wonderful pictures of the Republican candidate for president being nice to children. But the children lived in squalor, in an atmosphere of guns and drugs, and nobody knew precisely what the candidate intended to do about it.

In the next morning's newspaper, there was a news story saying almost nothing about Bush's visit to Baltimore— because what was there to say involving actual news?—and a column by me sarcastically thanking Bush for coming to town and wondering when he might like to talk about the things he had seen here.

But the day offered something more to me.

It marked out, once again, distinctions in how people get their news. It said, once again, how the news values of television and newspapers differed dramatically. It pointed out, once again, the different ways the same story is reported by different news organizations.

Those differences matter.

For the last several decades, all the public opinion surveys say that most Americans turn to television as their primary source of news. In fact, a 1996 national study by the Pew Research Center for the People and the Press found that sixty-five percent of all adults said they regularly watched the local TV news (while only forty-two percent regularly watched network news).

Those figures held. In October of 2006, the Radio and Television News Directors Foundation released figures from their Future of News Survey saying that sixty-five percent of Americans chose local TV news as one of their top three sources for news, while twenty-eight percent named newspapers and twenty-eight percent chose national TV news. The Internet was one of the top three choices for eleven percent of those surveyed. Two-thirds of the public said they had never read a blog or didn't know what they were, and less than five percent had ever watched news on a small screen device such as a mobile phone or handheld electronic device.

Cable news had come of age, but cable's overall viewer numbers were still stunningly low whenever America was not at war. The Nielsen Media Research organization said *Fox News* had about eight hundred thousand viewers, and CNN had about six hundred thousand. MSNBC had a few hundred thousand viewers, and CNBC, about a hundred thousand.

Meanwhile, in post-literate America, newspapers had heart attacks and died. In Baltimore, once home to three dailies, the two afternoon papers had gone out of business within a year of each other. Television seemed to be shoving them out of a new generation's very consciousness, and later the Internet arrived to shove them ever further. Weary souls who once came home from work and read about the important events of the day now found it easier to turn on the tube and get what purported to be a more visual version of those same events.

This, as it turned out, was a lie. But it didn't seem to discourage people—particularly young people, children of an increasingly visual culture—from turning on their sets when seeking information. They discovered that TV was easier than reading. You just sat back and let sounds and images flood over you. And TV didn't bore you with a lot of details. If it did, you hit the remote control, which was even easier than turning a page.

Also, not to be minimized, TV was more fun than a newspaper. They had such nice people on the TV news, such entertaining, apparently informed, well-dressed, well-coiffed people. We welcomed them into our homes, and they talked to us as if they knew us. Sometimes they told us little details about their lives. Sometimes, the people delivering the news seemed even more important than the news itself. When the people who run local television news discovered this, they did a remarkable thing. They kept calling it the news, but they kept getting further away from any self-conscious need to cover actual news.

It was enough to show pictures and let them stand for the news.

For local television, pictures of George Bush earnestly telling children that he loved America counted as much as the unexamined misery in these kids' lives. Pictures of a presidential contender satisfied television's need for the look of seriousness. Pictures of him talking to children satisfied viewers' emotions, if not their intellect.

When I walked away from North Chester Street after Bush left, I told myself: One of these days, I've got to write about the emptiness of all this.

One summer afternoon three years later, that day arrived. I was told my contract was not going to be renewed at the end of the year. In my sadness, I found solace. For the next five months, I could sit in the newsroom at WJZ and quietly take notes on everything going on around me—a nightly front-row seat at the inner world of TV news. Then I followed up those hours with a series of interviews that help make up this book.

1

Dancing as Fast as They Can

The voice on the newsroom intercom arrived like an alarm clock trying to jangle its way into a reluctant consciousness.

"Denise Koch," it said. "We need you."

I was standing in Koch's little office, where the two of us were talking about the personal feistiness of a former Maryland congresswoman, out of power for eight years, who was running to snatch back her old seat. She was at least seventy-eight years old, a fact I had inconveniently mentioned on the air. The former congresswoman did not appreciate this. On the campaign trail one night, in her playful Mammy Yokum way, she threw a couple of pretty good bare-knuckle punches into my midsection. It was her way of showing she was still a tough little cookie.

"But you took it like a man," Koch laughed.

"With this body?" I said, patting a soft belly where there had once been a washboard. "I'll take her best shot and never get up."

"Denise Koch," the voice on the intercom said again, this time even more urgently. It was coming from the TV station's control room. "We need you right away."

Now Koch's eyes flipped open in alarm. The clock said 5:15 p.m. Koch was a six o'clock news anchor at WJZ, and they needed her somewhere out there—but where?—to deliver some tidy little sixty-second story about impending war for the five o'clock broadcast.

Koch, sucking air, arms flailing, bolted around her desk and charged into the newsroom, leaving behind all entertaining thoughts of the seventy-eight-year-old former congresswoman's punches to the mid-section and all other matters not pertaining to the next few moments of her life standing in front of a television camera.

"Where?" she cried to a couple of young writer-producers bent over computer keyboards. "Where am I going?"

The writer-producers were bright young lads not far removed from their college days. In the hallowed tradition of all local television news, which rewards on-air talent with sizable money and leaves chump change for the off-air scrubs, they had these marvelously impressive-sounding job titles to compensate for their microscopic pay checks. Writer-producers, indeed. They looked at Koch with complete ignorance.

"Newsroom or studio?" Koch said.

The bright young lads shrugged their shoulders. Koch looked behind them, to an elevated little office of an executive producer named Mitch Friedmann, who was short, curly-haired, and frequently given to Vesuvian eruptions. He liked to split the air with high-decibel curses over life's major problems, such as soup that had chilled. But this time he hid his exasperation behind a studied look of deference to the station's senior anchor.

"Studio," he said.

"What's it about?"

Friedmann's eyes scanned his printed five o'clock rundown.

"Iraq, I think," he said. "You got about thirty seconds to get in there."

Iraq it was. The president of the United States, George W. Bush, growing impatient with Saddam Hussein, was threatening to drop bombs on him. Ambassadors from the United Nations were urging calm. Bush said Hussein was an evil man. Demonstrators were protesting what seemed like the beginnings of combat in the Middle East. A year after the September 11 terrorist attacks, with American troops already combing Afghanistan, with the Palestinians and the Israelis blowing each other up almost daily, and with Hussein allegedly stockpiling weapons of mass destruction, the world was a nervous place.

Koch, bolting through the newsroom now on shaky heels, cried, "Oh, my God." She knew none of the day's newest details. Something about Iraq, that's all she had. The clock was ticking, and now it showed about fifteen seconds left. Nobody had told her it was her turn to front for a Middle East piece. She hadn't seen any script, hadn't talked with anybody about it, and hadn't seen any video. And now she was going on camera before thousands of people gathered by their television sets to hear the news that would ultimately send America to war from the primary authority figure on their favorite local TV news program.

"Oh, my God," Koch cried again.

Her voice fluttered like Oliver Hardy going down a flight of steps. You could hear her as she exited the newsroom and rushed down the hallway past the full-length mirror the anchors used for last-minute checks of their hair. Directly above two heavy studio doors, a light flashed: On Air. Koch yanked open one of the big doors and bolted into the studio as one of the five o'clock anchors, Sally Thorner, peered into the camera, pursed her lips earnestly and declared, "Denise Koch has been tracking events in the Middle East, and has this report. Denise..."

Koch, arriving in front of a chroma-key background just in time to clip on a tiny microphone, handled it fine. She is a professional broadcaster, and this is what they do.

Calmly reading from a TelePrompter script, she related the president's newest threats, the UN's latest objections, the protests from foreign leaders and from Americans worried about a new war. She was poised, and she appeared fully authoritative. She might have just come from talking to a high-ranking State Department official, instead of joking with me about the disgruntled former Maryland congresswoman. She never even paused to catch her breath. Half a world away from the crisis in the Middle East, the crisis at WJZ-TV, in Baltimore, passed in the minute it took to deliver the story. All was well.

Back in the newsroom, the two young writer-producers paused to watch the report on a TV monitor above them. One of them stifled a yawn. They learn fast. Nations might be marching to war, but this was simply one more news story reported in the usual way.

When Koch walked back to her office a few minutes later, we glanced at each other and rolled our eyes with a familiar, "if-the-public-only-knew" look.

"It'd make a great TV sitcom, wouldn't it?" She laughed sardonically.

But Koch, a fourteen-year veteran news anchor, was smart enough to understand: it would be a sitcom posing as a news program for an audience that was too conditioned, or too indifferent, to see through the facade.

And it was posing seven days a week, much in the same manner as hundreds of local TV news operations all across America.

They commit fraud and pronounce it to be journalism. They put on a television program and give it an empty word: news. They do it the same way in Baltimore as they do in Boston or Detroit, or Phoenix or Los Angeles. While declaring themselves reporters and editors (and "friends you can turn to"), they put on a program disguised as news and resist the temptation of actual journalism.

They do it with a small collection of on-air reporters who perform a corporate charade. They pretend to cover entire metropolitan areas. They go through the motions of covering entire states. They feign insight into governors and mayors and county executives, police stations and courthouses, neighborhoods in cities and suburbs, state legislatures and city councils, private and public school systems, business communities, political campaigns, economic systems, traffic jams, sports teams, weather reports—and, when the situation arises, crises in the Middle East.

They do it with too much air time to fill and not enough personnel to fill it. Local operations that once put on thirty minutes of news now give us as much as three hours each evening, a process by which they give viewers more and more of less and less. They do it with reporters, photographers, producers, and technicians sometimes dancing so fast you can practically see sparks coming out of their shoes. They promote themselves ceaselessly as full-service news organizations, when in truth they play an artful con game. And they do it with shadows and mirrors created by general managers so consumed by financial statements that their programs present the look of news but utterly diminish and distort the actual events of the day and short-change all who watch.

At local TV news operations across the country, they do it in such a similar fashion that it has become a kind of journalistic McDonald's. Not only do they look alike, but they've sold millions of customers who imagine they are digesting nourishing information nuggets.

And the people behind the counter, offering up these morsels, know what empty calories they're serving. But they also understand the rules: Try to change the menu, and find another livelihood.

As Denise Koch walked into her office, I strolled back to my desk. It was October of 2002, and I had just started my twentieth year doing commentary on this program, WJZ-TV's *Eyewitness News.*

I wrote a few hundred words each day about local issues, each piece encapsulated within television's familiar ninety-second confines. The job was not difficult. At about twenty minutes past six each evening, I appeared on camera and read aloud what I had written maybe an hour earlier. I broadcast these commentaries five nights a week, after I had finished my job each day as a metro columnist for the *Baltimore Sun*.

In my self-congratulatory moments over those television years, I told myself I was offering valuable little nightly insights in a maze of colorful but empty pictures. I am a reporter, not a performer. But, in my gloomiest moments, I saw myself as part of the same general broadcast fraud I saw around me. It wasn't the daily news, just the daily distraction.

Instead of news, television offered the appearance of news. Instead of honest presentation of overseas reporters, there were nightly "fronts" by local anchors pretending to have worked the stories themselves. Instead of local reports with texture, there were ninety-second "in-depth" pieces. Instead of serious investigations, there were cheap imitations, with the word "investigation" casually slapped on like a used-car bill of sale for unwary customers. Instead of story telling, there were slap-dash collections of meaningless sound bites by reporters rushing about to cover enough ground for three different broadcasts. Instead of character insight, there was a repertory company of casual stereotypes: the angry poor person, usually black; the official voice of political or police authority, usually white; the distraught mother of a crime victim, usually black; the missing pet, and the family in search, usually white. All stories were reduced to emotional shorthand, and the emotions were so shallow that they evaporated in the transition from one segment to the next.

I sat next to Suzanne Collins, who was the station's most tenacious reporter. She spent hours combing through court records, police blotters, campaign finance reports. She exposed bungles by prosecutors, laziness by bureaucrats.

For this, management considered her an oddball reporter whose value was suspect. What good were investigative reports in which boring documents held the key? Television news wanted dramatic pictures—the burning building, the police chase viewed from a helicopter—not numbers on printed pages. It wanted viewers at home, already caught between their suppers and their children throwing tantrums, to stop everything and pay attention.

Across from Collins sat Alex DeMetrick, the best writer in the building. When ecologists embarked on a Chesapeake Bay cleanup, hoping to assist endangered wildlife, DeMetrick called it "an apology on behalf of one species to another." He wrote like that. He understood science and technology and turned a phrase like a poet. Thus, he was regarded as a guy going nowhere.

"Alex will never make it big in this business," an assistant news director named Michael LaMothe told me one night. LaMothe was an idealist speaking with a bitter sense of irony. "He thinks good writing's important. He doesn't put himself into the story enough. You gotta dance a little for the folks at home."

"Maybe he has too much integrity for that," I suggested.

"Will you cut that crap?" LaMothe said. In television, it was important not merely to tell the story, but to show one's own role in the production: the reporter as gallant fighter/humanitarian/court jester/good neighbor. DeMetrick's personality was too sober for such empty theatrics, and LaMothe had become too cynical not to vent about it openly.

Behind Suzanne Collins's desk was Pat Warren's. Warren had been a weekend anchor but was removed. She was perceived as "not nice enough." She could be a little abrasive; television doesn't like abrasive, unless it is seen as performance schtick. Once, as weekend anchor, Warren got into trouble because she asked a reporter a question on the air, and the reporter hadn't a clue. It was an easy question, but Warren had broken an unwritten rule: All on-air questions to reporters should have the appearance of spontaneity, while not being even slightly spontaneous. Warren was intelligent and tough, and she had a low bullshit threshold. Everybody in the room knew when things were eating at her.

A few nights after Denise Koch ran breathlessly into the studio for her Middle East report, Warren was assigned a follow-up story. President Bush was now raising the decibel level on threats to invade Iraq. Nervous United Nations officials were meeting in overtime sessions to figure out a response. Iraqi streets were erupting again.

When Warren arrived at the station that morning, an assignment editor named Tanya Black handed her the day's order.

"We've got file footage of Iraq," Black said, "and a network feed from the UN. You can read some wire copy over the footage. And then go to Washington."

"Washington?" Warren said. "The UN's in New York. Why am I going to Washington? It's two hundred miles from New York."

"Newman wants it," Black explained, pursing her lips to keep her darker thoughts to herself.

Jay Newman was the station's general manager, an obsessive-compulsive micro-manager with a basset hound's face and the attention span of a three-second sound-bite. He was known for firing off dozens of computer messages each day to his news director, and telephoning her repeatedly within the confines of each broadcast. Newman didn't talk to people, he hovered over them like some bird of prey until something else caught his attention and he flitted off, sometimes in the middle of people's sentences. Once, on vacation in Cancun, he hooked up a telephone line so he could listen to each broadcast and critique it. Newman presided over every nuance of the newsroom operation. The station's veteran news director, Gail Bending, now ran her department in name only.

On this morning, Newman wanted Pat Warren in Washington, which is barely an hour's drive from the station, in order to commit routine fraud. He also ordered reporter Sharon Lee to get reaction to the Iraqi situation from ordinary citizens in Baltimore most of whom still had no information at all beyond what television itself was beginning to report.

When I looked up from my desk that evening at a newsroom monitor, there was Warren. She was in Washington, as everyone could tell. This was because of the wonderful scene behind her. It was the U.S. Capitol building. This was an old shorthand gimmick, the way all movies about Paris have the Eiffel Tower seen from a hotel window. The background establishes both location and mood. The U.S. capitol said to everyone: Important business is happening here, and this station is all over it.

Merely by having the building behind her, Warren looked authoritative and involved, as an anchor delivered the words TV news considers magic: "Reporting live from Washington..." Then Warren delivered her ten-second live introduction and went to her package—the network-supplied tape with Warren's voice-over that she had recorded over the original reporter's voice before she left Baltimore that morning. In this case, it was pictures from the UN and from Iraq. Nobody was supposed to notice: Neither the UN nor Iraq was located in Washington, D.C., where Warren was.

In the course of the day, had Warren actually interviewed high-level politicians in Washington? Nah. Had she interviewed government insiders? Nah. Her assignment was strictly to stand in front of a famous building recognizable to all.

Nobody watching the show was supposed to notice these distinctions. The capitol glowing behind Warren was to imply the great drama of the moment, and to bestow legitimacy, to make it seem as though Warren had spent these last hours talking to the great leaders of the world—even though Warren had been nowhere near any of those leaders.

The entire story, for all of its international importance, ran ninety-seven seconds. When it was finished, Warren could be seen on the right side of the TV screen, with the lights of the capitol still glowing behind her, and WJZ anchor Vic Carter was seen on the left side of the screen, sitting in the studio in Baltimore. He thanked her for the report. Then Carter said, as though he had been speaking intimately with President Bush himself, "The president leaves no doubt that if Iraq makes one false step...it means war."

In his next sentence, Carter then declared, "Sharon Lee now continues our *Eyewitness News* team coverage with local reaction to today's major developments."

Lee, Carter announced, was stationed at the "WJZ Outback." The phrase was said quickly. It sounded as if Lee might be stationed somewhere exotic. What in the world was an "outback"? Some place in Australia? An Outback Steakhouse? Wherever it was, we were going there directly from Vic Carter's apparent intimacy with the president of the United States.

In fact, Lee was "out back"—meaning, she was standing in the station's back yard, in the dark, by its parking lot. She was there strictly for dramatic evening atmosphere—and for logistics. When her ninety-second video-taped package finished—it was local people, in rapid little sound-bites, grunting concern about possible war—there was Lee in the Outback again. Only now, she took up the bottom half of the right side of the screen. Pat Warren, still standing in front of the capitol building, had the upper half of the right side. And, in the studio, there was anchor Vic Carter.

He thanked them both for being part of the station's "team coverage." The two reporters nodded their heads. Instantly, they were all replaced on-screen by Denise Koch, who declared, "Check in with WJZ's *Eyewitness News* for complete team coverage on the U.S. showdown with Iraq. Count on us to update you on all breaking developments."

Massive death and destruction might be just around the corner, but WJZ would still find time to call attention to itself, and to link its "team coverage" to the war effort over and over. "Count on us," indeed. Again, Newman's orders: Push the product at every given opportunity, sell it hard, stage it as though we were really covering it and not just fronting for other people's work. When Sharon Lee came back into the newsroom, I asked, "Why were you out there in the cold like that?"

"Newman," she said. "It looks more dramatic if we're outside."

"On a freaking parking lot?"

Lee shrugged her shoulders; viewers didn't know it was a parking lot. "Plus," she said, "he wanted the three boxes."

The boxes—anchor Carter in one, reporters Warren and Lee in the others—made it look as though WJZ had personnel blanketing the area. *Eyewitness News* was everywhere, in Washington, in Baltimore, all over the place. At the UN, and in Iraq, too. That was the implication, anyway: We've got the news blanketed.

In fact, it was a typical weeknight at the station, with typical staffing. This meant, for the six o'clock news, there were two anchors. There were two weather reporters. There was a sports reporter.

And there were seven street reporters—seven people who actually left the confines of the studio to cover local news. These were the same reporters also doing the same stories for the four o'clock and five o'clock shows—in slightly modified forms, so that viewers would think they were watching actual updates.

How did the station deploy these seven reporters to best cover all the important news of the day? Well, there was Pat Warren with her ten-second intro in Washington, and Sharon Lee "out back," each assigned to lend her alleged expertise to events in the distant Middle East.

Reporters Alex DeMetrick and Katie Leahan were in different locations—in Virginia—for updates on two serial snipers who had terrorized the region. The terrorizing had ended two weeks earlier, but no matter. And there was Suzanne Collins, reporting from Annapolis on the possibility of imposing the death penalty in Maryland on those same two serial snipers—if Virginia didn't execute them first.

That left exactly two reporters to cover all of the news about the two million people who live in the Baltimore metropolitan area, the station's primary viewing audience. One was Mike Schuh. He was dispatched to cover a rush hour traffic tie-up downtown. And there was Tim Williams, offering a feature on the Navy-Notre Dame football game, to be played in Baltimore the next day and, not to be overlooked (and the *Eyewitness News* team did not overlook it), to be shown on WJZ.

Seven reporters to cover all the important business of the day.

Two reporters actually doing stories about Baltimore.

Was it a slow news day? Not quite. Among the day's actual news: With a new Republican governor elected three days earlier, the Democratic mayor of Baltimore worried openly about economic support for his city. A stunned Speaker of the Maryland House of Delegates, knocked out of office by a political novice, was frantically asking for a recount of votes. Public school officials admitted they'd overspent their budget by $10 million. Baltimore police announced new measures to cut the city's frightening number of homicides. A twenty-seven-year-old suburban man was sentenced to thirty years in prison for stabbing his father to death while high on drugs. Gambling interests met with racetrack executives about bringing slot machines into Maryland. Advocates for the poor were worrying about diminishing health coverage. A twenty-year old Baltimore County man was sentenced to life in prison for rape and attempted murder, and said he'd been denied a fair trial because he was black. The Maryland Court of Special Appeals convened to hear arguments in the case of an "escort service" for high-profile sexual clients. A suspected drug dealer was killed in a high-speed police chase. School officials transferred fifty teachers, a remarkable move considering it was two months into the school year.

Also, a certain seventy-eight-year-old woman who had punched me in the mid-section and was, strictly by coincidence, defeated in her bid to get back her old U.S. congressional seat, announced she would not be running for office ever again.

All of these stories were reported in the day's local newspaper, the *Baltimore Sun.*

Not one of them was reported on *Eyewitness News.* For that matter, they were almost entirely overlooked by all other television stations in town, as well.

For those who value the life of legitimate journalism, such preposterousness is nothing new. In a 1998 *Columbia Journalism*

Review piece, "Does Local TV News Need a National Nanny?,"
Lawrence Grossman, former president of NBC News and
PBS, remembered organizing a New York citizens' group
years earlier to challenge the license of WPIX-TV.

"Among other egregious practices," Grossman recalled,
"the station labeled old stock footage as on-the-scene reports
of citizen protests in Eastern Europe, described army publicity
film shot in Fort Belvoir, Virginia, as coming 'via satellite
from the Central Highlands of Vietnam,' and identified audio
reports called in from a pay phone on Forty-Second Street as
'live from Prague.'"

That was thirty years earlier. By the summer of 1998, a
non-profit group called Media Watch declared that local TV
news across the nation tended to be "severely unbalanced, with
excessive coverage of violent topics and trivial events."

The words echoed almost every other study of local TV
news. As Grossman noted, "Last year the *Detroit News* reported
that in the Motor City, 'Crime and violence constitute by far the
largest share of the coverage,' taking up an average of forty-
three percent of all newscasts." A study by the nonpartisan
Center for Media and Public Affairs in Washington, D.C., said
that crime, weather, accidents, disasters, soft news, and sports
accounted for the majority of stories on newscasts.

"Add in time for credits and commercials," Grossman
noted, "and you get a total of twenty-four minutes and twenty
seconds per half-hour newscast—and that leaves just five
minutes and forty seconds to cover all other 'serious news'
about government, health, foreign affairs, education, science,
the environment..."

And yet there is this: We watch it, and everybody calls it
the news. We watch it, despite all evidence of its emptiness.

A 1999 study by the Project for Excellence in Journalism—
an affiliate of the Columbia University Graduate School of
Journalism, working with a group of TV news journalists,
university scholars, and professional researchers—cited local
news operations that "increasingly produce more with less,

creating a culture of superficiality and haste."

A 1995 study of the local news in fifty major markets by the Rocky Mountain Media Watch found that crime and disaster news made up more than half of the coverage on local broadcasts. Fluff—celebrity news, teases, anchor chit-chat—took up thirty percent.

A 1993 *Washington Post* look at local newscasts in five big cities found the percentage of stories on crime, sex, disasters, accidents, or public fears took up anywhere from half to three-quarters of local newscasts.

When did I start to notice such things at WJZ? Maybe it was that slow Memorial Day when a building collapsed. Early reports were unclear if workers were inside. Assistant news director Michael LaMothe cried, "Let them be trapped, let them be trapped, oh please, let them be trapped."

Or maybe it was that night when producer Grant Morrow, hungry for a lead story as air time approached, was told that a bus with handicapped kids careened off a mountain, killing three and injuring twenty others. Morrow replied, "Stop trying to cheer me up."

Newsrooms are inevitably places where gallows humor reigns; LaMothe and Morrow were two decent, sensitive people, cited because they were mocking the traditional underlying imperative of local television: If it bleeds, it leads.

But that was the least of it. Though LaMothe and Morrow were bemoaning a business that had lost its professional compass, they made their remarks long before local TV learned its worst lesson: how to disguise its emptiness with new sleight of hand—and new layers of fraud.

2

Going Snowblind

The first time I walked into WJZ-TV, the place offended me. I was accustomed to working in scruffy newspaper offices, where the desks were brought in during the Roosevelt years and retained all original dust. This was known as atmosphere. On newspapers, reporters considered pen and paper their survival equipment. At the television station I saw people having high-level discussions about their neckties.

But money changes things. I started out at a newspaper called the *News American,* in the summer of 1966, making $50 a week. The take-home was $38.98. The specific numbers linger like a wound that never quite heals. A year later, full of youthful audacity, and informing the editors that I was engaged to be wed, I asked for a $20 raise. They gave me $18.50 but held firm on the last buck and a half. They figured $68.50 a week was enough money for any man to start a family.

I should have noticed the start of a bad trend. One afternoon seven years later, in the spring of 1974, I learned a couple of things: I had just been nominated for a Pulitzer Prize (which I did not win, strictly on merit) for a story about courthouse corruption. And, on this same day, a politician I'd recently exposed for taking illegal money resigned from office under pressure. This was pretty exciting. Then I got home and my wife greeted me at the door. "Big shot," she said, "take a look at the family checkbook. The gas and electric company is cutting off all power if they don't get paid in the next ten minutes. And Equitable Trust called to say we're late on the car payment."

This is the way it could go in the newspaper business, which is one reason print people have such an instinctive hatred of television people. In the eyes of all newspaper people, the TV types pose in front of cameras, make too much money, and imagine themselves terribly important because their faces appear each evening from the scene of elaborately staged press conferences.

I shared this hatred of everything television stood for, right up to the instant they sat me down and started talking money. They asked a question I had never in my life previously heard: Could you work for this much money? It was 1983, but I thought about 1966 and the fifty bucks a week at the *News American*. The words echoed in my head: Could I work for this much money? Then I thought about the wonderful raise to $68.50 on which I had once walked down the wedding aisle.

Could I work for this much money? Yes, I could. I thanked them on behalf of myself and my family. The gas and electric company stood up and applauded on my behalf. Equitable Trust did cartwheels. I told myself this would be more than enough money. I told this to myself right up to the moment they asked me to sit in front of a camera and somebody mentioned, "You know how many people will watch you tonight? Probably half a million." And this number, like the others, never went out of my head.

What was I doing?

I didn't belong here, but here I was. On the night of November 11, 1983, I sat next to anchor Jerry Turner in a chair in the WJZ studio to deliver a television commentary about the death of the mayor of Baltimore's mother. Tululu Schaefer was her name. Her son, William Donald Schaefer, sixty-four years old and elected that week to a fourth term as mayor, lived with his mother his entire life, and now she was gone, and on this night, in one of my first commentaries, I figured it was appropriate to say a few words about her.

But where were my words?

There were three cameras in the WJZ studio, and a stage manager named JoAnn Lawlor who would point and tell me which one to look into. The game, I had learned in my first few appearances on the air, was pretty simple. Some time during the day, I would write my commentary on a special TelePrompter typewriter. This typewriter had extra-large lettering. The typed commentary was then pasted onto a long roll of scripts, like some vertical Torah, and placed into a studio TelePrompter.

From there, the game got even easier. As you looked into the camera, there was your script, rolling right in front of you like a life preserver. If you could read, you would not sink.

If, in fact, your script actually appeared in the TelePrompter.

On Jerry Turner's left was Al Sanders. The two anchors' television skills had made WJZ one of the powerhouse stations in the whole country. Their ratings were often higher than the combined ratings of their competitors.

Turner, fifty-five, was silver-haired and self-assured. He was authoritative at all the important times but quick to laugh on-camera when the moment called for it. Viewers were charmed. Sanders, forty-three, was African-American, round-faced, self-deprecating, and funny. The two men clearly liked each other and were comfortable in each other's company. On any newspaper, all these would have been considered nice but slightly superfluous qualities. On a television station, they were the stuff of which general managers can build reputations as Einsteins.

But what was I doing here?

I was a career newspaper guy who stumbled into the place by a couple of accidents that tell us a little about my own work but a lot about the nature of American broadcasting. I'd built a decent local reputation as an investigative reporter at the *News*

American. Then, in January, 1976, I started writing a column. There is a difference between a reporter and a columnist. A reporter says: Here are the facts I have found. A columnist says: Here are the facts, and here is what I think about them. A columnist is a reporter with a visible opinion. That distinction represented the beginning of all change in my professional life.

One morning about eighteen months after I started writing the column, my telephone rang. It was Alan Berrier, the news director at WCAO radio. In Baltimore, there was a time when those call-letters meant the world in radio. WCAO was the rock and roll station with which almost everyone in my baby-boom generation had come of age. Roughly half the Baltimore-area listening audience tuned to the station's most popular disc jockey, Johnny Dark, while all other stations divided whatever audience was left over.

But a new kind of Dark Ages was beginning. WCAO was an AM station, and all across the country, AM was trying to reinvent itself. Its former listeners were now turning to FM stations. FM had stereophonic sound. The AM band did not. From New York to Los Angeles, AM was thus beginning to transform itself into so-called information radio, a world that would one day be populated by Rush Limbaugh and assemblages of imitators across the country.

For now, WCAO wanted to dip a little toe into what were still chilly waters.

"I like your stuff," Berrier said. "We'd like you to come on the air for us."

"I already have a job."

"Keep the job. This'll take you a few minutes a day."

"No," I said. "I don't know anything about broadcasting. I'd make a fool of myself."

Berrier snorted. "It's easy," he said. He'd been in the business for about fifteen years, as newsman and disc jockey. Now he shared a morning drive-time show with a fellow named Lou Roberts—Louie and The Bear, they billed themselves—while overseeing the station's news department.

It was a news department in name only. It consisted of one announcer in the early morning, one at mid-day, one in the late afternoon. It was a rip 'n' read operation: rip wire copy off the machine, and read it over the air, and try to sound as if you know what you're talking about. Or have someone pick up a morning newspaper at the local 7-Eleven on the way to work, and let an announcer relate some actual reporters' stories on the air as if they were his own. This is the essence of nearly all reporting at American radio stations to this day.

For WCAO, Berrier's phone call arrived at a time when listeners still tuned in mainly for the music. But their numbers were falling like a safe thrown from a window. Berrier figured I might help to build a new, more serious audience. I figured I'd already done enough talking in my life. One time in college, I took a required course called Intro to Speech. I got exactly six words into one speech and all other words left my head altogether. I stood there like the village idiot and remained, over the years, dumb struck at the thought of public speaking.

"You don't have to memorize anything," Berrier said. "Just do commentaries like your column, and read them over the air."

I thought about that for a moment. The column changed pace all the time. If I wrote about politics one day, I aimed for something else—neighborhood stuff, characters, cops, whatever—the next day. In fact, some days, I wrote about broadcasting. I tended to be less than flattering.

"Sometimes in my column," I pointed out, "I criticize radio."

"That's fine," Berrier said. "Come on the radio and criticize radio. We believe in free speech. Free speech is very important."

"Nah," I said, "I don't think I could."

Then he mentioned money. It wasn't very big money—$25 a broadcast to start, five times a week—but it would supplement a newspaper salary that was still, in the summer of 1977, less than $25,000 a year.

"You know, you're right," I said. "Freedom of speech is very important."

Berrier told me to try writing some sample commentaries at home. He wanted them to run about a minute. After you write it, he said, read it aloud and time it.

I wrote a commentary the length of my newspaper column and read it aloud before an audience comprised of my kitchen clock. It ran more than three minutes. I started removing things: adjectives, adverbs, brilliant turns of phrase, entire sentences. This got me down to about two minutes and forty-five seconds.

This was not like newspaper writing. This was shorthand, it was journalistic haiku. The art of the one-minute commentary, I soon discovered, was to keep it simple. Take one topic, make one point about it, and get out. And keep the language simple. In the newspaper, you could play with the sophisticated simile, the graceful metaphor. If the reader doesn't get it, he can read it again. On the air, though, the graceful metaphor drifts away, and the confused listener cannot say: Would you mind repeating that?

The commentaries were taped each morning, and they worked well enough that WCAO began running them three times a day. They ran for four years. But they were a small, puny voice at a time the station needed to bellow some new sound across all its hours. The ratings continued to fall, as did revenues. One morning Berrier walked me from a little recording studio into a hallway.

"The general manager's pretty upset," he said. "The ratings keep falling. He says we've gotta get rid of some people doing commentaries."

This bothered me, since I was the only person doing commentaries. It was radio's way of saying the party's over.

But, not wishing to lose the fabulous $25 a day, I found another party. Since several stations on the AM band were going through the change-over to talk, I contacted WBAL, the biggest radio operation in town, a 50,000-watt monster trying to forge its own new identity against the blast of FM's new musical muscle.

The general manager was a man named Al Burke. He presided over WBAL for thirty-five years. In radio terms, this made him Ruler for Life. Burke knew my work. By this time, I'd been hired away from the *News American* by the *Baltimore Sun*, the city's prestige paper. Burke hired me to do the same kind of free-lance commentary I'd done at WCAO.

I had the job for two years, and then Christine Craft entered the American consciousness.

Craft was a television news anchor at KMBC, the ABC affiliate in Kansas City, Missouri. She was, by many accounts, pretty good. Within the limited range of skills the local anchor job calls for, such as pronouncing all street names properly, she was fine. But her television station brought in an outside consultant, the way broadcast stations do. The outside consultant said, "Get rid of this woman." Craft was judged to be not young enough (she was thirty-seven), not pretty enough (a newspaper account later said she had "wholesome, outdoorsy good looks"), and not deferential enough to her co-anchor. The co-anchor was male. Craft was fired.

For this, I wrote a column in my new newspaper, the *Baltimore Sun*, in which I vented on behalf of women and other sensitive souls, decrying the warped, distorted, sexist values these outside consultants attempted to impose on broadcast stations and, by extension, on American culture.

It was such a wonderful column that it got me fired from the radio station the day it appeared.

The column ran in the morning, and in the afternoon I went to WBAL to record my daily commentary. I never made it into the studio. I was called into the office of John Grimes, an executive who said he was speaking on behalf of Al Burke, the general manager. Burke, he said, could not be disturbed at the moment. Grimes, rubbing his hands nervously, said Burke had read the newspaper column that morning.

"Oh, yeah?" I said.

"Yeah," Grimes said. He looked down at his hands, which he kept rubbing together briskly, as though trying to remove something from them. "The one about the outside consultants."

"Uh-huh."

"I don't know if you know this," Grimes said, "but we have an outside consultant in the building now."

"Oh, yeah?"

"Yeah," Grimes said. "And he says we have to let you go."

Now I knew what he was trying to rub from his hands: my blood.

"But, why?"

"Well," Grimes said, "he says you don't fit in here any more."

And that was the end of my radio career. A few days later, I was allowed into the inner chambers of Al Burke's office to plead my case before final sentencing. But this was strictly for show.

"Son," Burke said to me, "I'm paying this consultant a lot of money. If he tells me I gotta let you go, and I don't listen to him, then I'm just wasting all that money."

What was I doing here?

What was I doing in a business that hired and fired people so casually, and for reasons so unrelated to the job itself? By this point, I'd worked on newspapers for seventeen years. Nobody in a newsroom talked about circulation figures, about advertising rates, about outside consultants. When people talked shop, they talked about insensitive editors. Or they talked about stories they were trying to break.

In radio, they talked about ratings. They brought in consultants. The quality of journalism counted for nothing.

I decided I was finished with such a business.

Then, a few weeks after the WBAL firing, I went grocery shopping and bumped into a fellow I knew a little bit. Years earlier, while I was a freshman at the University of Maryland, this fellow was a graduate student there. His name was Richard

Sher. He was the Intro to Speech instructor when I'd gotten six words into my final speech and then utterly forgotten every word.

When Sher left college teaching, he went to work for WEAM-radio, in Arlington, Virginia. The ratings were so good, the station had him hosting three different shows under three different names. Sometimes he was Richie Sher. Sometimes, Dick Drake. Sometimes he was Russ Wheeler. Sometimes, he used one of his shows to promote another one of his shows. He had alternative egos doing alternative voices.

After a year, he moved to nearby WAVA, an all-news station. He was named news director there. The title was somewhat more impressive than its reality. He had a reporting staff of three. The *New York Times* it was not.

A year after that, he was back doing disc jockey work at WEAM. Three years later, he was news director at WCBM in Baltimore. This time he had four people in the entire newsroom. After two years at WCBM, Sher went to WRC in Washington to be news director. It was the same deal, a handful of people allegedly covering an entire community—only this time, the community was the nation's capitol. The *Washington Post* it was not. So much for the journalistic stature of radio news.

The career path of broadcasting being what it is, Sher moved again. He spent four years at KNBR Radio in San Francisco, then flew back to Baltimore one weekend to see his mother. He decided to call Al Burke at WBAL. Burke offered him a job as news director. Sher and his wife, Annabelle, and their three young sons packed their bags and flew three thousand miles back to Baltimore.

Six months later, Burke called Sher into his office. Sher had half a dozen people working in his newsroom—a big number for a local radio station—and he was making all of them crazy.

"Son," Burke said, "I'm gonna have to let you go."

"Why, Al?" Sher said.

"You've tried to turn our news operation into a Cadillac," Burke said, "and we've been doing very well as a Chevrolet."

Sher walked out the door and made plans to get out of broadcasting. Then a phone call arrived from Jerry Turner. The two men had met a couple of times.

"Come over here and talk to these people about a job," Turner said.

Thus began another of the legendary careers in Baltimore television. Over the next three decades, Sher became WJZ's best-known street reporter. He hosted a shrill weekly news panel show, called *Square-Off*, that ran for nearly twenty years. He anchored the noon news each day, and he anchored the weekend evening news. And for six years, he hosted a morning chat show called *People Are Talking*. His co-host was a young woman named Oprah Winfrey.

When I bumped into Sher that morning at the grocery store, he greeted me with the good-natured confidence of a man in the midst of his very own legend. I, having just lost a sizable piece of my income to the Christine Craft crusade, greeted him like a shlemiel.

"Hey," he said jokingly, "when are you gonna let me make you a TV star?"

And I, not so jokingly, said, "Now."

What was I doing?

Several days after meeting Sher, Dick Reingold called my house. Reingold was the news director at WJZ. "Write a sample commentary," he said. "We'll put you in front of a camera and let you read the thing, and let's see what you look like."

I already knew what I looked like. I didn't look like television news. I had a beard, and it was already starting to turn gray. And I had some hair, but not as much as I'd had just a few years earlier. I was thirty-eight years old, and now they wanted me to sit for a screen test like Lana Turner. It occurred to me that I was about to make a terrible fool of myself.

As it happened, I did. I wrote a piece about a lanky young fellow pumping gas at a Crown station across the street from Baltimore's Poly-Western high school complex. He had dropped out of school. Now, on the first day of the new school year, he gazed across Falls Road and watched as all these kids with their dreams still in front of them gathered for opening day. The guy at the gas station was still in his teens, but his dreams already seemed behind him.

I finished typing the piece and walked down a hallway with Reingold and entered a studio. I recognized the set from the evening news. There were four empty seats.

"Pick any one," a cameraman said. I went for the sports seat and looked into a camera as someone pinned a microphone to my necktie. In the camera's lens, there was the commentary I'd written a few minutes earlier.

"Relax," Reingold said. "In two weeks, you'll be so full of yourself, you'll be wearing sunglasses in your own living room."

I laughed uncomfortably at the Hollywood image.

"Look down," a cameraman said.

"Huh?"

"Every few paragraphs," he said, "look down at the desk, as though you're checking your copy. If you keep staring straight ahead at the camera, it makes people at home feel threatened, like you're staring at them."

"In five," another voice said, "four, three..."

I got through the piece all right. I heard a cameraman say, "Pretty good," and then Reingold said, "Good."

I have since seen the videotape of the screen test. It is awful. As I look into the camera and begin to talk, I feel the need to gesture physically to help make my point. My gesture is a tilt of the head and a tilt of one shoulder. By the time I finished my ninety seconds in front of the camera, the slight tilt had become a head about to topple like a boulder from a mountain cliff. As a television person, I made a very good newspaper typist.

But they liked the contents of the piece, and figured they could work on my posture. A few nights later, Reingold took me to dinner with Paul Yates, the station's general manager. We never talked about television. Yates wanted to pick my brain about Baltimore. He had a television station dominating all others, with a method so simple that all the collective intellect in local broadcasting had failed to notice it: It was the home town station.

He had Jerry Turner, who had now been there for two decades. He had Al Sanders, who had now been there more than a decade. He had Baltimore natives such as Richard Sher who anchored the top-rated noon news and Bob Turk, the popular weatherman, and Maria Broom, who'd grown up in Baltimore and was a culture hero for her consumer reporting, and for being a high-profile African-American role model. Unlike a lot of stations, WJZ tended to hold onto their on-air people. The longer they stayed, the better they knew the turf. The community seemed to appreciate this.

In me, Yates saw not just a guy to broadcast commentaries, but a local presence. He asked about my history in Baltimore. I'd grown up in two places: the Latrobe Housing Projects, in the shadow of the State Penitentiary, where my family lived on the GI Bill after World War II; and then middle class Northwest Baltimore. I was a public school kid. I was a University of Maryland graduate. I was part of the community. These all counted with Yates.

The other stations in town seemed to run people through a revolving door. They were here, and then they went somewhere else. For all their surveys and all their high-priced consultants, the other stations didn't seem to grasp a simple fact: Television involved invitation into people's homes. And people don't feel comfortable with strangers. The WJZ strength was its steadiness of personality, its employment of people who sank roots into the community they were covering. My roots were already here. And people knew it, because they'd been reading me in the newspaper.

But, now that it actually came down to it—to sitting in a studio, in front of a camera, with half a million people watching—what was I doing here?

On the night of November 11, 1983, I intended doing a commentary about the death of the mayor of Baltimore's mother. By this time, I'd been on the air for a few weeks and was beginning to get the routine down: Write the piece on the TelePrompter typewriter. When the six o'clock news arrived, sit in the studio and look into the proper camera. Then read the piece as it scrolled through the TelePrompter.

On this particular night, Jerry Turner introduced my commentary. He said funeral services would be held for Tululu Schaefer, with whom the mayor of Baltimore had lived all of his life. Then he said, "In his commentary tonight, Michael Olesker says Mrs. Schaefer had a profound effect on the mayor of Baltimore."

As I watched Turner, I should have seen something was wrong. He was not looking into any camera. He was looking down at a stack of papers in his hand. I noticed none of this.

I looked at him and said, "Jerry, she was a lovely woman." And then, gracefully, I turned in my chair to look into the appropriate television camera to find the words to my commentary. What I beheld, instead, was a sea of white.

My first thought was, *I knew I should have typed it darker. The print is so light, I can't even see it.* Whereupon I realized, there was no print. If I continued to stare into this sea of white, I would go snow blind.

Now a revelation occurred to me: I must be looking into the wrong camera. I began to turn my head from side to side, peering into each of the three studio cameras, increasingly frantically, so that people at home must have thought my head was on a swivel. The same thing appeared in each of the cameras: nothing.

A copy of my commentary sat on the desk, directly in front of me. But I was too frozen with fear to reach for it, and too full of dread that people at home would see me hold it up to read from it and think: "He doesn't know anything, he's just reading. Jerry and Al don't have to read. They just know this stuff."

From the left corner of my eye, I could see Turner and Sanders. They were gesturing frantically to the photographers in the studio: Where is Olesker's commentary? No one knew.

All we knew was that some idiot had forgotten to put it into the TelePrompter. I saw the stage manager, JoAnn Lawlor, making calming gestures as she stood between two cameras. She looked like someone on an aircraft carrier trying to steady a rookie pilot as he attempts to land his jet in the middle of a ferocious Atlantic.

A number flashed repeatedly in my head: half a million, the number of viewers who watched the six o'clock news, all of whom were now perceived as vultures waiting to leap upon my slightest mistake.

And now I knew what was happening to me: I was having a nervous breakdown in front of all those people. And, in my moment of crisis, I knew exactly what to do. I would look into one of these cameras, and I would say, "Folks, I don't need this job, and I don't need this aggravation. And I'm outta here." And I would make one of the great exits in the history of television.

This thought was immediately followed by a second: Wait a minute, they pay me for this. Not $50 a week, nor even $68.50, but an actual living wage.

And I managed, the way a dying man is supposed to see his entire life passing in front of him, to recall the general essence of the commentary and stumble through the high points of it.

We broke for a commercial. I took off my microphone and rose disconsolately to leave the studio, certain that my first words to Alan Berrier, of WCAO-radio, had finally come true: "I don't know anything about broadcasting, and I would make a fool of myself."

Then Al Sanders looked up at me.

"That's the best thing that could have happened to you," he said.

"How do you figure that?" I asked.

"If you can handle that, you can handle anything," he said.

Over the next nineteen years in television news, WJZ and I would put that theory to the test.

3

Ready for Your Close-Up

"They told you about makeup, didn't they?"

"Huh?"

"Makeup," said Jerry Turner.

Makeup had not occurred to me. A few weeks before the TelePrompter fiasco, in the last hour before my first television broadcast, I was thinking of many things, all related to my upcoming public humiliation, but makeup was nowhere on the list. Turner held up a small leather case and unzipped it. Inside were makeup creams and blushes and applicators. It looked like my ex-wife's pocketbook. I reminded myself that I had been married and was raising two children, reassuring myself that I was not a guy who wore eyeliner.

We were sitting in Turner's little office off the WJZ newsroom. Turner was the biggest thing on Baltimore television and a legend among local TV news operations across the country. For a couple of years in a row, *TV/Radio Age* named him the number one local anchor in America. *Broadcasting* magazine named him one of the top ten. *Advertising Age* called him the most dominant individual on any newscast in America. He and Al Sanders were named one of the top three news anchor teams in the U.S. by *Electronic Media* magazine.

What made them the best? Who knew? But it had not even dimly occurred to me that makeup might play some part of it. I hadn't come out of that particular school of journalism.

I wanted to tell Turner about the night I'd spent in an abandoned West Baltimore church, with a desperate street junkie, so I could write authoritatively about the heroin tearing apart a man's life. I wanted to tell him about getting arrested once by cops angry about police corruption stories I'd written, and how I'd spent the night in jail before a judge tossed out the case. I wanted to tell him about prosecutors and grand juries that had demanded I reveal confidential sources or go to prison, and I had faced them down and won. I wanted to tell him what a tough guy I was, and tough guys don't wear makeup.

So I looked him in the eye and declared, in a voice that cracked like a saltine, "Makeup?"

"Yeah," he said lightly. "You're probably Max Factor tan number two. Most of the white guys use that. Come on."

He walked me across the newsroom to the men's lavatory. We stood in front of a large mirror with a row of lights ringing the edges.

"You'll have to get your own stuff," he said. "But this'll get you through tonight."

He reached into his makeup kit and pulled out moisturizer. He pulled out base. He pulled out concealer and powder and eye shadow, some of which he dabbed and patted all over my face.

"Stay still," he said when I pulled back reflexively.

I felt like the Victorian virgin whose mother gives her advice for dealing with the wedding-night bed: "Just close your eyes and think of England." I thought, *If I were a newspaper reporter getting a look at this, I would write the most riotous story about one alleged newsman helping another alleged newsman get ready to report their big stories by putting on their makeup.* I felt like a fool. I felt I was debasing myself as a reporter, and as a man.

"That's not bad," Turner said when he finished.

I looked in the mirror. Actually, it wasn't so bad. It looked like I had a pretty nice tan. I looked at Turner. We looked pretty damned heterosexual for a couple of guys who had just applied makeup in the men's room.

I followed Jerry into the newsroom. He was a man utterly at ease with himself, if not with his own name. His real name was Jerry Joiner. It seemed a slightly shaky starting point: a television news person, purporting to tell it like it is, who wouldn't even tell his real name.

Turner had grown up in Meridian, Mississippi, and graduated the University of Southern Mississippi with a music degree. He drifted to Chicago and California and blew the horn in a variety of dance bands and pumped gas between gigs. Along the way, he had enough assurance to date the actresses Janet Leigh and Lana Turner. He drifted back to Mississippi, where he worked on a couple of small newspapers and stumbled into a new business, a radio-TV outlet, WTOK. He told them he could create a news department for them. He bought a used Chevrolet panel truck, painted a lightning bolt on the side and installed a two-way radio on the dash for remote broadcasts. It was the beginning of a career. He moved north to Norfolk, Virginia, where he was news director at a radio station, and then to a TV station, WYEX, in Richmond. By the time WJZ hired him, as a weekend reporter and producer of commercials, he had lived a little.

He had personal dash that translated as authority. For local TV, this was like finding Peter Jennings. WJZ, beginning to expand to a half-hour show in the late 1960s, gave him a shot at anchoring. By then, he'd changed his name from Jerry Joiner to Jerry Turner. It rolled off the tongue better.

A producer named Paul Gluck, watching Turner's popularity mushroom over the years, later marveled, "He never had any sense of self-importance, the thing that distances celebrities from other human beings. He wasn't the pope moving through the masses, he was Jerry bopping through the crowd."

He understood the deal he'd made. In exchange for fame and pretty substantial money, he had to pretend at adult seriousness. On nights when big news broke, he could work a story as well as anybody if pressed into service. His name alone brought big shots to the telephone.

But the truth was that on most nights he was a grownup who read aloud for a living. He covered no stories, broke no exposes, analyzed no complex public business. He sat in front of a camera and recited from a TelePrompter. But it was the way he did this, and the way he looked, that mattered.

As Turner rose to remarkable levels of popularity, WJZ hired one of the country's top TV news consultant outfits, McHugh and Hoffman, to analyze its on-air people. By this time, Turner's early evening broadcast far outdistanced its competitors, and the eleven o'clock show drew roughly twice the numbers of its competitors.

The McHugh-Hoffman report was strictly confidential. But it stated the obvious about Turner: "He is a very attractive individual with a good physique and is well groomed; a concerned newsman who delivers the news in a light, sometimes humorous, uncomplex but comprehensive manner; a warm, charming, affectionate person."

So much for Edward R. Murrow. The Battle of Britain demeanor wouldn't do on a nightly basis, not when you were delivering thirty-second items about lost puppies and traffic backups. Warm and charming counted, and so did grooming and physique. These were the values of local TV news.

Turner was part of the second generation of local anchors. The first generation, arriving when the networks had Walter Cronkite, Chet Huntley, and David Brinkley, was defined by those such as Jim Jensen. He anchored New York's WCBS from 1964 to 1995. The *New York Times's* Frank Rich once described Jensen as "a shining light of the Golden Age of Testosterone... With his deep Midwestern baritone, rangy good looks and a humorless, macho manner that suggested he could reach out of the tube and slug someone, he laid down the news with the authority of—well, if not God, then at least Charlton Heston at full Old Testament throttle. Was Jensen actually an old-school journalist...or was he, like Ted Baxter, merely an empty suit behaving like a stuffed shirt? Did he have any knowledge or insights to back up the headlines and wisdom he dispensed? It mattered not."

When Jensen died, Rich wrote, "What really did him in was the changing world of local TV news. The '70s brought the proliferation of *Eyewitness News*—happy-talk broadcasts devised by consultants like Frank Magid Associates. In the new local news, there was no Top Dog but an egalitarian 'team,' assembled to win over the full diversity of Nielsen demographics. There were jokes and casual repartee, to flatter viewers into thinking they were part of the TV family. There were no authority figures, no stentorian voices. On the new news, no one even pretended that journalism was a required skill."

Jerry Turner was part of that generation that followed Jensen's entrance into local news. What mattered wasn't the modest journalism background he had, but his intangibles. He was a delightful man, and clearly comfortable in his own skin, and so everybody around him felt comfortable. Viewers sensed that, when the broadcast ended, Jerry would go out for a beer with the guys—and that, if a lady showed up, he'd know how to show her a good time.

In a business where anchors flitted from one market to another every few years, the station signed him to a ten-year contract, and then signed Al Sanders to a five-year deal. Aside from ballplayers, Turner was probably the closest thing to a matinee idol that Baltimore could claim in that era. He wasn't a father figure so much as a hip uncle. To watch him was to hang around with the most popular guy in town.

It was happening for him in the manner it happened for TV anchors all over the country, only more so: They were reporters in name, but well known mainly for being well known. In Turner's case, he seemed to eventually transcend the news. He made the news seem more important by good-naturedly associating with it. The news, around him, seemed a social climber.

He understood the power that it implied. When the wire services first reported a meltdown at the nuclear power plant at Pennsylvania's Three-Mile Island—about an hour's drive from Baltimore—news director Scott Goodfellow and executive producer Skip Malkie argued for Turner to interrupt programming and announce the potential dangers.

"We need to go on the air right now," Malkie said, "and let everybody know."

"Let me tell you something," Turner said. His demeanor was calm, and he did not intend to pull rank. He was, by nature, self-effacing. But this was something else. "If Jerry Turner goes on the air with this story," he said, speaking in an unaccustomed third person, "there's gonna be panic across this state. Every road in Maryland will be clogged, and people will get hurt."

As they debated, the networks broke into the day's programming to do their own report. But Paul Gluck, producing the news that day, remembered, "Jerry understood the strength of his own image. The story probably had less gravity coming from Frank Reynolds." Reynolds was merely ABC's anchor.

Turner rarely left the confines of WJZ once he arrived there. His job was to show up at three in the afternoon, write a few fifteen- or twenty-second stories boiled down from wire copy, look over the day's other stories—or, "script," as it was known in the trade—written for him by producers, and then anchor the shows at six and eleven. That was it. On the rare occasions that he ventured outside, his mere presence changed the atmosphere.

Once, as reporters awaited the resignation of Vice President Spiro Agnew at the old federal courthouse in downtown Baltimore, Jerry joined them. If history was about to be made, the station wanted its star photographed in the midst of it. As a media mob gathered on the courthouse sidewalk, traffic on adjacent Calvert Street slowed to a near standstill. Drivers honked their horns and passengers leaned out the window to wave at the tall, silver-haired Turner, who was their glamorous back-fence neighbor.

"Jerry," they called out to the embarrassed Turner. "Hey, Jerry."

Once, during an explosive time in the city's public schools, he ventured out to cover a school board meeting. The superintendent, Dr. Roland Patterson, had become a racial dividing line. There were hundreds of people at the meeting that night, many hollering angrily at each other.

Then Turner walked in. All of the yelling stopped. Spontaneously, the crowd rose to its feet to applaud him. He seemed to have arrived specifically to part the rough verbal seas. In fact, though, he was there hoping to do what any news person does: let a story unfold without getting in its way.

But it was too late for that; he was already too famous. He apologized for intruding and asked everyone to please return to business. With his benediction, they returned to their differences, but with a more self-consciously civil tone. Nobody wanted to look like a jerk in front of royalty.

He had an aura about him. For the first fifteen minutes of each broadcast, his demeanor was so serious that he seemed to age in front of everyone. The bags under his eyes seemed to deepen, and the voice was funereal. But by the time the weather segment arrived minutes later, and it was time for occasional banter, his demeanor changed utterly. He had endured the difficult moments, and as loyal viewers we were relieved to see his mood lift. It was safe to relax now; if Jerry was happy, we could all be happy.

Off the air, he was delightful. Sometimes he would sit in the newsroom with a fake arrow through his head, like the comic Steve Martin in his early days, while helping to piece the show together. If the big guy was cutting up, then everybody could.

The other stations in town struggled to find Turners of their own. But they missed the point. Instead of letting someone develop naturally, getting to know the community they were covering, they shoved them out of town when ratings failed immediately to approach Jerry's. And the anchors, so busy being big shots, never grasped the essence of the job: They were newsmen, but they were delivering the news in the intimacy of people's homes. They tried to out-Cronkite Turner, who never pretended to be Walter Cronkite. He just wanted to be Jerry Turner.

In Baltimore, as in countless American markets, there came a revolving door of anchors at other stations. On the CBS affiliate, WMAR, they gave one fellow, George Rogers, twin titles: anchor and news director. His background? He'd previously hosted *Shell's Wonderful World of Golf.* Rogers was replaced by Dennis Holley, who then left town after a radio disc jockey made a wisecrack about him. Holley sued the disc jockey, and won, but then the town snubbed him as a poor sport.

Holley had a co-anchor named Bill Markham. When Markham's contract came up for negotiation, he told the *Baltimore Evening Sun* TV critic Michael Hill that he would give him the scoop when he signed. But negotiations suddenly broke down, and Markham quit. When Hill asked why, Markham offered an explanation that showed his complete divorce from reality.

He said management had decided blue shirts looked better on him than white shirts. "Oh, yeah?" Markham said. "I just bought a bunch of new white shirts. You want me to wear blue shirts, you're gonna have to buy 'em for me." Management refused. Markham, the devoted newsman, took a powder. On such whims, local television news history was made.

This was a time when the country was still remembering images of Ted Baxter, the nitwit anchor on the Mary Tyler Moore situation comedy. It was also a time when newspaper critics, feeling threatened by the mushrooming power of television, lost no chance to slash at any symbol of TV's shallowness.

Sometimes TV's own people handed critics the swords to flail away. Charles Kurault, CBS's teller of sweet stories from America's small towns, spoke to the Radio and TV News Directors Association one year. He told them about traveling the country in search of stories. He said it had given him the chance to watch local TV news in city after city.

"The broadcast news business," Kurault told these news directors, "is riddled with glib, highly-paid poseurs who wouldn't last two weeks as cub reporters on a local newspaper. I am ashamed that, thirty years into the television age, so many of our anchormen haven't any basis on which to make a news judgment, can't edit, can't write, and can't cover a story."

For the most part, he said, people who succeed in TV news do so "not by being good, but by being pretty." He said that virtually all of the local news programs he watched across the country had one thing in common.

Hair.

"That's what I've noticed most," he said. "Hair. Hair carefully styled and sprayed, hair neatly parted, hair abundant and every hair in place. But I can't remember that much came out from beneath all that hair. I remember the style, but not the substance. And I fear that the reason may be that there wasn't much substance there."

He mentioned Ted Baxter. "I can't watch the *Mary Tyler Moore Show*," he said, "without a shudder of recognition. I know that sensible, professional news director who's terrified of what his idiot anchorman might say next. I know that anchorman, in love with himself and his image, who wouldn't know a news story if it jumped up and mussed up his hair."

Jerry Turner never seemed like one of those guys, nor did his co-anchor, Al Sanders. They seemed intelligent and mature and aware of actual news. Other anchors did not. In my newspaper column—before I took the TV job—I would point out local anchor idiocy when it was irresistible.

Once, Baltimore had been stunned by snowball killings: suburban teenage boys taunting an elderly man and his wife, pelting their home with snowballs and breaking their front windows, until the poor old man inside, Roman Welzant, reached for a gun and killed one of the boys.

Welzant was charged with murder, but a jury called it self-defense and acquitted him. Rich Hollander, a reporter for WBAL-TV, the NBC affiliate, reported the verdict live from the courthouse. Then he threw it back to the studio. WBAL's co-anchor, Mike Hambrick, handled it there.

"The verdict is not guilty," Hollander reported.

"Rich, will there be an appeal?" Hambrick inquired.

Uh...by whom?

By Welzant, perhaps wishing he could go to prison instead of seeing his pathetic plight validated? By the prosecution? Surely a man of Hambrick's official stature—and surely most adult citizens—understood that you can't re-try a person just declared not guilty.

Hollander, grasping for a way to explain that there are no appeals by prosecutors, but not wanting to make his anchorman look too air-headed in front of thousands of viewers, explained that, of course, there is no double jeopardy in American jurisprudence.

"All right," Hambrick said, nodding somberly, as though this arcane point of criminal justice met with his distinguished approval. "Thank you for that report."

It wasn't entirely Hambrick's fault. He was just one of those young men who had become an anchor because of a deep voice and shellacked hair, and considered a good barber the extent of his professional needs.

Meanwhile, WMAR tried various disguises to make themselves look like a serious news operation. For a while, the on-air news set included a couple of rows of reporters sitting at their desks directly behind the anchors. The reporters had telephones and pens and paper on the desks. The idea was to make it look like a working newsroom where exciting stories were still being pieced together as viewers looked on.

The problem was, by air-time, almost all the real work had been done. So all these reporters, forced by management decree to remain at their desks for the entire program, had nothing to do but sit there for an hour and pretend to be occupied. As the unblinking camera looked on, self-consciousness became the rule of the day. When enough of them complained, management sent a memo offering advice: "Call your mothers or write letters to boyfriends. Just look busy." Appearance was all.

Often, these news anchors were not helped much by their own stations' promotional ads. In one spot, WBAL's Hambrick was seen spraying his hair. Some of the spray got in his eye. This was intended as self-deprecating humor. It was an acknowledgment that Hambrick was stiff; he was cold. The spot gave him a "regular guy" look.

Did it have anything to do with news? Nobody at his station cared. They were selling personalities. If people bought the personality, they could overlook such blunders as the courthouse questioning after the snowball-killing verdict.

One of Hambrick's co-anchors was Stan Stovall, who was a conscientious body builder in his off-hours. WBAL built an advertising campaign around this. Edward R. Murrow turned in his grave. In one promo, Stovall could be seen wearing a loincloth and lifting weights. A voice-over declared, "Stan Stovall is one of the strongest newsmen in the country. He pulls his weight—and then some." As a medium declared its own dumbbell mentality, Murrow turned again.

Before I joined the TV business, I delighted in writing about such nonsense in my newspaper column. Partly, it was an act of self-defense. If television was the wave of the future, I had to shovel some sand to stave off the tide.

Millions of people whose post-work rituals once included a contemplative journey through the home-town afternoon newspaper now had new habits. Instead of reading, they turned on the tube. Instead of Walter Lippmann's ponderings, they had NBC's Chet Huntley and David Brinkley, or CBS's Cronkite and Eric Sevareid. The generation that had survived World War II and Korea now watched Vietnam erupting before their very eyes each night on the television. Who needed columns of print explaining the war when there were real soldiers slogging through real jungles right before your eyes?

Everybody told my generation the future was visual, and the written word passe. Those of us who still believed in print had our hopes lifted when a couple of young *Washington Post* reporters, Carl Bernstein and Bob Woodward, unearthed Richard Nixon's Watergate scandal. Maybe newspapers were still important. Maybe the kids coming up behind us would realize the importance of serious reporting and start subscribing to newspapers and, not coincidentally, save a generation of newspaper people's careers.

I was still working at the *News American* during the Watergate scandal. The night Nixon resigned, about a dozen of us worked long past midnight to put together a special edition. This was where we belonged; this work was the way we defined ourselves. We were newspaper reporters, and we wanted to spend this moment of history doing something we would remember.

Nobody wanted to go home. Finally, with nothing left to do until morning, a group of us walked through the damp night air to Burke's Tavern a few blocks from the paper.

We weren't kidding ourselves. We knew we hadn't contributed anything important to the coverage. We were there that night to offer local reaction, and analysis, and hoped to contribute in some small way to a moment in history. But there was something else shadowing the moment.

"You know what bothers me?" said an editor named Lou Linley. He was big and beefy and muttered into his beer. "I'm afraid, years from now, I'll tell my grandchildren, 'I helped put out the newspaper the night Nixon resigned.'"

"And they'll say, 'Who's Nixon?'" I said.

"Nah," Linley said. "They'll say, 'What's a newspaper?'"

Then everybody stopped talking for a while. It felt as if we were riding a dinosaur during its final death twitches. TV seemed to be striking at us like some great meteorite that would obliterate us all. So every time I criticized TV in the newspaper, I felt I was implicitly reminding readers: This is where you get the real stuff. Pay no attention to those actors in your living room.

Also, I wrote these columns because TV news, by its own comic qualities, seemed to welcome it. When the Stovall weight-lifter ad appeared, I called Malcolm Potter, WBAL's general manager, and asked him to defend it.

"Viewers watch news for lots of reasons," Potter said. "Some watch it for the content, some because they like the people who deliver the news. We think we have nice people, and we want viewers to know it."

Potter was throwing it in my face. Yes, he was saying, we know that the news itself is only part of the show—and what are you going to do about it?

WJZ played the same game. In its promos, Jerry Turner comforted a child in a hospital bed. (The cameras just happened to be there at the time.) Al Sanders stood on a pier next to a tugboat while a voice declared, "Hard working people pulling the world within reach for you." Richard Sher and Oprah Winfrey, the noon anchors, cavorted with a troupe of ethnic dancers. "That's what friends are for," the commercials said.

But what were reporters for? Were they there to be our friends, or to bring us the news? At TV news operations across the country, the answer was a mix.

And now, on my first night at WJZ, I stood there in the newsroom with my face all made up, attempting to become a part of this process that I found so objectionable.

I looked around the newsroom and checked the clock every few seconds. Only a few people were there. Most reporters had taped their stories and gone home for the night. Technical people had moved down the hall to the control room, with its huge board of electronic buttons and monitors. Turner and Al Sanders were taking last-second looks at their copy.

As he walked past me to head down the hall to the studio, Turner patted me on the shoulder. "Keep one thing in mind," he said. "Be yourself. If you try to be somebody else, they see right through it. And they resent it."

Sanders was a few steps behind him. "You'll be fine," he said. He winked at me and kept going.

I was a little worried Sanders might have held a grudge against me. Several years earlier, when I was doing investigative stories at the *News American*, a reporter named Joe Nawrozki and I wrote a series about the Baltimore police intelligence unit. The police commissioner, Donald Pomerleau, had turned the unit into his own private force. He had undercover cops spy on a long list of people for arbitrary political reasons. One of the names on the list was Sanders.

When I confronted the commissioner, he said he'd had Sanders tailed "to find out who his sources are." I called Sanders to ask about it. I'd never spoken to him before. When I told him about the list, and Pomerleau's response, he seemed astonished.

"Sources?" he said. "I haven't got any sources."

"You don't?" I said.

"No, of course not," he said. "I know that's a terrible thing for a reporter to say, but I don't. I stick a microphone in front of people, and they talk into a camera and we put them on the air, and those are the only people I talk to."

He was still a street reporter, and honest enough to admit the obvious: TV news made its mark with pictures, not with digging beneath the surface of things. There was nothing covert about it. It was all image: the distraught mother crying over her teenage son killed in a drug deal, followed by those nice anchors offering words of comfort before the commercial pitch from a local Chevy dealer.

By the time I started working at WJZ, and Sanders was Turner's co-anchor, the station's ratings were about as dominating as any local news operation in the country. Sanders was the perfect television partner. Turner was suave; Sanders was gracious and comforting. Turner bopped when the moment called for it; Sanders made fun of his own weight. Turner was serious for the hard news; Sanders clearly led with his heart. And, most visible of all, Turner was white and Sanders was black.

Psychologically, these were still the post-riot years in Baltimore. The city still recalled the fire and rage after Martin Luther King's assassination. What followed the riots was a different kind of upheaval: thousands of people, mostly white, moving out of the city to suburbia; the public schools emptying of all but a small number of white children; the city, once majority-white, becoming two-thirds black; and racial considerations touching everything.

In such an atmosphere, the sight of two men working together, and clearly enjoying each other, seemed to symbolize calmer possibilities. Maybe we could work things out. When the station ran promotional spots of the two men, they never involved news; it was Jerry getting coffee for Al, and Al getting coffee for Jerry, and the two of them delighted that they'd simultaneously attempted to surprise each other in the same way.

Both on the air and off, what seemed to matter to the two men wasn't race, but the things they had in common. They were contemporaries who enjoyed the traditional manly pleasures of their generation: sports, good music, a good smoke, and a good drink. To talk about race was an annoyance—you were either a man, or you weren't; you were dependable, or you weren't. This was something to build on. To watch them was to enjoy the comfort they took from each other and imagine it as a role model for the whole town.

Sanders had grown up in St. Louis, where his name was Al Gay. "I knew, real early, that I'd be changing that name," he would joke. He graduated Harris Teachers College in St. Louis and worked in radio. Scoop Sanders he called himself for a while. He had a presence on the air: gentle, mature, non-threatening in a time of racial unease. In Baltimore, his best stories tugged at the emotions. He won an Emmy for a feature story on the family of a child born without a brain. He did a sensitive series on welfare troubles. Jerry Turner thought he was terrific and wanted him as a partner. The only problem was, Turner already had a partner. Her name was Oprah Winfrey.

Long before she became America's Sweetheart, Oprah was brought to Baltimore because executives at WJZ understood the medium was changing. As they expanded their evening newscast from thirty minutes to an hour, it was too much for one person to anchor the entire program. Since Jerry Turner was white, his co-anchor should be black. And, since Turner was male, his co-anchor should be female. It did not matter that Oprah Winfrey of Memphis, Tennessee, knew nothing about Baltimore, or that she was only twenty-four years old, or that she had almost no reporting experience. For television news, she was perfect.

But the deck was stacked against her. Even before she hit town, WJZ ran a childish series of promotional spots, asking, "Do you know what an Oprah is?"

"Ofrey?" the people in the commercial would answer.

"Ofrah? What's an Ofrah?"

In hindsight, no one could imagine CBS introducing its anchor years earlier by asking, "Do you know what a Cronkite is?" The spots demeaned Oprah and the entire notion of news anchors as serious figures.

To make matters worse, there were the implied professional slights to everyone around Oprah. Reporters who had struggled for years for an anchor position resented being passed over, and resented all the attention she was getting. But they resented her quietly. Television is a nervous business. There are too many people for too few jobs. The men who'd brought in Oprah also had control over everybody else's jobs. In television, all on-air people have personal-service contracts, which can be dropped every few years So, rather than aim their anger at management types, critics aimed at Oprah.

Then it got worse for her. Management thought her nose was too flat, and her eyes too wide apart, and her chin too large. It seemed to mean nothing that she'd just competed for Miss Black America. They wanted to change her hair and her style of speaking. It was amazing. They'd hired this woman they obviously liked, and then tried to change her to somebody she wasn't. They sent her to New York for a special hair treatment. Her hair ended up in the stylist's basin. She returned to Baltimore with her head wrapped in a scarf and her confidence utterly shattered.

One day she sat in the newsroom and looked toward heaven. Then she intoned comically, "I don't know why it happened, Lord, but I know you've got a reason."

When she was paired publicly with Jerry Turner, Baltimore practically had municipal cardiac arrest. Here was this young woman from Nashville, introduced to viewers previously accustomed to inviting only the elegant Turner into their homes. The chemistry never clicked for a moment.

He was forty-nine; she was a quarter-century younger. He was the perfect combination of authority figure and next-door neighbor. She was a stranger who knew nothing about Baltimore. He was a gentleman of the old school, a touch of the southern patrician figure, but with working class empathy. He was friendly, but also protective of his stature as Baltimore's reigning anchor.

Oprah was open and ebullient. She wore her hair in an Afro. She was self-mocking and ingenuous and eager to be liked. In the newsroom one day, she was asked, "Did you go for the Miss Black America title?"

It was a little test. If she boasted about it, she had no sense of nuance. If she joked, she understood she was in a business where everyone had an ego.

"Yeah, honey," Oprah laughed, putting a hand on a hip, "but I've got the black woman's behind. It's a disease God inflicted on the black women of America."

She had an unpretentiousness that should have translated across the airwaves but did not. For all her free spirit off the air, a curtain descended when the camera turned on. She and Turner seemed to sit in separate studios instead of two feet from each other. They barely made eye contact. In the world of local TV news, where viewers consider you their neighbor as well as their reporter, this went over dreadfully. Many, intensely loyal to Turner, sensed the stiffness on the air, took sides, flipped the dial. The drop in ratings sent a chill through the executive offices at WJZ. Somebody would eventually have to take the fall.

Then came the clincher. The critics call it Happy Talk and the TV people call it cross talk, but everybody knows what it is: the little ad lib patter between anchors. It is supposed to be a relaxed look at the people who bring the news, calculated to make those at home feel part of the extended-family intimacy.

One night, Oprah joked on the air that Jerry was old enough to be her father. She meant it to be amusing. Nobody thought it was, especially Jerry. This woman had to go. When she showed up that Friday morning, she was called into the general manager's office.

"You're not anchoring any more," he said. "Starting Monday, you'll do the five a.m. cut-ins."

When the morning cut-ins were finished, Oprah would handle the noon news. Her natural ebullience disappeared. Reporters leaving the building would find her sitting in her car, weeping, unable to summon energy to start the engine.

Then one day, somebody got an idea. They put Oprah and Richard Sher in a room, and they talked about an idea for a morning talk show for the two of them. The talk show would one day change the culture of American television.

The one who replaced Oprah as co-anchor, at Jerry Turner's insistence, was Al Sanders.

"You'll be fine," Sanders said now. I looked up as he and Turner headed from the newsroom to the big studio down the hall. For the next forty minutes, I sat in the newsroom and waited to be summoned. I felt like a man awaiting surgery I looked at my script every twelve seconds or so, attempting to commit it to memory in case the TelePrompTer decided to break down.

I told myself it would be all right. I'd written my first piece about a kid named Leon. I'd met him that day at Calhoun and Baker streets, in West Baltimore, standing outside Douglas

High School. I asked why he wasn't inside. Leon said he was running a little late for school. It was two in the afternoon. He shuffled between foster homes, and nobody particularly cared about him, and the city had thousands of kids like this. It was also a city with the highest school dropout rate in the country, and the public schools seemed utterly bewildered about reaching them.

I figured it wasn't a bad piece. It had a few facts and figures, and it was personalized and passionate, and it covered an important subject. About forty minutes into the show, an executive producer, Eileen Fredman, nodded to me and said pleasantly, "Why don't you head in there now?"

After that, it was pretty simple. I sat next to Turner, who introduced me as the station's newest addition. I talked about Leon and the schools, and in ninety seconds it was over and we went to a commercial break.

I walked out of the studio feeling huge relief. I'd gotten through it alive. I felt I had talked about an important social issue to a large audience. I was reminding them about young people in trouble, about lost potential, about the crisis in the schools.

When I got back to the newsroom, a couple of people said I'd been fine. Then they handed me a packet of material. Routine stuff, they said. I didn't look at it right away. I headed for my car feeling pretty good.

I thought: I can make TV news a little more serious than it's been.

I thought: I'm doing something important in the life of the community.

I thought: There's not such a big difference between newspapers and television. We're both trying to do the same thing. We're trying to inform the public, and keep alive a healthy flow of information.

When I got to my car, I opened the packet they'd given me. Routine stuff, indeed. It was pages of type-written instructions, prepared for the station by the Frank N. Magid consulting firm. It was all about being an effective television news person.

One set of instructions was titled "Hair for TV News."

The other was titled "Makeup for TV News."

It was TV's way of saying "This is the make-up of a real reporter."

4

Reporting from Baghdad

It goes on.

Night after night, across the Persian Gulf War in the winter of 2003, the bombing and the pretending goes on. The bombing is real, but the local television coverage is strictly pretending. It pretends to an intimacy, and an expertise, it does not have. I think of Edward R. Murrow, reporting live for CBS from the rooftops of London during the Blitz. In Iraq, buildings are blown away, and WJZ pretends they have special, close-up insights. I think of Charles Collingwood, reporting for CBS from the littered beaches at Normandy on D-Day. In the Persian gulf, countless lives are lost, and WJZ implies that its own people are all over the story. No local broadcast operation, in the midst of World War II, would have taken the words of Murrow or Collingwood, and inserted the voices of its own reporters.

But something has happened in modern broadcasting, which is the extension of the thing that started in my last years at WJZ, when the general manager Jay Newman turned a broadcast covering local news into a program that pretended to cover international events—events about which its own reporters knew nothing more than any other citizens and did not leave the building to find out what it did not yet know.

In the aftermath of the September 11 terrorist attacks, Newman came down from his office and moved all over the newsroom. He trotted out his biggest guns. He sent his news anchors to front for stories about which all reporting, all interviewing and analyzing and photographing, and all personal endangerment, had been borne by reporters half a world away. And he attempted to let WJZ take implicit credit for it.

Night after night the station's anchors delivered ten-second live introductions to video packages prepared by network correspondents. The audio version of those network video tapes was removed, as was all reference to the original reporters. And the voices of WJZ's anchors were inserted—in the parlance, "retracked"—over the original reports. Whose actual language was used in the retracking? The original reporter's language, which was now magically transformed into the voices of WJZ's anchors.

One after another they stood there, first Denise Koch and then Vic Carter, and then Sally Thorner and Kai Jackson. Each one was said to have been "following events" in the Middle East. The implication was WJZ is involved; *Eyewitness News* has its own people working all angles of the troubles. But they never left the building, never picked up a telephone to pursue a source or did any manner of reporting beyond mouthing someone else's work.

Sometimes it wasn't just the anchors who were forced into this charade. Sometimes, if big stories broke inconveniently, street reporters accustomed to covering traffic backups or robberies found themselves pressed into action to report the latest they had "learned" about events in the Middle East.

"Look at this, it's like a bus station," Richard Sher muttered one night after he had been pressed into last-moment service on a terrorist bombing in Kenya. "They call out your name and say, 'Let's go, we need you to jump on this one.'"

One night when I still worked at WJZ, I sat in the

newsroom and watched the usual process. Having finished her five o'clock anchoring duties, Sally Thorner left the studio and strode down the hall into the newsroom, where she called out, "Do we have copy?"

"I'm writing it for you now," an executive producer, Mitch Friedmann, called back.

A moment later, as Thorner slipped on a microphone and stationed herself in front of a newsroom camera, Denise Koch announced from her six o'clock anchor desk that there was breaking news from Baghdad, "and Sally Thorner has the full story." Thorner, though she had just finished anchoring the five o'clock, now stood in the busy newsroom as though she might have gotten off the phone with Middle East sources only a moment ago. She then voiced-over a video package from Baghdad, replacing the previously recorded sound of some network reporter's original story.

When she finished, she threw the coverage back to Koch in the studio, took off her microphone and walked toward a couple of reporters sitting nearby in the newsroom.

"What's new?" she asked. The war was already behind her.

"Back from Baghdad already, Sally?" asked reporter Tim Williams, smiling puckishly. Thorner looked confused. Was there a joke? Of course she hadn't been to Baghdad. She read words that were typed for her in a TelePrompter. This was the way things were done. Sally had reported the news on the television. Therefore, she was a reporter. Williams, not wanting to argue with Thorner, shook his head: Let it go, nothing important.

But it was and it went beyond the nightly charade. By devoting so much of its time and manpower to its second-hand coverage of events in the Middle East, the station was utterly neglecting its primary mission: covering the news in its own community. Local stories, when covered at all, were now reduced to fifteen-second blurbs boiled down from wire copy. The Baltimore metropolitan area had become an inconvenient afterthought as the station attempted to make itself look worldly and plugged in during overseas tensions.

And there was no journalistic reason for the subterfuge.

CBS, WJZ's network parent, had a hundred correspondents dispatched to the war, according to newspaper accounts, feeding stories back to all its affiliates throughout each day. (NBC reportedly had 125, and ABC had as many as 200 in the region.)

In an honest broadcast of the war, WJZ's anchors would have said, "CBS's reporter has filed this story..." Or they would have cut back the coverage, allowed CBS (or any of the cable news stations) to handle the war, and given local viewers a look at local news, for which the station had at least a modicum of expertise.

But they didn't do it that way.

This wasn't about the war; it was about WJZ's involvement in the war. It wasn't about America responding to international terrorism; it was about getting viewers to identify WJZ, and not some other station, with the coverage of that terrorism.

It was about theater.

And that sense of theater had been years in the making, and I remembered backstage glances I had gotten long before I entered the business. And I began to connect yesterday with today.

I was a student at the University of Maryland when the country was coming apart. You could see it on the network television news each night. In the South, demonstrators for racial fairness went up against police who had snarling dogs and fire hoses. With each police dog, with each act of violence, a nation watching what it had previously never seemed to notice now tuned in and chose sides.

Meanwhile, from Vietnam, we saw men blown to bits on our television sets. We watched the bodies carried away on the nightly news while eating our dinner. At colleges across the country, students demonstrated against the war and the

Selective Service system that was reaching onto campuses. This conflict, too, could be seen on the nightly newscasts.

But none of this drama, in my time, came out of College Park. The unofficial campus slogan was "Support apathy." Nobody seemed to care enough to organize a protest. There was a half-assed Students for Democratic Society table in the Student Union, but whenever I walked past it, there was no sense of the SDS anti-war explosiveness like other campuses.

And then, for a moment, this changed.

I saw it change one afternoon as I walked through the Student Union on the way to class. There was a crowd at the SDS hallway table. There were loud, angry words about the war in Vietnam. The confrontation seemed familiar, though I'd never seen it here. It was the same scene I'd watched repeatedly on the television news: angry college kids confronting each other about the war.

Then, on the edge of the crowd, I spotted a television camera crew. One of the Washington stations had assigned a story on campus unrest. The TV crew came to nearby College Park and instinctively went to the SDS table for type-casting. As the little crowd increased, so did passions. It looked like the things seen on so many nights on so many network telecasts, which had served as dress rehearsals. Here was the chance for these kids to act out their own parts for the camera.

The great debate lasted as long as five minutes.

Then the television camera was turned off, and so was a bright television light. The camera crew, having gotten the drama they wanted, went away. The cries of the crowd died immediately. In moments, the SDS area was empty, and I never saw another such debate on campus unless cameras hovered nearby.

Something was in the air that nobody had fully anticipated. It wasn't just a country going into political convulsions, but the eye of the television camera watching it, and sometimes egging it on. Television was making two enormous discoveries in this time: new electronic gizmos to make transmission easier and faster, and the huge sums of money to be made by producing relatively cheap news programs and weaving advertising through them.

But it was already becoming a business that sometimes caused the news to happen. They turned on a camera and brought out every passion (or every latent exhibitionist) within its range—and did not know what to do once they had made this discovery, except exploit it.

In April of 1968, in the aftermath of Martin Luther King's assassination, there were riots in scores of American cities as black people heaved off generations of pent-up rage. At the *News American*, where I worked by then, all available reporters were sent into the streets and police stations and courthouses for four days and nights to write about the massive looting and arson and killing. The smart reporters also connected it to the history of injustice and cruelty that had preceded it.

But something else was going on, involving the coverage of these calamities.

On the third night of the riots, the *News American's* city editor, Eddie Ballard, sent me to a street near West Baltimore's Pennsylvania Avenue where a building had been set afire and an allegedly angry crowd was gathered.

"See what's going on," Ballard said. He was a former police reporter who had worked his way up. He had Eisenhower's round face and a cigarette hanging from his lower lip.

I was twenty-two years old and too stupid to feel threatened. When I got to the street, I saw what looked like an empty storage building afire. Neighborhood residents, all of them black, sat on nearby front steps and passively watched the thing burn. Nobody moved from their steps; nobody expressed any emotions when I got out of my car. There was no volatile crowd. These people were exhausted and emotionally drained by three days and nights of violence.

As I walked along the sidewalk a few people looked at me, but nobody moved. We watched the fire together. In a few moments, a TV news van pulled up. A cameraman and a fellow holding a bright light got out of the car. As they pointed the camera at the burning building, people rose from their front steps.

"Burn, baby, burn," yelled a man heaving a rock toward the fire.

A few others, shaking off their own lethargy, joined him. They were acting out the thing they had seen so many times on television in the previous days and nights. They were getting their little piece of the action. Now more people heaved rocks and bottles at the flames, and more called out epithets, and the air was charged with something that resembled rage.

This lasted until the TV camera and the light turned off. Some people, about to heave rocks at the fire, stopped in mid-throw as the light died. They went back to their front steps and sat down as the TV crew pulled away and calmly watched the building turn to embers. And so it went in the televised riots of 1968.

In the face of this, newspapers had to dig deeper into the meaning of it all. It wasn't enough just to tell what was happening. TV could get to the story and tell it long before we could. They just had to set up a camera and microphone. We had to get back to the paper, write the story, put it through printing presses, load it onto trucks, and send the trucks out for deliveries when the next edition came out.

But we could explain what some of it meant. And we could investigate things that the TV people couldn't (or wouldn't) take the time to investigate.

For a couple of years, reporter Joe Nawrozki and I had a pretty good run of investigative stories. Sometimes we dug for weeks before we wrote anything. We sifted through records, and worked sources, and pieced things together. Years later, when I listened each night as television news boasted of such things as "Eyewitness News Investigates," I wanted to reach for their throats for cheapening such a notion.

Even in my investigative reporting days, in the 1970s, television was reaching for its own parasitic cut of the action. Once, while I investigated a federal law enforcement agency, I took a telephone call from a source in the agency's intelligence unit. He mentioned an attorney we both knew.

"You talked with her today," my source said.

"I did?" I said. I'd had a lot of conversations that day.

"Just before noon," he said.

"How do you know?" I said.

He recited my conversation to me. He said the federal agency was upset with the stories I had been writing, and wanted to know who was talking to me. So they put a wiretap—unauthorized, illegal—on my phone. My source was there when they did it. This was an era of considerable federal abuse of electronic eavesdropping equipment, and congressional hearings investigating such abuses, and when I wrote the story about my wiretap, the *News American* ran it on the front page and newspapers around the country picked it up.

Also, ABC-TV sent reporter Frank Reynolds to Baltimore to interview me for the national news—and the *News American*, delighted over national publicity, encouraged me to cooperate. Reynolds and a photo crew arrived late in the afternoon, when the paper's final afternoon edition had already been put to bed for the day. This did not matter. When the ABC photographer scanned the newsroom, all kinds of remarkable things began to happen.

Reporters whose stories had already been filed suddenly threw fresh sheets of paper into their typewriters and typed as if fighting deadline pressure. Actual words did not matter. The paper's business editor left his office to scan the financial wires for the first time in years; it happened to be located directly where the TV camera was pointing. One reporter leaned over a nearby desk to get into camera range, gestured dramatically, walked away and then circled back to the same spot. Other reporters picked up telephones and talked into them while taking notes. No one was on the other end of those telephone lines.

Then, hearing that the famous Reynolds was in the building, an advertising layout woman who worked one floor above the editorial offices came bounding into the room. She shouted, "Where is he? Where's Burt Reynolds?"

And these were people of a certain sophistication. Many of them had been around television cameras in pursuit of stories. But here was a chance to be seen across the country—and they wanted to be seen doing what people in a newspaper office are supposed to be doing.

When Frank Reynolds sat me down to answer questions, I tried to focus on the wiretap. Important issues were at stake. So was my reputation. Words came out of my mouth, but my brain was preoccupied.

Later I wondered: If I was so disheveled at such a moment, what is the power of a television camera for people who are not accustomed to it?

And what is the power of that theater for those who are watching it?

5

The Lady and Her Bird

By the time I arrived at WJZ, the station had dominated the local ratings competition for about a decade. Baltimoreans talked about Jerry Turner and Al Sanders as though they were members of their own households. But there were important supporting players, remarkable because they constituted not so much a staff of reporters as a cast of characters, each playing a well-defined theatrical role in a continuing dramatic series.

The thinkers at the station understood something. It was generally unrelated to traditional journalism, but had plenty to do with the new television style of journalism, which was inventing itself as it went along: Viewers want people to root for. In the midst of daily fears and frustrations about the world around them, they want familiarity, which breeds comfort and then trust. Television asks viewers to commit an act of intimacy, inviting characters into living rooms and bedrooms each night. In making such a gesture, who needs strangers?

Behind Turner and Sanders was a weather man, Bob Turk, designated for advertising purposes as the Sunshine Kid, who could have been anyone's good-natured younger brother or cocker spaniel. Turk got the job by walking off the street and auditioning. He had no previous experience with weather-casting, but so what? The best known weather act in Baltimore was the team at WBAL-TV, Rhea Feikin and her partner. The partner was a puppet called J.P. The puppet knew as much about the weather as Feikin, who knew nothing at all. (Is that hurricane heading our way? Let's wait for the puppet to tell us.)

Turk was an outdoors type, and he was likable. He had grown up in suburban Baltimore and worked for a while for local government. He had a wide Jerry Colonna mustache and a high-pitched laugh, and a pet dog he'd bring on the air occasionally. Unlike the puppet J.P., the dog did not attempt to forecast the weather. But he helped establish Turk's image: Bob was kind to real animals. He was nice; he was solid.

In this, he contrasted with the station's sportscaster, John Buren, who wore Hawaiian shirts and broadcast his teases from a "Sports Palace" office decorated in a miracle of Elvis Presley memorabilia, tabloid newspaper front pages, and kitschy sports artifacts. Buren saw sports as a good-time lark and not a series of religious rituals. He played it mainly as a joke. Sometimes he seemed like Bill Murray doing his "Saturday Night Live" lounge lizard bit. He preferred running video of a geek dropping a pop-up to a Cal Ripken home run.

"I don't do sports," he would say to those who complained. "I do television." During each football season, he invited Hall of Famer Artie Donovan in for weekly on-air sessions. But Donovan was a good-natured raconteur as likely to talk about funny characters as he was to discuss football. And, as a throwback to the glory days of the Baltimore Colts, he was a reminder to viewers: This is the hometown station.

"Artie makes Baltimore feel good about itself," Buren said. Every Friday, he had the good sense to introduce the big buffalo, and then get out of the way. Donovan charmed viewers for more than a decade before the arrival of the tone-deaf general manager Jay Newman.

On his own, Buren arrived on the set each night carrying his written copy, his comb and brush, and a pocket mirror, which he propped in front of himself during the commercial break while he went through various ministrations. First came fastidious attention to his eyebrows and eyelashes. Then, the ritual combing of his hair.

"My hair," he would announce on occasion, "is my life."

It was quite laughable, except for this: what everyone else did in the privacy of a dressing room, Buren did in front of others. He'd been around the block a few times—nine stations before he hit Baltimore: five months in Roanoke, then on to Raleigh-Durham, then six weeks in Norfolk, then stopovers in Lynchburg, Evansville, Washington, D.C., Atlanta, and San Francisco. He understood what the business was about and ran with it. All guilty concerns over vanity, he wore on his sleeve.

He wore his opinions there, too—at least, when he was off the air. He thought professional athletes were generally idiots, and avoided them whenever possible. When Baltimore tried to get an expansion pro football franchise, Buren sat in a chair just off-camera and whispered a desperate prayer: "Please don't let it be Baltimore, please don't let it be Baltimore." If Baltimore got a new team, it meant more work, that was all. When the city later landed the Cleveland Browns and turned them into the Baltimore Ravens, he was happy the station didn't make him cover road games.

One day, rumors surfaced that a local businessman was trying to land a pro basketball team for Baltimore. I figured Buren would dread the thought.

"Nah," he said, "no trouble. The league sets up all the interviews before games. There's nothing for anchors to do."

"What about going on the road?" I asked.

"Are you kidding?" he said. "They don't send me on the road to cover the defending Super Bowl champs. You think they're gonna send me to cover a bunch of overgrown carjackers?"

When the Baltimore Orioles hired Davey Johnson to manage the club, Buren's on-camera interview included this question: "What about those drinking rumors, Davey?"

He lasted sixteen years at WJZ with such an attitude—despite lots of complaining from viewers.

"I like the complaints," said Natalea Brown, the news director through Buren's early years there. "We want viewers to like some of you and hate some of you. That means they're talking about you."

Buren was half of the station's team of two sports reporters, a standard number for most local television operations. (Newspapers have considerably more. The *Baltimore Sun*, for example, had sixty-five people on its sports staff at that time.)

"And anyway," said Natalea Brown, "who cares about sports?" The station's surveys said less than ten percent of its viewers tuned in specifically for sports. And this was before the time of ESPN and cable's saturation sports coverage, where the serious sports fans could turn.

Also included in the WJZ cast was an elder statesman, George Bauman, who had lived in Baltimore his whole life and handled whatever occasional political news the station deigned to carry. But politics was devalued because it contained so little visible blood.

There was Frank Luber, who had been a radio announcer on the city's big rock-and-roll station and thus arrived with name recognition. One producer referred to Luber as "The Happy Rotarian," a Baltimore guy who grew up and made it in front of the home folks. There was Marty Bass, a feature reporter/weather man who wore a toupee because consultants told him he had to, and one day took it off without the world coming to its end. There was Richard Sher, all over the place with his "People Are Talking" show with Oprah Winfrey, his noon news anchoring, his "Square-Off" public affairs show, and his nightly homicide stories.

And there was Maria Broom. She joined the station in the mid-1970s, just before Oprah Winfrey, and was an instant sensation. Never before had a black woman appeared on any Baltimore news program. But her background provides part of the strange casting process of local TV news across the country. Broom was hired to be a television reporter without possessing an ounce of reporting background. Why? Because, in television news, journalism has always been considered optional.

Broom grew up in Baltimore and attended Morgan State University as a dance major. She won a Fulbright scholarship and studied dance in Berlin. When she came home, she worked as a stewardess for Pan Am Airlines. She happened to be in Miami when a news crew from WPLG-TV boarded her plane for a story on airport security. They wanted to interview the captain and a stewardess.

"You ever do any television?" the TV reporter asked her.

"No, I'm really a dancer," she replied.

The TV reporter was black. In that time, stations were just beginning to hire blacks, but WPLG's token black female had just taken a job in Chicago. There was an opening. Nobody said it was an opening for a black, but everybody knew that it was.

"Think about it," the reporter said.

The piece on airport security went network. The station's news director liked what he saw in Broom's interview. She was pretty and smart. And she was black. He called and offered her a job.

"No, no," she said, "I'm a dancer."

"We'll train you to be a reporter," the news director said. "Give us three months and we'll have you on the air."

The money was good. Broom decided to take a chance. The full training, such as it was, took one week instead of three months. Then she was on the air, a dancer-cum-airline hostess passing for a reporter. She found out it was not like studying for brain surgery. A few months later, full of confidence, she went home to Baltimore and applied for a job at WJZ.

At her interview, she would remember years later, she was asked, "Did you major in journalism?"

"No," she said.

"Did you study it?"

"No."

"Can you write?"

"No."

"No?"

"Not really. But I can read."

That meant something. Shortly after Broom's arrival at WJZ, competitor WBAL hired a young woman named Sue Simmons. She stuck around for a few years and then went to New York's WNBC, where she would anchor the evening news for the next few decades. When she left Baltimore, a reporter asked what her strengths were. Simmons had no illusions.

"I'm pretty, and I can read," she said.

Maria Broom had matching abilities. "I still had very limited skills," she recalled years later. "But I was black, and I had a nice bush. It was a time of big Afros. I was a picture of the modern black woman. So it was like a movie. They said, 'We're going to make you a star,' and then they did."

When Broom was beginning to make it big, I was writing newspaper pieces about Maryland's prisons. You could go into any institution and find countless inmates with Broom's picture in their cells. They cut them out of *TV Guide* and *Ebony* and *Jet*, magazines where the station had taken out advertisements promoting their new star.

Billboards around town proclaimed, "Viva Maria." Viewers who hadn't yet figured out the nomenclature approached her, crying, "Hey, Viva." The station called her segment "People Power." The billboards, with a smiling Maria peering down, declared, "Now Baltimore has someone to talk to. Viva Maria."

"I was what they gave the black people," she said, looking back. "Everybody had a niche. That was mine."

Her "People Power" unit took letters from viewers and tried to help them with manageable problems: welfare distress, faulty department store appliances, a dying youngster who wanted a basketball signed by the Harlem Globetrotters.

In Baltimore, such stories made her a folk hero. At WJZ she was part of this popular wave that was sweeping over everything. But Broom lasted only a few years. The station decided to pull her off of "People Power" for a fluffier "Feelin' Good" health segment. She decided she would rather dance. So she retired from TV news and spent the next quarter-century as a dance teacher in Baltimore and an actress on HBO's *The Corner* and *The Wire.*

When I got there, *Eyewitness News* was going strong but the grumbling could be heard off-stage. When the ratings arrived every few months, they showed the station with massive numbers and its competitors, WBAL and WMAR, panting to stay within sight. There were newsroom parties whenever the ratings came out, catered buffet lunches with bubbly talk of good times for all.

I had never seen such a thing in any newspaper office, and found the self-congratulation unsettling. The office was missing something at its absolute heart: a sense of understanding its job. There was nobody running the news who particularly understood news, or cared about news as the community's business. It was seen as a product. These were people who had studied television production in college, and were consumed by the daily process of producing. They were bright people— but their intelligence, and their insights, had almost nothing to do with uncovering actual news and almost everything to do with the technical business of putting together a complex electronic broadcast each night.

At WJZ, the chain of command was breathtakingly simple. There was a news director who oversaw all newsroom and technical operations and met regularly with the general manager, who oversaw the combined newsroom and business divisions. There was an assistant news director, who handled whatever work was too much for the news director to handle. There was an executive producer for each news program, who oversaw the work of the shows' producers.

Editorially, that was it.

In my time in newspapers, I worked for a series of editors who had one thing in common: they worked their way through the ranks as journalists, covering stories, cultivating sources, learning about the various neighborhoods and police districts and school systems.

If these editors had a problem with something I wrote, we talked about it. It was not always an easy process, but it was a civilized one in the best sense of it: We tried to think things through. Out of their sense of things, and mine, we tried to find the best version of the truth on short notice.

In my nineteen years in television news, such an editorial give-and-take did not happen even once.

I wrote my commentaries, and somebody in the newsroom with nothing else to do made certain the words showed up in the TelePrompTer at airtime.

That was it.

For nineteen years, five nights a week, there was never any discussion. Nobody in a position of editorial authority questioned anything before it went on the air. Who would question it? These were people whose background, and whose abilities and interests, simply lay elsewhere, and whose experience—in news, in television, in life—was just beginning.

Each day when I checked in with the six o'clock show's producer, I would ask, "Anything in mind?" This was a nineteen-year empty ritual. It was my way of showing a little respect for the nominal position of authority while knowing the response ahead of time. It was always the same: "Nothing here. What do you have in mind?"

The producers had other concerns. It was their job to put all the elements of the show together, to format the stories and decide how much time they would get, to coordinate reporters and photographers and handle some of the writing. Those handful of newsroom people above the producers—the news director, the assistant news director, and a couple of executive producers—had other worries.

When they heard me reading my commentaries, live, was the first they knew what I had written, what politician I was skewering, what school official's competence I was blasting, what police official's integrity I was questioning.

It is this way around the country.

Not only is there a lack of editorial control in local television news, but those in position to exercise that control have no credentials when called upon to exercise any. In a 2000-01 survey of 368 television anchors, producers and news directors, Syracuse University broadcast journalism instructor Chris Tuohey reported some stunning news about these people—producers—who handle the nuts-and-bolts newsroom decisions each day.

One respondent, news director Ellen Crooke of WNDU in South Bend, Indiana, said that key decisions on what gets covered "are in the hands of people who have very little experience in journalism...and have very little knowledge of the community and what's important and what affects people... The entire reputation and liability of your station is in the hands of somebody who just came out of school."

One respondent recalled having to convince a young Kansas City producer that the death of Frank Sinatra was a lead story, not a twenty-second voice-over in the second block of the broadcast. Another respondent simply said, "Children are producing our newscasts."

In a 1999 *American Journalism Review* piece headlined "Help Wanted: Newscast Producers," Lou Prato, a Penn State journalism professor and former TV news director, wrote, "While there's a glut of reporters fighting for jobs in TV newsrooms, there's a big help wanted sign for the less glamorous but equally important job of newscast producer. Producers are so scarce that news directors in all markets frequently hire candidates who are barely qualified."

A news director at WWMT in Kalamazoo, Michigan, Mike Rindo complained, "It's like mining for gold in a mud puddle because they're in such demand." Producers tended to move quickly to larger markets, or to find a profession that pays better.

The lack of perspective, and of history, could be stunning. One day in the newsroom I noticed two young writer-producers talking across their desks.

"Let's ask Olesker," I heard one of them say. "He'll know."

I assumed they were discussing local politics and weren't certain about a name. One of them, a woman who had graduated from Baltimore's prestigious Goucher College several years earlier and drifted into television, approached me a little shyly.

"We were talking," she said, "and we didn't know."

"Yeah?"

"When was World War II?"

The two of them were writing history that was heard on the air each evening, but somehow an entire world war had slipped out of history's march of time.

As WJZ burned away all ratings competition in Baltimore, Jerry Turner and Al Sanders basked in the glow. But off-camera they tended to fume. Slipping off the set each evening during the weather and sports segments, they would grab cigarettes, inhale deeply, and vent.

They vented about the station crushing the competition with the same night-after-night formula: a series of catastrophes punctuated by the anchors' cheerful banter. "Every night, there's nobody alive by the end of the show," Turner would say. He meant the endless string of homicide stories. It wasn't that crime was unimportant. It was the way the damned business was showcased every night, so that the program's opening fifteen minutes seemed to take on the aura of a hysterical man running down the street with his throat cut.

But there was no perspective attached to the endless blood, no attempt to look seriously at the narcotics fueling the violence, or the decayed housing and crumbling schools leading to hopelessness and rage, or the exodus of thousands of families from the city's troubled neighborhoods. The crime stories were entities unto themselves; never was there an underlying texture, never an attempt to explain what events meant—beyond the nightly minute and a half now handed over to my commentaries.

"Go out there, Mister Michael," Turner would laugh, imitating an Evangelist preacher. "Go explain to us the meaning of it all. But don't go longer than ninety seconds."

That was television's unofficial time limit. Anything beyond ninety seconds was considered a flirtation with viewers' psychological conditioning. Over years of watching television news, they'd been numbed by a procession of stories reduced to mere fractions of a minute. Fifteen seconds for school problems, thirty seconds for court decisions. To stretch a story beyond that—particularly a commentary, where there was no supporting video to hold them—was to risk losing everybody's attention, at least according to the prevailing thought.

What counted most to TV news was the look of things; what counted to WJZ was looks, plus emotion. Emotion, as much as fact, drove all stories. Late one afternoon, one of the state's largest law firms announced plans to pull up its long-time Baltimore stakes and relocate in suburbia. It meant the loss of more than a hundred jobs and considerable city prestige, and seemed a troubling symbol in a time when businesses were deserting downtown Baltimore at a frightening pace.

That same afternoon, though, a telephone tip arrived about a Howard County woman whose parakeet had flown the coop some weeks earlier. The woman could be seen each day, standing on her deck, whistling and singing for the bird's return.

The problem was, at that hour of the afternoon, the station had only one available photographer and one reporter. Only one story could be covered. On that night's news, the plaintive sounds of the Bird Woman of Howard County got nearly two minutes of air time. The law firm threatening to leave town went unmentioned. Also unmentioned, night after night across an entire era, was the exodus from the city of scores of businesses and thousands of families.

"Every night," Al Sanders said, "the same crap."

"Easy, big fella," said a stage manager named Walter "Skip" Ball, trying to lighten the moment as they broke for commercials one evening. Officially, Ball's job was to communicate with the control room down the hall and shift between the three cameras in the studio, coordinating all flow of reporters, stories, and last-minute insertions or deletions from the show. Unofficially, his job was commiserating with Turner and Sanders to keep everybody cool when the camera went on.

One week, the station ran a series called "Remaking Your Man," in which reporter Frank Luber was subjected to a new indignity each night during a ratings sweep period. One night he had his hair styled. Another, he had a facial treatment.

Though the biggest news stories were getting ninety seconds, Luber's pieces were getting far more. The night he bought a new suit, the piece ran four minutes and twenty seconds. Heads of state had been assassinated and gotten far less time. Wearing his new ensemble, Luber wrapped up one piece by stopping strangers in the street to ask, "How do you like my new suit?"

When the package finished, Al Sanders, having had enough, looked into the camera and told viewers, "Thank goodness we only have two more nights of this."

Not quite. As if now embracing truly serious journalism, he and Turner went to a story about weatherman Bob Turk receiving an award for being nice to his dog. When that piece finished, viewers were treated to an incestuous piece of self-promotion—a video package—about the station's news crew winning a doughnut break sponsored by a local radio station.

When they came back from the doughnut story, Turner declared, "Isn't this wonderful?"

"We only bring you the biggies, folks," Sanders said.

Later, off-camera, Turner slammed a hand onto the desk, while Sanders leaned back and fanned himself with a stack of papers, as if trying to cool himself off.

"Jesus," Sanders said, "if you've got the personality battle won, then what the hell do you have to lose by putting on some serious stuff?"

He was stating the obvious as modestly as he could. The town loved Jerry and Al and had very little use for the competition. All the numbers showed it. So why not do something worthwhile with the popularity? Why not talk, for example, about the continuing flight of businesses out of the city instead of the flight of a single parakeet from suburban Howard County? Or hire some more reporters and photographers so you could handle both stories?

But they were caught in a conundrum for which neither they nor an entire industry has ever found a satisfactory answer: If pseudo-news brings ratings, and ratings bring advertising dollars, how do you toss out a proven winner and risk it on possible failure?

The beleaguered news director, under the thumb of a general manager whose only allegiance is to ratings and profit margins, isn't going to fight for change. Nor will executive producers, focused on coordinating editorial and technical operations. And producers, young and inexperienced and consumed by trying to fill an hour each day with the efforts of a handful of on-air reporters, never even consider such a possibility.

Instead, there is this:

One night on WJZ's eleven o'clock news, viewers watched a ten-year-old girl stand in the doorway of her East Baltimore rowhouse. Shivering even in the hot glare of television lights, she described how she and her eleven-year-old girlfriend were abducted from a recreation center and taken to a park, where they were tied up and slashed with a knife and razor, and somehow managed to escape.

"What was it like?" a reporter asked the little girl.

The child wore a bandage around her neck where her abductor had slashed her throat with a razor blade. Her lower lip trembled. The girl said she was ordered to take off her clothes. The television reporter held his microphone up to her mouth. The girl said her abductor wanted a kiss. The TV camera caught the tremble of her lip. The microphone edged closer. The girls would not give the abductor a kiss, and would not take off their clothes, and so the man began to cut them, the ten year old said.

Her eleven-year-old girlfriend was not seen on the TV screen, as she was lying in a bed at Johns Hopkins Hospital with five stab wounds in the back and razor blade slashes on the throat. There were no cameras at the hospital, because officials would not allow them.

The mother of the ten-year-old girl, standing in the doorway of her home, could have thrown the TV crew out also, but she did not. As I watched the story that night, I cringed. In a traumatic time, the mother wanted to put her little girl on television to show the world what her daughter had gone through. But in what should have been a time of private healing she exposed her child to a second violation: sixty seconds of trembling shared with the metropolitan area.

But if the mother's judgment was mistaken, she at least had the excuse of irrationality in a time of shock and anger. WJZ had no such fallback. They put the child's face on television and took away her privacy in order to juice up ratings numbers.

The news director was Dick Reingold, by inclination a decent and intelligent man. When we talked the next day, Reingold started to rationalize the story, and then he stopped. There was no reasonable, civilized explanation.

"The mother was angry," I said. "But news people are supposed to stay clear-headed."

"Exploitation isn't our style," Reingold said apologetically. "We've been accused of it, but it isn't our style."

He mentioned timing. The reporter who had been assigned the story telephoned the eleven o'clock producer for advice. He felt a little queasy. The producer, in the classic television manner, was a kid with limited news judgment and limited life experience. "Go with the story," he said. There were no other newsroom consultations, no editorial board meetings, and not a moment of soul-searching. It was ten o'clock at night. There were no other management people in the building—a fact that is standard procedure seven nights a week for the late news, at WJZ and hundreds of stations around the country.

When I talked to the reporter who did the story, he said he was given one directive: Don't use the little girl's name—as though that preposterously flimsy gesture would keep viewers in her own neighborhood, or her own school, from identifying her when they saw her face.

A thin line is walked every day in the news business. Television has it the toughest, with its small staffs and not enough guidance from people in high places, and the profound impact of the moving picture. Strangers come up to these television reporters, seeking one moment in the spotlight. All of this has to be weighed against the demands of time and space. At WJZ that night, they had an exclusive with a little girl whose mother wanted to put her on the eleven o'clock news. Sometimes, even mothers can be wrong.

"We had half an hour to go before broadcast," Reingold explained, "so the decision had to be made quickly. You have to make those kinds of decisions every night, sometimes every minute, and they're often very hard ones. This was a hard one."

I started to let it go, but one last thought occurred to me.

"By the way," I said, "when did this abduction take place?"

"A week ago," Reingold said.

"Wait a minute," I said. "A week ago?"

"Yeah."

It was a week for the mother to think things through. It was a week that had gone by without anybody else getting near the story. And there wasn't a reason in the world not to wait another day to think about putting this little girl on the air to re-live, for thousands of strangers, what it was like at the hands of a sexual predator.

Never mind Reingold's "half hour to go before broadcast." They had far more time than that to come to their senses. But, on a night when the news was slow, and there was (as usual) one reporter on hand to find a story to lead the eleven o'clock broadcast, and one young producer making the decision back in the newsroom, it was too much to turn away when a mother offered her ten-year-old daughter on a silver platter.

It was the story of a child's violation—by a strange man, and then by television itself.

Dog Days

In my retirement from broadcasting, I am haunted by images. They appear on my television set each night, and they purport to represent some version of the truth, but they do not. They are promotional spots showing television anchors looking like actual reporters. At a stretch, these commercials might be defended as colorful metaphors implying the serious work of real reporters; but in truth they are a sham on which a television station creates a fraudulent belief system for naive and trusting viewers.

The images are promotional spots for WJZ's *Eyewitness News,* in which an announcer's strident voice declares, "The Eyewitness News team...covering breaking news...live in the air...live on the ground..." while the station's primary news anchors are seen going about their alleged business.

Vic Carter covers a story while peering down from a helicopter. No one is supposed to ask how Carter could be seen so clearly from so far away in the sky. Sally Thorner streaks through the streets to corner a source. No one is supposed to notice that in real life Thorner never leaves the studio. Anchor Denise Koch interviews a uniformed police officer at the scene of an incident.

In the memory of all who have watched these anchors over the years, such events never actually happen. The promotional spots, drummed into viewers' heads repeatedly over the course of each day, are works of imagination based on nothing. They are the station's attempt to plant a notion: that their anchors are serious news people who hit the streets each day for actual news gathering, and then bring back what they have learned to broadcast on the evening news.

It is all a fiction, the anchor as superhero. Later, when these anchors are fronting for news stories written and reported by others, the notion has been planted: We have seen these people at work, in helicopters and on busy streets where they speak with authority figures. And this is what they have found out.

In truth, the only time these anchors go outside the building is to shoot promotional spots showing them outside the building. They are people who never leave the office but pretend to see the world.

In the early days of local television, for all the farcical nature of the news, the station at least had the grace not to sell the anchors as something they were not. Jerry Turner and Al Sanders were shown as a couple of guys who just wanted to get each other coffee. Nobody confused that with actual reporting. They were friends—and in that era, when viewers were charmed by the mere newness of local television news (and by two men whose friendship had crossed racial lines), it was enough.

But the modern promos were a direct result of years of TV manipulation, in which image was projected and sculpted along perceived marketing needs, and those images drifted farther from pleasant commercial vignette toward some cynical vision of journalistic reality.

In the case of WJZ, three of its four evening anchors— Vic Carter, Sally Thorner, and Denise Koch—almost never left the station to pursue stories. The fourth, Kai Jackson, covered stories for the eleven o'clock news, usually involving little more than a brief live introduction to a sixty-second story orchestrated for Jackson by a newsroom producer. The notion of putting an anchor in a helicopter was laughable. So was the thought of sending any of the other three anchors out of the building to do any of their own reporting.

What was important, though, was leaving viewers the impression that such things happened—particularly, in the modern fraudulence, when the general manager, Jay Newman, decided to stress the anchors to the point of diminishing all other on-air people.

And the images haunted me because they captured, in seconds, that vast expanse between the thing television news promised and what it actually delivered.

Somewhere back in the 1970s, television executives made two discoveries that changed their world. They now had technical capabilities to deliver news reports far beyond the confines of a studio, and they could make enormous money doing it. But they had to make a soul-searching decision, which ultimately took about twelve seconds: Did they want to make the foundation of the business journalism itself—or ratings? Did they want to gauge success on the basis of their reporting—or on sheer popularity numbers?

When they made ratings their god, the ballgame was over.

Instead of news, there was melodrama that was only occasionally the stuff of importance. Instead of news makers as the most vital people in a broadcast, it was those who brought us the news makers.

The thing that prevailed, because it was pushed so hard every night, was a cult of personality. The stations offered their viewers a five-part series on the secret fantasies of their anchors. It was a sexy time, but less sexy than advertised: Jerry Turner alleged that his fantasy was to be a jet pilot; Al Sanders, a railroad engineer. Thus, the station got a double boost: first, the hint of sex in the "secret fantasies" promos; then, when their alleged fantasies turned out to be so mundane, they were perceived as comforting. Look, these anchor folks could be our neighbors! WJZ's competitors, meanwhile, offered similar fluff.

For television, there is the constant temptation to cash in on the obvious: The reporters appear in thousands of viewers' homes. These viewers come to think of them as famous friends. For any local news operation, it is tempting to cash in on this familiarity and let journalism take a back seat.

I felt such temptations myself.

As a columnist with my photograph in the newspaper three times a week, I had always gotten nice feedback from readers. But within weeks after I started doing television, the magnitude of response jumped enormously, and then jumped again when the station conducted market research. Viewers liked what I brought to the newscasts so much that after a few years the station decided to include me in its stock opening each night. There I was, lumped in with Turner and Sanders.

I had never experienced so much feedback—and feedback of a certain kind. Everywhere I went, I was known for being known. It didn't particularly matter what I might have said, what editorial positions I might have taken—I was on television. That was the thing that mattered. And two things happened in my head: enormous gratitude that the time of $50-a-week pay checks had now vanished and a sense of emptiness that things were going so well with so little effort on my part.

The commentaries were about 250 words long—less than one-third the length of my newspaper columns. Once I'd made a few phone calls, and checked on facts, it took me ten or fifteen minutes to write them, and sometimes less. Never in my life had I done so well for working so little. So the station put together specials for me to anchor; on Maryland's new governor, on Baltimore's new mayor, on the closing of Memorial Stadium. Each spring, Marty Bass and I would broadcast opening day of the Orioles Season, and horse racing coverage from Pimlico Race Course the week of the Preakness Stakes. I knew plenty about the Orioles. About horse racing I know next to nothing. It didn't matter. I could talk about the economic impact of horse racing in Maryland and fake my way through the rest of it.

"The thing is," I said one evening to Jerry Turner, "this is a lot of good stuff happening for doing very little."

"Shh," he replied, laughing at this great secret. But I noticed, not for the first time, a cautionary sign he kept in his office: "There are two great tragedies in life: Not getting what you want. And getting it."

Soon the station began running my commentaries early in the newscast—again, in response to viewers—and, after I delivered them live each evening, they were re-shown on the following morning's newscast, bringing in a whole new audience.

And then the station began running commercials about me.

One afternoon I was ushered into a conference room to meet with several advertising people hired to film the promotional spots.

"We want to capture the essence of who you are," I was told.

"You want me holding a pen and paper, interviewing somebody?" I asked.

The creative types chuckled indulgently.

"Nah," one of them said. "Something that stands for a connection to Baltimore."

What emerged were colorful spots showing a kid on his way home from school, with my voice-over describing what it was like growing up in Baltimore, and how we've all gone through changes over the years. At the end of the spot, there's the grown-up version of me. I'm on the telephone, comically telling my mother, "Okay, Ma, I'll comb my hair," as Jerry and Al wait for me to join them on the air. The message wasn't about reporting skills; it was about familiarity, about establishing me as a long-time local guy, about having family that still lived in the same town. Though I was an actual reporter by profession, the image makers believed the home-town connection was important to stress.

I noticed the impact of my promos almost immediately. I was now stopped literally dozens of times a day. Some people reminded me to comb my hair—as though they had overheard an actual conversation between me and my mother. Invariably, they were polite and friendly, and the greetings became a kind of good-natured therapy.

Occasionally, it was also weird. One day, as I checked some records at the city's Municipal Building, a man asked for my autograph and scrambled for a piece of paper I could use. He pulled an old photo from his pocket and turned it over for me to sign.

"How should I make it out?" I asked.

"To Ralph," he said.

Out of curiosity, I turned the picture over. It was the man's dog.

"What's your dog's name?" I asked.

"That's Ralph," he said. "He'll love this. He watches you all the time."

When such things happen, and happen every day, you begin to get a sense of an audience. They turn on the news for information, but they turn to a specific station for something else: the faces of the people they know, people who seem to have a connection to their community. Television thus has a decision. They can cash in on that trust, or honor it by delivering what the medium promises.

In Philadelphia, in the 1990s, one TV news operation conducted audience research on its on-air talent, asking viewers to name ten long-tenured reporters—from any of the three network-affiliated local news operations. Then, name the anchors from those stations.

Viewers were able to name all of the anchors—but they couldn't name more than a handful of reporters. What this told station executives was a couple of things: Reporters who cover actual news might be important—but not nearly as important as anchors; and even the longest-tenured reporters did not register in the public's consciousness.

So, when WJZ began running promotional spots on me, and putting me in the nightly opening, this was an explicit statement: They were investing in my stock, and anticipated viewers investing their emotions.

The emotional connection, by the way, did not mean that viewers had to agree with me. In fact, there were nights when many of them wanted to reach through their screens and throttle me.

One December, shoppers in Prince George's County complained to owners of a mall about a Santa Claus there. This Santa was black; the complaining shoppers were white. In my commentary that night, I wrote about people forgetting the values of Christmas. I said they should remember that Santa Claus isn't real, he's a symbol of the spirit of good cheer and brotherhood, which transcends skin color.

Scores of phone calls flooded the newsroom, none about the racial point I had tried to make.

"My kid was watching TV and you said Santa wasn't real," the first voice hollered in my ear.

"My kid thinks I'm a liar," said the next one. "I've been telling him Santa's real, and you just said he wasn't."

All calls that followed remained true to that theme. I'd blown the lid off every tot's Christmas fantasy. I had forgotten a fundamental difference between newspapers and print: Little kiddies weren't reading newspaper columns, but anybody can be sitting by the TV set, and words can be heard by all.

Always, in the first fifteen minutes of the evening newscasts, there came the spillage of blood and gore.

"If it isn't bloody, I don't want it," an executive producer named Janet Fedor would trill merrily. Fedor was a sensitive woman making the best of a bad situation. She knew what the bosses wanted and kept her head down and complied. The trilled words became her comic mantra.

"What fun's a fire if it isn't fatal?" producer Grant Morrow would ask, pretending to be disappointed one night when a camera crew came back with footage of a burning building that included no charred bodies being carried out. It was black humor as defense mechanism. At least Fedor and Morrow had the luxury of private jokes. They didn't have to read the stories in front of an entire community each night.

But here were two highly successful men, Jerry Turner and Al Sanders, popular beyond their dreams, embraced by their audience as few news anchor teams in America—and still facing nightly professional frustrations. They were captives of their own success. They were intelligent adults who knew a con job when they were part of it. They were men who had grown up reading newspapers and following the broadcasts of Edward R. Murrow and Eric Sevareid, and knew what news reporting could be.

By the time I arrived, in 1983, Turner had been a fixture for two decades. For many viewers, he seemed bigger than the news itself. This was a fact known to all political elements.

One evening Turner took me aside and said, "You know, they asked me to run for office."

"They did?" I asked.

"Yeah. Some big-money guys. They got me in a room and laid out the whole thing."

"Republicans?"

"Yeah," he said.

It was a little unclear what office they had in mind. In Maryland, the Democrats had a lock on most offices, but in Turner, the Republicans knew they had someone with instant name recognition, and community trust, and outsized stature. He described several party veterans laying out their plans for him.

"They said, 'You get elected, and this guy becomes racing commissioner—if you're comfortable with that. And this guy gets the liquor board position—if you're comfortable with that.' That was the phrase they kept using. I was just the front man for their moves."

"What did you say?"

"I said, 'I don't feel comfortable with any of this.' And I got up and walked out."

He shook his head in befuddlement. "Isn't that awful?" he said. "You know, I'd probably win. And the thing is, I don't know anything. I mean, what the hell do I do? I sit up here and look into the camera and read the news. But that's all I know." He sighed in wonder. "And that'd be enough."

Like anchors in every market in the country, he and Sanders understood the essential nature of their jobs: They were journalistic hosts. They were maitre d's for the evening's main courses. They could wear serious expressions and speak in earnest, concerned voices, but they were still just fronts for other people's reporting. Though it was true that, when deemed necessary, Turner could pick up a telephone and reach anyone in the state to work a story, on most nights it was simply not deemed necessary. He and Sanders's professional (and financial) value was mainly computed in ratings numbers, since their only visible skills involved the ability to read, to talk for a few seconds with reporters doing live shots from the street, and to chat comfortably during the lighter moments of the show.

So behind the angst about empty news coverage was a deeper psychological anxiety that nobody talked about. It was an impostor complex, a fear that somebody would realize the flimsy foundation on which their high-profile careers were constructed. It is this way at every TV station in the country. Political money men might want to sell such an image to unsuspecting voters, but in their hearts, Turner and Sanders knew better.

Turner, in particular, was a child of the Depression. When he finished college in 1947, it took him five years to discover broadcasting. In between, he worked for a little while at a railroad yard.

"My father hired me," he said, "and fired me."

He laughed as he told the story one afternoon in his little office. But there was a message in the tale: He understood insecurity. And he understood, after the seriousness of working at a railroad yard, what a flimsy gig this really was—and how professionally vulnerable he was to some rising young street reporter with a little too much attractiveness and initiative.

Reporters didn't have the anchors' stature (or their money), but they performed visible work for a living. Therefore, any reporters with drive, and an affinity for the camera, were apt to be a threat.

For all their stature, Turner and Sanders were sensitive to their vulnerability and protective of their turf. They were generous when praising good work, but aware of it when someone might be interested in usurping their jobs. In this sense, no one seemed more threatening than Richard Sher.

Sher had energy spilling out of his pores and confidence and camera-presence and ambition. Turner and Sanders looked at him the way Caesar gazed upon lean and hungry Cassius. Turner, in his mid-fifties, had a silver-haired grace; Sher, about forty, was silver-gray. Turner would joke, "I've got three years left on my contract, but only two years' worth of hair left." In television, such things mattered. Sher's hair was full and bushy, the picture of aggressive youth. The *Baltimore Sun's* gossip columnist, Laura Charles, always referred to Sher as Turner's "hair apparent." For nine years, whenever Turner or Sanders was off, Sher was the substitute anchor.

Turner's stature was undeniable, but so was Sher's breathtaking daily output. He co-hosted an hour's talk show each morning: *People Are Talking*, with Oprah Winfrey. Who needed Jerry? Not Oprah. The show was a huge ratings hit, and Richard and Oprah were the town's chummy interracial TV sweethearts. When they finished *People Are Talking*, they co-anchored the noon news each day. This, too, topped the ratings. One night a week, Sher hosted a public affairs discussion show, *Square-Off*, that tumbled into raucous shouting matches. It was popular enough to last nearly two decades. As soon as Sher finished the noon news each day, he started his reporting chores, munching on a sandwich he'd brought from home while heading off in an *Eyewitness News* van. Usually he handled the day's big murder story. He knew it would give him the lead spot on the evening broadcast.

"I've been to more funerals than Sol Levinson," Sher would say. Levinson had one of the city's big funeral parlors.

Sher seemed to be everywhere. But his reporting style could veer over the top. Families, in his reporting, did not merely grieve for murder victims. They grieved for victims whom "they loved very, very much." If there was a child available, Sher held the child's hand or planted a kiss. These gestures became part of his taped package. Some of it was a gregarious nature, an honest empathy, but part was his understanding of the station's image, and his own: They were the community's friends.

Turner and Sanders sometimes rolled their eyes at this. But in Sher, Turner also saw a younger version of himself, and he felt crowded by it the same way he'd felt threatened by the younger Oprah, who had succeeded wildly in spite of him.

But this was only part of it. Nearly every night on the set, Turner and Sanders grumbled and fumed at the bloody crime stories, the shameless kitten-caught-in-a-tree stories, the endless pandering. For years the station had a policy of Person-on-the-Street interviews, local reaction to big stories.

Invariably, the interviews were meaningless. Those interviewed tended to be inarticulate and barely aware of the story in question. But the interviews came from more slippery motives. For one thing, they were easy time-filler. For another, in a time of viewer backlash against "experts," the station was giving the common man a shot. And the dumber the answers, the more they were considered not empty air time, but comic relief. Or, on occasion, outlandish drama for its own sake.

But it raised a question: Where was the division between show business and actual journalism?

Late one afternoon, a tape editor sidled up to Turner as he sat in the newsroom. "You gotta see this," he said, leading Jerry back to an editing booth. When they slipped in, the editor rolled raw tape: footage of one of the station's reporters interviewing the grieving mother of a young man who'd been killed in a street fight the previous day. In the standard procedure, a photographer had shot more footage than the reporter could fit into any ninety-second package. On the editing room screen now, there were scenes that had been photographed but carefully tossed aside for obvious reasons.

Here was the reporter asking the mother about her son. The mother started to respond. The reporter stopped her.

"It's all right if you want to cry," the reporter said, putting a comforting arm around the woman's shoulders. Then the reporter asked the question again. This time, the mother wept copious tears. The tears became part of the finished product on that evening's news.

When Turner saw the raw tape, he let out a noise somewhere between a howl and a heart attack. He put his hand over his mouth, as much to muzzle the sound as to sort out his own confused feelings. Yes, this was naked manipulation of someone's emotions. Yes, it was stage-managing of the story. Yes, it was deliberate taking advantage of someone in a state of shock and grief.

But, at its core, it was what TV people considered a "moment," a few ticks of the clock that seemed to offer something that newspapers, for all their words, and all their high-flown analysis, could not offer: the sight of apparently natural human emotion. On that evening's news, the poor mother would be seen awash in tears, and no viewers at home would see the prompting behind her sobs. And what was the big deal? Surely the mother had cried real, unprompted tears at some point. Television wanted a glimpse of those tears— even if it had to order them up on cue.

"Surprised?" Turner was asked as he walked back from the editing booth.

"Not really," he said, shrugging. "It happens." He remembered another reporter's raw tape. Given an answer to a question, the reporter said, "Give me the same answer again. But, this time, say my name first." Viewers never saw the off-camera coaxing. In the final product, they witnessed what appeared to be a friendliness between the reporter and the person he was interviewing, in which first-name intimacy seemed perfectly natural. After all, the reporter was a well-known part of the community. This familiarity validated that fact. Friends call each other by first names. The reporter was your friend.

In fact, Turner could sometimes offer his own professional compromises. One night I wrote a commentary about a boy who had overcome physical handicaps and inspired his family and friends. In the standard give-and-take, Jerry read the brief introduction to the piece and said, "In his commentary tonight, Michael Olesker looks at a boy who refused to quit."

"Jerry," I said, looking his way while the camera caught both of our profiles, "he's really a great kid."

"I know," said Jerry, smiling delightedly.

The response stunned me so much that I nearly said, "You do?"

He didn't, of course. He had no idea. But, who was hurt in such a benign little gesture?

It was Jerry reinforcing the kid's courage, lending his special stamp of approval. But it was also Jerry attaching himself to the brave kid, latching on to some of the boy's plucky aura. As I turned to read my commentary off the TelePrompter, I marveled at the instinctive shamelessness of the gesture. But I also understood why so many viewers felt so warmly toward this man, and this station, and I wondered how the difference between truth and apparently innocent lying could be reconciled.

Nearly every night, the off-camera groaning commenced with the A section, that block of stories between the show's open and the first bank of commercials. Inevitably, it was non-stop crime, brightened only at the very end of the section by a light "kicker." Heaven forbid viewers be depressed when the commercials arrived.

"Oh, I could have been at CBS by now," Al Sanders would moan comically. Then he would point a finger at me. "But nooo. You had to quote me accurately."

He meant the incident from some years earlier, when the city's police chief had claimed his undercover operatives weren't tailing Sanders—they only wanted to know who his sources were. And Al had been honest enough to say, for public consumption, "I haven't got any sources."

In that moment, he'd pulled the curtain away and allowed a peek behind the scenes. And so, while he and Jerry enjoyed their popularity, they also knew there was an element of putting one over on people. They were a couple of guys fronting for a glorified headline service with moving pictures. And, almost from the earliest days I spent at WJZ, they wore their misgivings—and their confused emotions—on their sleeves. They were two enormously good-natured, affable, unpretentious men who were delighted with their commercial success. But, on the subject of news coverage, they grumbled on the set, and in the newsroom, and with colleagues.

But I never knew of them taking their complaints to management. In newspapers, arguments between editors and reporters are a constant. The perception—and I think it's a fair one—is that better journalism comes out of honest debate. But newspaper people have a luxury not granted to broadcasters: They are judged by their work. In television news, on-air people have personal-services contracts, which are renewed every few years. And the renewal is based on ratings more than anything else.

So there is reluctance, even among the most secure people, to challenge management. And, always, there is the cloud of ratings hanging over everyone's heads.

Not long after I arrived, the station hired Suzanne Collins away from WBAL-TV, the NBC affiliate on the other side of Baltimore's TV Hill. Collins had been an intern at WBAL and won a full-time job in the classic manner. They sent her to Three Mile Island after the nuclear power plant there broke down. President Carter was holding a press conference. Collins, lacking any kind of White House credentials, bluffed her way past the Secret Service.

WBAL, appreciating her moxie, gave her a job producing investigative reports. In other words, she did the legwork, the digging through records, that led to on-air reporters pretending the serious work was completely their own. In one of her first efforts at WJZ, she produced a piece on teamsters filling out phony hours in their log books.

Jerry Turner was to front the piece. Jerry loved the idea of investigations. But the more he thought about it, the more he worried. There were an awful lot of truckers.

"We don't want to go upsetting any large groups," he fretted.

Large groups meant potential ratings; ratings meant popularity. And never mind all that idealistic stuff about journalism, and all those nights bemoaning the station's lack of substance. What if we lost viewers because of a miserable piece about a bunch of slightly larcenous truck drivers?

Finally, with mixed emotions, Jerry said, "Let's go." The piece drew a big favorable reaction. Jerry took his bows, and in the newsroom he gave credit to Collins. But even this man with huge ratings had been slowed down by the eternal TV conflict: wanting to show actual reporting but not wanting to risk even momentary threat of popularity loss.

As a fellow who was proud of my reporting background, I naturally wanted to bring something to my new profession. I suggested story ideas to people in charge. I shared Turner and Sanders's concern over content. Where I'd once laughed at TV's piffle and poked fun at it in the newspaper, I was now a part of that package.

One morning I went to East Baltimore's blue collar Highlandtown neighborhood, where the owners of the Esskay meat-packing plant had closed their doors and moved out of town. Esskay was a Baltimore fixture for generations. The company now said its plant was outdated. Employees, knowing baloney when they saw it, called it a lie. They said the company wanted cheaper labor, wanted to break the company union, wanted give-backs and couldn't get them, and so they let the building run down until it was unusable.

The impact on East Baltimore would be huge. There were about 500 workers at the plant, and they spent some of their money in neighborhood places such as Santoni's Groceries and the Lucky Spirits Bar, and in stores all along Eastern Avenue's commercial strip.

In my mind, here was a story that captured an essential part of Baltimore's character: a big city with a small-town feel, a city of neighborhoods. In Highlandtown, working class families settled in over generations. Now that stability was badly shaken. In the coming years, in fact, the face of the neighborhood would change: with the Esskay money dried up, businesses across the area felt the pinch. Eastern Avenue, once bustling, became scarred by empty stores. The half-century old Patterson movie theater closed, and the Patterson bowling alley struggled to stay alive. Many former Esskay workers found jobs in suburbia, and moved there to be closer to their new employment.

When I left the neighborhood, I went to WJZ and told a few newsroom executives what an important story the Esskay closing was. They looked at me with blank stares.

"Anybody there get shot?" an assistant news director asked, looking up from his desk.

"Shot?" I replied. I could feel the blood rising in me. "Listen, you can lose your life in other ways."

The assistant news director shrugged and said, "It's not *Eyewitness News.*"

"What's that supposed to mean?" I asked.

"Why don't you do a commentary on it?"

Which I did—but that misses the point. Here was a chance to show viewers why neighborhoods began to deteriorate. We could show the plight of hundreds of working people with their jobs snatched away from them. And, not to be minimized, to show those remaining in Highlandtown that the station really did give a damn.

But we didn't—not enough to send a reporter and photographer into the neighborhood, not one time over the years, to talk about the impact of the venerable Esskay plant closing its doors and kicking a community in the teeth. Nor, when the area began to come back, did the station send anyone to cover that either.

Unless somebody there got shot.

Over the last two decades of the twentieth century, the city of Baltimore's homicide rate reached epic proportions. In one fifteen-month stretch, forty-three of the victims were children. The wail of distraught mothers was as familiar on the TV news as the flash of police lights.

One night I drove slowly along the city's Greenmount Avenue, a rough east-side stretch riddled by narcotics traffic and the crime that sprang from it. Along Greenmount from Twenty-Eighth Street down to the Maryland Penitentiary, a distance of eighteen blocks, there were scores of children. Some were toddlers, some were teens. They sat on front steps, rode bikes, danced to music audible or not. Some had visible parents and plenty did not. Beneath a billboard, a skinny girl who looked about nine years old strolled with a two-year--old child in her arms. The billboard said, "Save A Dream. Thurgood Marshall Scholarship Fund." Marshall, the former Supreme Court justice, had grown up only a few miles from here. His photo on the billboard should have shielded its eyes from such a scene.

Then it dawned on me: This was a school night—and it was eleven o'clock. It was also a neighborhood plagued by violence in a city where children were falling from bullets and the television cameras were there when hysterical mothers wept over their dying babies. But why did the cameras have to wait for such moments? Why weren't there stories capturing the ordinary nightly scenes? Scenes like children, strolling about when they should have been doing homework or sleeping, who showed up the next day in school exhausted and unprepared and unable to do their work, and thus ensured the next generation of the permanent economic underclass.

"What do you want us to do?" an executive producer asked when I suggested the story. "Sit there and wait until somebody gets shot?"

"No," I said. "The shooting isn't the point. The point is what leads up to it. It's the violence that doesn't result in blood; it's just people's lives coming undone."

"It's not *Eyewitness News.* You want it reported, do a commentary on it."

I turned away, caught between anger over the casual dismissal of the story and personal concern. Management people didn't like to be challenged. Turner and Sanders knew this every time they vented to each other but never took their complaints any higher. The bosses ruled by implied intimidation. They knew how on-air people worried about their jobs, and how tough it was to find on-air employment. I wanted to challenge the status quo, but I didn't want to lose my paycheck in the process.

One day I went to Criminal Court to hear testimony about a thirteen-year-old boy who was killed by a stray bullet. He'd been running the streets with some friends. Now one of the friends, eleven years old, took the witness stand. The boy wore a sweatshirt and sneakers. He was asked, "Did you give a statement to police?"

"Yes," the boy said.

"Will you read the statement to the jury?" he was asked. He was handed a transcribed copy of his statement.

"No," said the boy. No, he would not read it.

"Can you read and write?" he was asked.

"No."

"No?"

"A little bit."

"Can you read the word 'cut?'"

"No."

"Can you read letters?"

"Yes."

Now the attorney pointed to three consecutive letters on a page: C-U-T. The boy read the letters aloud, one by one.

"And what do those letters spell?"

"I don't know."

With great amounts of diligence on both his part and the public schools', the eleven-year-old boy had somehow made it all the way to the sixth grade. He was marched into court as part of a small procession of kids produced in the city: kids moved from one foster home to another because their own families had come undone, kids lacking any sort of moral guidance who quickly became part of the city's predatory class, kids who reached the sixth grade in school and still had no ability to translate words on a printed page.

I went back to the WJZ newsroom and gently suggested a story about such youngsters. How were they being passed through the various grades without any visible evidence of learning? What happened to such kids once they reached the criminal justice system, as so many of them did?

The bosses weren't interested. For one thing, they weren't allowed to bring cameras into court to show the kid on the witness stand unable to read. For another, where was the blood? For another, it would take too many hours, and too much manpower, to track down enough people to make the story work. When you only have a handful of reporters, you don't have the luxury of waiting around to get a sense of texture.

"It's not *Eyewitness News*," I was told. The phrase had now become a refrain.

But what in the world did it mean?

7

Lingerie News

In the beginning there was Al Primo, who taught local TV news the most basic lesson in marketing itself, and then watched the lesson go bad. He invented the thing that became *Eyewitness News,* an idea so stupefyingly simple that not a single genius in local television, anywhere in America, had conceived of it until the late 1960s.

Primo was news director at KYW in Philadelphia at that time. His idea was instead of having three people—one each for news, weather, and sports—deliver the entire news broadcast, the station would use every available body. Actual reporters (or reasonable facsimiles) would be sent out on stories and then relate these stories on the air. They would have beats, so they could gather information. They would be ethnically identifiable personalities who could cover news of interest to minority audiences (and, not coincidentally, attract viewers with similar minority backgrounds). They would even, for a time, dress alike. This way, they looked like a team. You could root for them, like a hometown ballclub.

In no time at all, the idea was so successful that it became a national cliché: hundreds of look-alike, sound-alike local news teams across America with their uniformed anchors, their earnest reporters out in the streets sticking microphones in front of important community figures previously seen only in newspaper photographs, and their good-natured "happy talk" leavening the evening's tragedies.

To read some of the early *Eyewitness News* internal memos is to be stunned by their simplicity. They talk of sending out reporters "to cover stories and talk to the people on the scene who were involved in, or had witnessed, the event."

In other words, do what reporters had been doing since the dawn of the written word. Primo described this as "the human drama of the coverage." Not only were viewers getting the event as it occurred, seen through the eyes of a reporter who was on the scene, they also got a very real reaction from an individual who was affected by it.

The words are astonishing. They are basic Intro to Journalism stuff being handed down as though they were stone tablets brought down from Sinai.

But then it went further. The reporter would bring the story back to the station—and then present it, live and on the studio set, with the anchor. The idea was "to increase the reporter's visibility. There [is] an intentional linkage between the individual reporter and the story...In many cases... the beginnings of creating a stronger personality for the reporters."

A stronger personality for the reporter? To what end? In the old journalism ideal, the reporter remained apart from the story, a dispassionate, objective observer, low-key enough that all players could forget anyone was watching and act out their natural instincts. And the reporter, unobtrusively taking notes, would ultimately relate both sides of a story and let his audience make up its own mind about the facts.

To what end, this personality? The memo was clear: "In the interaction between anchor and reporter, the viewer sees that the talent is knowledgeable and friendly." Friendly! "We begin to see the personalities of the talent." Personalities! Talent! "The on-air players are no longer the simple flat images of the tightly produced and edited show, they now take on depth.

They are people."

So there it was. The news wasn't just about the news, it was about the people bringing you that news. In fact, if you had the right people, the news itself was secondary. If it was secondary enough, you might not even have to produce actual news.

Yet the system has its staunch supporters, including Paul Gluck, who produced WJZ's evening broadcasts in the early 1980s and later moved to Philadelphia television. Later Gluck headed public television in Pennsylvania. Public television's notion of news is sobriety to the occasional point of insomnia. In the modern era, where commercial broadcasting is reduced to seven-second sound bites and the hit situation comedies were the stuff of "Friends" and "Everybody Loves Raymond," Gluck moved to public television and felt the need to assure his new staff that he was not a frivolous man.

"My intention," he announced to his new staff at public TV, "is to uphold our standards. In fact, I want to do a World War II documentary. I thought we'd call it, 'Everybody Loves Rommel.'"

But Gluck brings sensitivity as well as a sense of humor when he analyzes television news.

"*Eyewitness News*," he said one night in Philadelphia, "is simple. It means telling passionate stories in human terms by reporters with empathy for the lives of people in their community. It's the least institutional kind of journalism, but it's the most contextual. Every story should, at its best, take a human being and, through the prism of that person's experience, explain the predicament."

Fair enough, as far as it goes. One person fits better into a ninety-second story than does an analysis of an entire institution. But one person's experience, as the model for all stories, can result in little more than a series of clichés.

"Obviously," Gluck says, "there are dangers. *Eyewitness News* brought us happy talk. It brought us theatrical TV that was a hoot to watch and a grand platform for talent, but you could lose sight of important stories. At its worst, it's silly.

But if you have enough editorially mature people, you strike a balance."

Several years after Al Primo's late 1960s brainstorm—which he subsequently took to New York and transformed WABC from a ratings after-thought to a powerhouse—*Newsweek* magazine reported a confidential memo sent to San Diego's KFMB-TV by Frank N. Magid Associates, a media consultant firm hired by the station to boost its ratings. KFMB was just beginning to employ the tactics of *Action News*, a spiritual cousin to *Eyewitness News*.

Magid's memo to KFMB said, "Unlike earlier concepts of 'what is news,' which defined the product as 'what people should know,' *Action News* is defined as 'what people want to know.'"

In other words, in the brief couple of years since Al Primo had put *Eyewitness News* reporters on the street, consultants such as Magid were telling their *Action News* folks how to report that news once they got there. Magid's advice did not come from nowhere. First, they questioned hundreds of viewers. From those interviews, they drew up a composite portrait of the typical viewer. Then came the scary part: analyzing the performances of a station's on-air talent to determine how they meshed with this composite viewer and his or her desires.

The Magid *Action News* memo urged extensive use of splashy graphics. It urged stories of less than ninety seconds. It specified cutting down on regular coverage of local government, which tended to be boring. Boring stories might be important, but they tended to drive away viewers, which led to driving away advertisers. Instead of boring government stories, the memo said, deliver fast-moving stories with "eye appeal." If the innermost secrets of government had to be revealed, keep the coverage brief enough that nobody had time to reach for the dial.

One afternoon in the WJZ newsroom, an assignment editor monitoring a police scanner called out laconically, "We've got an empty warehouse on fire, if anybody's interested."

The assistant news director, Don Dupree, called back,

"How high are the flames?" This is the simplest illustration of what the Magid people meant by "eye appeal." The story might be meaningless, but it hypnotized.

Meanwhile, in San Diego, KFMB took Magid's advice to heart. Its viewership numbers leaped past its two competitors. Its news director, Tom Keeney, interviewed by *Newsweek* magazine, credited the *Action News* format. He also noted, it made his station look just like *Action News* programs "in cities like San Francisco, Denver, and Detroit. But that's not necessarily bad, is it?"

That question would echo for the next three decades as local TV news operations from coast to coast took on the homogenized look of hamburger chains. You could move from city to city and hear the same buzz words and catch phrases— "news you can use," etc.—and see the same space age news sets, and watch stories selected on the basis of ratings instead of importance.

Ralph Renick, the news director at Miami's WTVJ in the 1970s, told *Newsweek*, "These [consulting] outfits are the greatest threat to news broadcasting in America. They're like the Soviet Army in World War II. They come in to liberate and end up an army of occupation."

The reason was simple. *Broadcasting* magazine estimated that a relative handful of outside consultants shaped the news in three-quarters of all the TV markets in the country, turning over their design and packaging to these consultants—and their concept of what constituted a valid news story.

Most consultants claim their job is only tangentially related to journalism. They say they are only trying to win ratings points, not influence coverage. In his classic study of TV news, *The Broadcasters*, Ron Powers called this a lie.

"The consultant's self-described role," wrote Powers, "is that of a combination elocution coach and cosmetician: he advises on the production values of a newscast, the attractiveness of the set, the 'atmosphere' among the 'personalities,' the lucidity of the writing. He may comment on the appearance of this anchorman or that sportscaster. He may—on the basis of his surveys of 'attitudes and opinions'—suggest some broad ranges of interest among the viewing audience. He may act as a sort of fine-tuned Nielsen [ratings] service, telling exactly who's out there, how old, how well educated, how affluent, with what cares and what concerns...but never, never, say the consultants, do we get involved in the journalistic process itself. Never do we intrude into the area of content."

Oh, really?

The *Eyewitness News* memos and the *Action News* memos are of a type. They take the ancient business of reporting and turn it into something a little more choreographed, more codified, more aware of—and subservient to—the whims of the marketplace than the business of journalism, while pretending they are not.

I was handed the *Eyewitness News* memo after I'd been told that one of my story ideas wasn't going to cut it.

"It's not *Eyewitness News*," it was explained for the umpteenth time.

"And what is that?" I asked. "I keep hearing that phrase, but what the hell does it mean, exactly?"

As I read the memo, I thought about the night I'd written my commentary on the handicapped kid who'd inspired his friends and family.

"A great kid," I'd said on the air.

"I know," Jerry Turner said.

The response was right out of the memo: "In the interplay between anchor and reporter, the viewer sees that the talent is knowledgeable and friendly." Even if they have to make it up. And who could blame them for showing friendliness toward a kid?

I thought about the five-part series on "the secret fantasies" of WJZ's personalities. It was right out of the memo: "The on-air players are no longer the simple flat images of the tightly produced and edited show. They are people."

I thought about the five-part series on Frank Luber's makeover. It was right out of the memo: "There is an intentional linkage between the individual reporter and the story...the beginnings of creating a stronger personality for the reporters."

I thought about the raw tapes back in the editing room, with a reporter telling a grieving mother, "It's okay to cry." And a reporter telling someone else, "Give me the same answer, but say my name first."

And I thought about those consultants, the Magids and the McHughes and Hoffmans, proclaiming they would never get involved in the area of journalistic content.

But there was something else about these consultants that lingered through the years. They were interested in on-air chemistry, in molding on-air talent to fit viewers' desires. Such a thing works when we think of these viewers as an audience— and not as an electorate, concerned for a brief hour with the serious business of the day and hoping that reporters serve as a check on community problems.

For twenty years in Baltimore, one of the most popular TV news people was Rudy Miller, who anchored at two stations, WBAL and then WMAR. Her background was theater. She was discovered by a news director while she lounged in a nightgown on a bed. She was shooting a mattress commercial.

Miller was the great discovery for WBAL when that station had visions of catching Jerry Turner. She came out of Tulsa, Oklahoma, and wound up doing dinner theater acting in West Palm Beach, Florida. But the dinner theater was going out of business, so Miller supplemented her income with the mattress spot for a department store.

The commercial was shot at a local TV station, WPEC. There was Miller, in a nightgown on a bed, when the station's news director happened to walk past. It was Bill Markham, later to distinguish himself in Baltimore by walking out of his anchoring job at WMAR over the deeply important issue of blue shirts or white shirts on the air.

"You think you might be interested in doing TV news?" Markham asked Miller.

"I've heard a lot of lines," said Miller, rolling her eyes, "but not that one."

"I don't have any women in my newsroom," Markham said.

That such a woman might have some background in news was strictly secondary.

"I'm an actress," Miller explained. "I don't even watch TV."

Then Markham mentioned money.

"Where do I sign?" said Miller.

It was as simple as that. Miller was bright, and she could enunciate, and she was broke enough to take the offer. She was perky as a college cheerleader and projected the wholesome aura of a soap bubble. The only things she didn't know were news, weather, and television. It was understood that she would learn all three well enough to fake it.

"Mostly," Markham said, "you'll be my weather person."

"I don't even know where the states are," Miller said.

"Honey, this is Florida," Markham said. "Just remind people the sun's shining, and it's miserable every place else."

She was a hit right away. Viewers responded to her well-scrubbed perky looks, and out-of-town stations from bigger markets quickly began offering jobs. Baltimore's WBAL hired her to do the weather.

Miller did it for a year and then fled to San Francisco, where she learned to branch out a little—not only weather, but health and science. She was learning to be television's version of a reporter: She could fake authority.

WBAL brought her back—as their news anchor. The job would last for a decade, but would end with a Christine Craft-like story in which Miller would take WBAL to court for treating her like someone less than a man.

Meanwhile, at WJZ, my job had become clear: I was to handle things that would otherwise go unmentioned—the stories that didn't translate visually, the stuff that was too "inside baseball" for the station's reporters, the news that would let the station look journalistically responsible without having to invest too much time or manpower. The stuff that wasn't, specifically, *"Eyewitness News."*

At heart, I was still just a newspaper person posing as a television person. I still felt funny putting on my TV makeup every evening. An assistant news director lectured me about my wardrobe, which tended toward Early Attic. One night I was summoned to an assistant news director's office after writing a passionate piece about prison reform. I was certain he would applaud a fine piece of writing. Instead, he declared, "Take a look at your makeup. You gotta put it on better than that." It was the last time I wore any. It was my little revolt against the cosmetics of television news.

And, always, there was that sense of fighting the clock— no matter how important the story.

It was the unwritten rule of local TV news across the country: Generally, the people running the show don't want any story (or commentary) to go longer than ninety seconds. They felt that was an audience's attention span. Does the name Pavlov ring a bell? The geniuses in TV figured that, after ninety seconds, viewers started salivating like Pavlov's dog for a change of pace, and never mind that they'd only gotten the barest bones of a story on which to gnaw.

In fact, viewers had been conditioned that way.

In 1963, when *NBC Evening News* initiated its half-hour nightly news, Reuven Frank, then the show's executive producer, issued a staff memorandum on the specifics of each story. Frank wrote: "Every news story should, without any sacrifice of probity or responsibility, display the attributes of fiction, of drama. It should have structure and conflict, problem and denouement, rising action and falling action, a beginning, a middle and an end. These are not only the essentials of drama; they are the essentials of narrative."

This became the structure of network television for the rest of the century and beyond, both for networks and local television news operations. And, as an instructional manual for building a newscast, it was fine as far as it went. Though Frank was calling for "the attributes" of fiction, he wasn't calling for fiction itself. Though he called for dramatic "structure and conflict," he wasn't necessarily calling for dramatizing or fictionalizing.

Except in practice. For, built into this rising action and falling action, this structure and conflict, this problem and denouement, was the structure of the unspoken ninety-second limit. Television-speak was journalistic shorthand.

As Edward Jay Epstein wrote in his classic look at television news, *News from Nowhere*, "News organizations select not only which events will be portrayed...but which parts of the filmed portions of those events, when recombined by editing, will stand for the whole mosaic. This necessarily involves choosing symbols."

Again, Frank: "The picture is not a fact but a symbol...The real child and its real crying become symbols of all children." And Epstein added, "In the same way, a particular black may be used to symbolize the aspirations of his race, a particular student may be used to symbolize the claims of his generation, and a particular policeman may be used to symbolize...the concept of authority. Whether the black chosen is a Black Panther or an integrationist, whether the student is a long-haired revolutionary or Young Republican, whether the policeman is engaged in a brutal or benevolent act obviously affects the picture of the event received by the audience. If over long periods of time the same type of symbols are consistently used to depict the behavior and aspirations of groups, certain stable images...can be perpetuated."

The problem was, within television's self-imposed limits of ninety-second stories, how does any news organization decide which symbols stand for which people? Which elements of rising and falling action? Which attributes of fiction? The medium wasn't leaving itself much room for maneuvering in such a limited time frame—and, over the course of decades to come, it locked itself ever more solidly into such narrow structures.

Over years of watching television, they had grown

conditioned to ninety-second stories—or less. Sometimes stories ran for thirty seconds. Sometimes, fifteen seconds. Earthquakes in Pakistan, assassinations in Africa, overthrows of Asian governments were sometimes wrapped up in a sentence or two.

It was television's way of coping with its own trappings. The set is turned on, and viewers watch not a series of news reports, but a montage of performances. For thirty seconds, a man sells Toyotas. This is followed by thirty seconds of children dancing around a Burger King, followed by adolescents on a beach drinking Coca-Cola. Who can bear to sit through a story about tax reform legislation after that? Our senses have been juiced up by all those bikini-clad beach nymphets selling Coca-Colas. How can the news give us more than thirty seconds when we've been programmed, again and again, for lumps of information in half-minute globs?

Our senses don't make conscious distinctions. We judge the television people on the basis of their performances, and not just the news they bring us. We turn on the set in habitual anticipation of the thing that we watch overwhelmingly: entertainment. If we aren't entertained—on some level—then we look elsewhere.

To let the stories run longer than ninety seconds was to risk viewers' restlessness. If they got restless, they might do the unthinkable: change the channel. And when remote controls came along, that meant tightening the screws even more. They couldn't very well make the stories any shorter, but they could make each sound bite shorter and punchier, to give the illusion of great action and saturation coverage, and to keep people with diminishing attention spans from getting bored.

At Harvard, a study was done of television sound bites, those snatches of video that are pieced together to make up the whole story. In 1968, the average sound bite on network news lasted forty-two seconds. By 1988, it was ten seconds. By 1992, it was just over seven seconds. Local TV followed suit.

Television was cutting information into easily digestible

little chunks, like a doting parent cutting a child's dinner. But savvy media types, such as politicians, understood this and responded accordingly. They knew what would sell. They learned to speak sound-bite English. They went for the cutting remark that would get them their little moment on the news. But in the process, the national dialogue became distorted. It got more caustic, more combative. Sometimes it sounded like a shriek in need of an idea.

8

A God Named Cal

These were the tough years for American cities, bracketed by the first of the urban riots and the last of the formerly middle class neighborhoods that fell to the drug dealers and the quick-buck real estate manipulators capitalizing on people's fears.

But where was television's sense of it?

In Baltimore, the mid-century population that neared one million fell more than 300,000 by century's end. Once the nation's sixth-largest city, it fell to twenty-fifth. A public school system that had flirted with racial integration in the post-war years had become ninety percent black, ringed by suburban public schools that were ninety percent white. In the city, 40,000 people lived in subsidized public housing, and another 34,000 waited to get in. Two-thirds of the region's poor resided in the city. Over twenty years, the city's tax base declined by one-third while the surrounding counties went up dramatically.

If the television news operations noticed any of these details, they kept it to themselves.

When Baltimore's high school kids took their college board tests, they averaged a combined 754—out of a possible

1,600. The school dropout rate, and the rate of teenage pregnancies, were the highest in the nation. The city's funding for public education was far less per student than surrounding counties, its textbooks outdated, its classrooms overcrowded, its teachers paid less than suburban teachers. One-quarter of all city residents were functionally illiterate. More than half of all births in the city were to single parents.

If the television news operations noticed any of this, they mentioned it in passing, in fifteen-second stories buried deep in the newscast. To show a human being not being able to read was not considered the stuff of nightly drama; to show the overcrowded classroom was not as stark as the adolescent dropout bloodied and lying in the street from a drug dispute.

In Baltimore, the homicide rate was among the nation's worst. The city was home to an estimated 50,000 drug addicts, who committed the vast majority of all street crimes. The jails and courtrooms were packed. And here was the difference: Whenever the television news executives noticed any of this crime news—well, they couldn't wait to show the screaming mother, the police car with the flashing light, the ambulance with its siren splitting the night air. Such scenes captured the look of drama. The carnage held viewers' attention so they didn't flick the channel before the commercials arrived. But the stations never looked at the patterns behind the troubles, or the texture that made up communities and existed simultaneous to the bloodshed.

It happens this way in Baltimore, and in Philadelphia, too, where Paul Gluck remembers his time at WJZ twenty years earlier and understands how the game continues to be played across the country.

"Here's what the critics have to understand," he said one night after finishing his public television duties there. "I don't think anybody in a newsroom says, 'Let's do eleven crime stories.' But they're there. They're dramatic, they're unfolding as the day goes on, and they have the passions of life affixed to them. Nobody says, it's less expensive so let's do crime stories.

Some of it's done because it's easy and people are sometimes lazy. You hear it on the scanner and you run with it.

"But here's the thing: It's very easy to be seduced by the action. You have seasoned, grown-up news people, and the adrenaline starts to flow, and you find yourself seduced. And when it's kids who are running the newsroom..."

His voice trailed off. In my early days in newspapers, I worked for editors who thought the best of all stories was the human murder. But television changed everything for newspapers. Since TV could get to the crime scene first, and break into regular programming if the story seemed important enough, newspapers had to learn to dig deeper and explain what things meant. But, in the decades since local TV news has come of age, the medium has not progressed much farther than its original destination: Catch the flashing police light, the grieving family, the outraged neighbors.

At WJZ-TV, the first things I noticed the day I walked into the newsroom were the television monitors. They were all around the place—on walls, on desks, rows of TV screens in every direction. But every one of them had the sound off. A cynic would say this captured the essence of the medium: dramatic pictures was all.

But the picture—and the message—sent out every night was one-dimensional: Baltimore was dangerous.

"Well, that's the problem," Paul Gluck said. "Crime, and the constant coverage, can destroy a community's self-esteem. I've seen it a thousand times. You go out to a poor neighborhood, and there's a thousand crime stories that TV's done, and maybe one story on some brave people who are trying to clean up the place. They're out there sweeping trash, and wondering if somebody's going to take a shot at them, and we never put that stuff on the air. We put on the crime, which damages pride in community.

"And a lot of that crime is minority crime. So, what do you do? Find crime in a white community? You have to evaluate it carefully. But if you evaluate it too closely, the story's gone. So you have to roll the dice, and send out your reporter, and hope you've got something meaningful."

Night after night, looking up to watch the newsroom monitors of all the local stations, I saw the same menu: shootings here, anguished mothers there, neighbors expressing outrage and grief against a backdrop of flashing police lights. That the preponderance of shootings involved one drug dealer plugging another drug dealer in the same limited number of neighborhoods went mostly unmentioned. A shooting was a shooting; a great visual was a great visual. Instead of follow-up analyses the night after a shooting, there was always some new shooting to cover, and some similar neighborhood where outraged citizens could mouth the same anguished platitudes.

Such stories reinforced the dread felt when people thought about the city: No one is safe there. Television's perception was different: We only report what we see.

But the medium willfully wore blinders. It saw what it chose to see, what it found easy to see. Baltimore was like a lot of American cities in the final years of the 20th century, struggling with crime and social change. But enormous changes were also arriving in the surrounding counties.

While the city of Baltimore's population had dropped so dramatically over the final half of the century, its five surrounding counties had simultaneously swollen from dirt roads and small schoolhouses to tract housing developments and highways and complex school systems and, not to be minimized, their own crime and social problems.

But television seemed barely to notice—in Baltimore, and around the country.

At WJZ, whenever I suggested stories from suburbia, I was met with blank stares. The suburbs were off on the far side of their consciousness and their sense of important geography. There wasn't enough drama out there. But it was more than that.

In a 1997 *Columbia Journalism Review* piece headlined "Why Local TV News Is So Awful," Lawrence Grossman wrote, "The typical TV station spans too much territory to be truly local, covering more than ten thousand square miles, overlapping cities, counties, towns, wards, election districts, boroughs, even states."

For example, Grossman noted, the NBC affiliate in Paducah, Kentucky, also serves parts of Missouri, Illinois, and western Tennessee. The CBS affiliate in Johnson City, Tennessee, covers not only Kingsport, Bristol, and the rest of northeast Tennessee, but southwest Virginia and western North Carolina, as well. New York's local stations also try to cover Connecticut, New Jersey, and Pennsylvania. Washington's cover not only D.C., but also Maryland and Virginia.

Baltimore TV stations purportedly cover the city, the five surrounding counties, plus any major stories happening across the state. This is mostly a fiction. At the *Baltimore Sun*, there were separate bureaus for each of the surrounding counties. At WJZ, the station relied entirely on *Baltimore Sun* coverage, and on coverage from county newspapers—and, on occasion, if the stories were sexy enough, the station would follow up those stories and claim them as their own.

In all my years in television, though, I do not think any station in town ever sent a reporter to cover any of the county councils. Probably, they would not know where the meetings were held. County executives—the suburban equivalent of the mayor—were interviewed a handful of times a year, at most. And neighborhood coverage was out of the question—unless it involved some sort of disaster.

In general, station executives accepted the problem inherent in any kind of suburban coverage—or any coverage at all that did not provoke general viewer interest: Remote controls. Newspaper readers not interested in a story can simple turn the page; TV viewers change the channel.

As Lawrence Grossman wrote, "In the age of zappers, the TV station that tries to cover a single community's civic, school board, or religious news risks losing most of its audience who live elsewhere. So local TV news concentrates on what will keep its entire coverage area tuned in—crime, scandal, heartwarming features, and local sports and weather...The TV viewer in Kingsport...is likely to zap the channel rather than sit through a news item about a school board meeting in Johnson City, which means not only turning it off, but worse, turning on the competition."

This means local television has to do two things: Find stories with general appeal, such as the weather, and find characters with general appeal.

In Baltimore, that meant certain politicians, such as William Donald Schaefer, the mayor who became governor. Or certain ballplayers, such as Cal Ripken. In his two decades with the Baltimore Orioles, Ripken surely got more air time than anyone else in the state. When he broke Lou Gehrig's consecutive-game record, the station turned it into a week-long pageant. It helped that the station televised some of the Orioles' games, but it was probably more important that he was a common denominator for the entire viewing audience. As long as Cal's picture was on the screen, nobody was going to change the channel.

But such coverage became part of a dreary repetitiveness— this stock company of familiar characters and endless reports about the criminal dangers of the city.

The story of the ten-year-old girl interviewed on the eleven o'clock news is a prime example. But there is another kind of story dictated by the need for quick-and-easy. It's the routine story that doesn't necessarily connect with reality—except that it creates a perceived reality that takes on an emotional life of its own.

One summer evening I watched the newsroom monitors show a demonstration out of West Baltimore. Angry people protested the killing—several weeks earlier—of a man named Jesse Chapman. On one channel, demonstrators gathered behind a reporter and hollered about poor Chapman dying from a police beating. On another, they called Chapman a martyr. They claimed to have a videotape of the beating of Chapman.

They were making a lot of noise. But if you looked closely, they seemed to be a small group that had gathered in close for the television shot to make their numbers look larger. I wondered how many they really were. Some shouted threats of trouble to come. I turned to an assistant producer and asked how we had gotten the story.

"They phoned us," she said. Once we had our reporter and photographer there, the story was a given. We weren't going to waste manpower and not have anything to put on the air. But the story itself didn't have the ring of truth to it.

I left the station and drove to West Baltimore. I got there fifteen minutes after the TV live shots showed what appeared to be a neighborhood on the brink of riot. But now, instead of loud demonstrators, there were people quietly sitting on rowhouse front steps. I remembered the riots of 1968, and the night those people tossed rocks at the burning warehouse while a TV camera rolled.

"What happened to the demonstrations?" I asked a few people now.

They rolled their eyes. The demonstration was for television, but the television cameras were all gone. As the TV stations told it, the demonstrators believed the martyr Jesse Chapman was beaten to death by police.

"Hmph," said a young woman sitting in a small group of people on her front stoop. "I don't know if the police killed him. But I'll tell you this. If they didn't, then his girlfriend would have."

A few people said there was a man named James Breakfield who saw the police beating from his window and videotaped it, a fact allegedly ignored by law enforcement authorities.

That was the claim I'd seen on television. I left the people sitting on their front steps and went looking for Breakfield. He was on Mount Street, half a block away, where anybody (including TV reporters) could have found him if they had bothered looking.

"What about this tape?" I asked.

"Yeah, I got it," he said.

"It shows the police beating Chapman to death?"

"Not exactly."

"What does that mean?"

"I saw the police beat him from my window," Breakfield said. "They took the life out of him. Three police whipped his head with some instrument, whipped the daylights out of him. It sounded like a sledge hammer. I know they cracked his skull. I saw the whole thing, and I told the grand jury."

"Did you show them the video tape?"

Well, no, he hadn't. Breakfield had taken out his recorder some time after the beating was over. He had some shots of poor Chapman being carried off to an ambulance.

It was pretty chilling stuff. The problem was: It didn't hold up. There was a coroner's report, easily available to any reporter for weeks preceding the demonstration. The report said Chapman did not die from a beating. It said he suffered "superficial injuries." It declared no evidence of "repeated blows or other significant injury."

What killed Chapman? "Acute cocaine intoxication complicated by asthma," the coroner's report said. What caused the cops to pursue him in the first place? Chapman, his system full of cocaine, tried to beat up his girlfriend, who ran into the Western District police headquarters with Chapman close behind her. There, with officers all around him, the insane Chapman tried to beat her some more, and then ran out of the building with police pursuing him until they caught him on Mount Street. As Chapman fought with them, they struck him and subdued him and then Chapman died there on the street.

Was any of this out of character for the deceased? Not exactly. In a neighborhood riddled with narcotics traffic, Chapman was one of its traffickers. Over the last ten years of his life, he had a rap sheet that also included malicious destruction of property, armed assault, illegal use of a handgun, and rape.

The problem was, such distinctions were not being made by mobs shouting in front of television cameras—nor by television stations that thought it more important to get an exciting live shot on the air than to do the routine work of any legitimate reporter before going with the story.

On Mount Street, I talked with one of the neighbors, Rodney Heard, a mortician.

"I don't think Jesse Chapman deserved to die," he said, "but he brought it on himself. You assault a woman inside a police station, listen, you might as well commit suicide. But you'll have young people getting worked up for the TV cameras over this drug abuser. And then when the TV cameras go away, they'll walk up the street and get right into the drug traffic. That's what they need to protest around here."

Television never stopped to consider such a thing. It got the pictures that it wanted, and then it went away. It set up Jesse Chapman up as a martyr, as proclaimed by less than a dozen neighborhood people who got themselves on television, and it set a tone for a city. For those who felt oppressed by police, it reinforced that notion; for those who saw the city as a dangerous place with screaming, irrational people, it reinforced that notion. When I went back to WJZ the next day, I brought up Chapman's name.

"Who?" said an executive producer.

"The guy from last night," I said. "That demonstration."

"Last night," the executive producer repeated dully.

"Right."

"Right. Tell me about what's going on the air tonight."

Jesse Chapman was not. He was now yesterday's business because someone else in the city would bloody someone new before this day was done. Or if not bloody them, then commit a crime of such freakishness, or such outlandishness, or such pettiness, that television would find it irresistible.

This was what infuriated Jerry Turner and Al Sanders every night, and caught them in the grip of such painful irony. Their careers were carried along by such coverage, even as the city around them came apart. And that coming-apart was sped along precisely by such coverage, which reflected a place much more dangerous, more politically polarized, and more randomly sinister than it really was.

The newsroom rationale was simple: We were putting on a television program. That it happened to be a program about local news was a slight afterthought. Primary thinking was always guided by ratings, which moderated profits, which touched careers. What led to high ratings? The thinking was simple: that combination of personalities (the anchors, plus community personalities such as Cal Ripken) and drama (cops and robbers) that made other television shows popular. If this combination happened to involve serious journalism, fine. If not? That was fine, too.

In all these years, television insisted on covering every easy, visually dramatic crime story it could find while expressing complete indifference to all other crimes—not the crime of legal statute, but of economic cruelty.

This was an era—the Bush-Clinton-Bush years—of vanishing health care and pension benefits. According to widely-reported U.S. census figures, the poor were paying sixty percent of their income on rent and utilities, which was double the government's "affordable" figure. One in four American children were officially classified as living in poverty—one in two among black children. By the early 1990s the share of wealth (more than forty percent) held by the top one percent of the population was essentially double what it had been in the mid-1970s. The average corporate chairman, who had out-earned his workers by forty to one in 1975, out-earned them by 200 to one in the 1990s. The 2.6 million Americans with the highest incomes had as much after-tax income as the 100 million Americans with the lowest incomes.

Surely, in such disparities, there were stories to be told. In fact, they were told—in newspapers, and in magazines, and on public radio. In local television, however, news directors shuddered at the prospect of such stories. They weren't visual enough. They took too much digging, and then too much explaining. Viewers would get restless.

I thought I saw a way to tell the story without losing viewers, and I took the idea to Gail Bending, the news director at WJZ. She withered me with a pitying stare.

"It's Cal," she said.

"So what?" I said.

"It's Cal," she said, as if closing the subject.

Cal was Ripken. In the spring of 1997, Bending had ordered up a story on Ripken signing a new Baltimore Orioles baseball contract.

I had no problem with mentioning the new contract. My problem was the station's excessive coverage, and deification, of any ballplayer and the conflict sometimes presented: In the station's eyes, Ripken could do no wrong. In the station's eyes, it was more important to do a package on Ripken than a story with some texture about life as it was actually lived in an American community.

Where this conflict came to a head, in my mind, was the moment when Ripken signed his new contract for millions of dollars—on the same day that nearly 300 employees of the city's London Fog raincoat manufacturer were notified that they were losing their jobs, and the station did not care enough to make this, too, a big deal.

In Bending's mind, Ripken wasn't just a ballplayer but a figure whose mere mention froze viewers in their tracks. Cal was a god, partly because he was a great, fan-friendly ballplayer, and partly because he'd grown up in nearby Aberdeen and was thus billed as a home-town kid. And partly because, seizing a good thing, the local media had exalted him as much as possible.

To me, the Cal coverage was sometimes exasperating. I understood marketing, but I also thought I understood perspective. Bending saw Cal as balance. We showed homicide stories, but we also showed this feel-good guy. We had a world that sometimes seemed chaotic beyond repair, but we also had Cal out there every day, season after season, symbolic of the center holding through it all.

He was, in fact, what Walter Lippmann had referred to as part of the "repertory of stereotypes." He had gone from being a mere ballplayer to a symbol of all that was good and wholesome in Baltimore. And we were going to ride that symbolism, and wrap ourselves in it as part of our own identity, especially since we carried some of the Orioles' games.

On this day, though, it peeved me because of the contrast in money—and in coverage.

The new Ripken contract would pay him $6.3 million a year, in a time when professional athletes' salaries (and ticket prices to support those salaries) were soaring beyond all previous recognition. Meanwhile, at London Fog where the layoffs were announced, the average worker made $6.90 an hour, which came to about $14,000 a year. Ripken would make about the same $14,000—each time he batted. At London Fog, there were 281 employees. Figuring $14,000 a year per worker, this came to $3,934,000 per year (about two-thirds of Ripken's new salary)—for the entire factory.

None of this would be mentioned in any of our news stories. And it wasn't that I wanted to criticize Ripken. It wasn't his fault that professional ballplayers' salaries were obscene. But for a serious news outlet, here was a chance to point out the cruel ironies of the marketplace. And it was a chance to talk about some other economic troubles routinely ignored by local television news: how Baltimore's labor force was steadily declining in numbers; how the city's unemployment level doubled the rest of the region's; how household income in the city was virtually unchanged over two decades, while it was swelling in the surrounding suburbs.

The London Fog layoffs came at a time of difficulty in the American workplace: the vanishing opportunities for blue collar laborers, the nearly surrealistic distance between the nation's haves and have-nots   not just the wealthy ballplayers, but also the corporate executives with breathtaking income.

How did the bosses earn such big bucks? By increasing company profits. How did they increase those profits? In a lot of cases, by eliminating jobs, or by bullying employees into taking pay cuts, by cutting benefits, by holding the threat of job elimination over their heads. At London Fog, they'd been listening to such threats for years. The result was people making poverty wages and then losing their jobs, anyway, because companies could find even cheaper labor overseas.

I called London Fog's corporate offices in Philadelphia, where a company spokesman named Kevin Brockenbrough said yes, it was the familiar modern story: It was getting too costly to produce goods in America. The work would now be done, he said, "in the Far East, in one of those Asian countries. I don't know how much money they make there."

In America at this time, the average apparel worker made eight dollars an hour. In Mexico, two dollars an hour. In Bangladesh, twenty-five cents an hour. In Baltimore, the average baseball ticket at Oriole Park was now going for nearly sixteen dollars, which would pay for $14,000 at-bats for those such as Cal Ripken.

Meanwhile, as London Fog's employees began to search for new work, the nation began weeding out the lists of those eligible for welfare payments. The idea was put these people to work. But where? The places such as London Fog were closing down, shipping the work overseas. London Fog's employees would be the newest ones on the welfare lines.

The answer, I suggested with tongue somewhat in cheek, was simple: They could apply for work at Oriole Park. There might be jobs there as ushers, as beer vendors, as ticket takers. The pay was minimum wage. But they could see what a $14,000 at-bat looked like.

That night, I said some of these things—as many as I could fit in on my television commentary—about the vast difference in American salaries, as personified by Ripken and the three hundred folks at London Fog, about the loss of manufacturing jobs overseas, about CEOs making two hundred times as much as their employees.

When I got off the air, the first call I took was an angry fellow asking, "Why are you putting the knock on Cal?"

I hung up the phone and decided not to mention this to Gail Bending.

9

Richard and Oprah

In hindsight, everybody claims they saw the dawning of greatness. They say they looked at Oprah Winfrey in her Baltimore awkwardness and sensed luminescence waiting to be discovered. Naturally the truth is elsewhere. Oprah thought she was just Richard Sher's sidekick. And he thought she was, too.

The only one with vision was Bill Baker. At this time, he was the general manager at WJZ. Baker arrived from Cleveland, where he developed a successful talk show called *The Morning Exchange*. In Baltimore, he blew town as often as possible. He went to one city and then another so he could sit in hotel rooms and do nothing but watch local television. He was looking for two people, somewhere out there in America, who could create a morning talk show for Baltimore.

After all those hotel rooms, he stumbled into the right people in his own building. He grabbed these two refugees from the news department and brought them into his office. In Sher, he saw someone smart and ambitious and energetic beyond measure. In Winfrey, he saw Sher's opposite: a woman going nowhere, due to the monumental stupidity of people around her who didn't recognize Miss America when she fell into their laps. Baker called her Opie. He had Allan Frank, the station's program manager, approach Sher.

"What do you think about doing a talk show?" Frank asked.

"What kind of a talk show?" Sher asked. He was wary. He had an image as a professional newsman. All performance, and all drama, were built on a foundation of broadcast journalism. This was Sher's legitimacy. He saw himself, one day down the road, as the second coming of Jerry Turner.

Frank mentioned celebrity guests who would drop by to hustle their newest ventures. He mentioned a studio audience and telephone calls from viewers, all the elements that would become standards of the modern format but none that sounded like a traditional newsman's venue. Then he asked Sher how he got along with Oprah Winfrey.

"I don't know her real well," Sher said. He thought about her disastrous pairing with Jerry Turner, and he thought about seeing her weeping in her car sometimes when she walked out of the station at day's end. But he also thought about her friendliness and her self-effacing sense of humor.

"Why her?" he asked.

"If we do this show right," Frank said, "it should have a white guy and a black woman. It crosses all lines then. And Baker likes the two of you together."

Sher liked the idea of more air time but wondered about the format. After all of his radio ventures on both coasts, he valued the career he finally seemed to be building. In his radio days, he'd covered Bobby Kennedy's funeral procession, Patty Hearst's kidnapping, the return of Vietnam prisoners of war and thereafter found himself fired over management whims. At WJZ, he covered all those nightly murders for the evening news, plus some touchy-feely stuff. His career possibilities seemed strong.

Sher had some remarkable TV qualities. His energy took people's breath away, and so did his instinct for a story. He could sit at his desk on his distant side of the newsroom and hear a police radio through the clatter. Others might seem oblivious, or too weary to check it out. Sher would leap to his feet in an instant, calling out specific neighborhoods and directions to get there. He knew these things because he'd been in Baltimore most of his life. He knew the city's rhythms and understood its neighborhoods. He seemed instinctively to know which stories were important for television and how to sell them hard, and he wanted a piece of all action.

Oprah was a different story. She was deflated by the awful Jerry Turner pairing, and the heartless attempts to remake her looks, and the demotions on the job. She thought it was time to leave town.

"Think about it," Allan Frank told Sher.

Sher went home and told his wife Annabelle. They both understood the station's thinking on gender and on race. Baltimore is a mixed city with all the modern emotional complexities about color. The TV news operations, trying to reflect this, wanted to balance their staffs racially. For Sher, the idea of a black woman and a white man sitting together on the air, and not making a big deal about the implications, was appealing. The question was, how would such a show mesh with his career as a news reporter?

One morning, he and Oprah were summoned to Bill Baker's office. Baker said he'd been sitting in all these hotel rooms around the country and looking at people on television. He said he knew what worked in TV and what didn't. He was a bright, self-confident man with a Ph.D. and a professorial air about him.

"I think you two could make it work," he said. "You're the best people I've seen anywhere."

He talked about television's changing audience. He mentioned young stay-at-home mothers who needed an intellectual challenge since they only had their babies to talk to all day. He said a call-in show with authoritative guests could help these women.

"You think it would draw an audience?" Oprah asked. "It sounds a little serious for an entertainment show."

Not entirely, Baker said. There would be fluffy stuff, too.

Sher thought again about his image. How could he move from hair stylists in the morning to homicides in the afternoon? In that era, serious broadcast people still tried to draw lines between news and overt entertainment.

Oprah thought about her contract. It was about to expire. The talk show could be her breakout vehicle, but maybe Baltimore wasn't the place for her. The past year had been brutal, and she thought about starting fresh somewhere else. Stations across the country were hungry for young black women. Baker knew this. A few days later, he called Oprah to his office.

"You and I have been through a lot together," he said. "It hasn't been easy, but we've stuck with you, and now you're a star." That was a little verbal tic Baker had, calling people his stars. Now, with Oprah's contract up for renewal and the talk show on the line, he was pouring it on for all he was worth.

"I'm asking you to stick with me a little longer," he said. "I don't want to be here without you."

It was a moving speech, and an unusual one. It was about personal loyalty, which is more rare in television than emeralds. Loyalty, Oprah understood. Baker was speaking her language, and it touched her. She signed her new contract that night.

And the next day, it was announced that Bill Baker had agreed to take a job somewhere else.

The show was called *People Are Talking*, with Richard Sher and Oprah Winfrey—in that order of billing—and it went on the air August 1, 1977, and lasted six years before Oprah went elsewhere.

In that time, Phil Donohue's program was the high-minded talk show model, but its success quickly gave birth to low-rent imitators. First came hybrids of news and features such as *People Are Talking*, which begat Oprah's breath-taking national success out of Chicago. But Oprah helped spawn the proliferation of those bared-teeth productions such as Jerry Springer, Ricki Lake, Sally Jesse Raphael, Geraldo Rivera, Montel Williams, Morton Downey, Jr., and Jenny Jones.

In the early talk show years, politics turned to pop sociology, which led to a generation of celebrity chit chat co-existing with whiners and sociopaths. Ricki Lake would offer "daughters who date older men and moms who say they can't stop them," which prompted Jerry Springer's "women who say, 'I had his baby and he kicked me to the curb.'" Then Geraldo Rivera provoked racial fist fights on his show, with his own battered face juicing the ratings. For those who did not yet find this crass enough, there was Jenny Jones introducing an unsuspecting young man to a homosexual admirer. The young man would respond to the admirer by shooting him to death.

People Are Talking was pretty innocent compared to what followed. But it still put Sher and Winfrey in two awkward camps. One day an actor from the soap opera *All My Children* appeared, and Richard and Oprah asked if one of the show's characters would marry another one. They saw it as a good-natured reflection of pop culture. Newspaper critics wondered, how can they ask such a fantasy question and retain a credible image on the news?

Oprah didn't care. For a while, neither did Richard. The show was so popular that it topped the previously indomitable Donohue in head-to-head ratings in Baltimore. Then, billing itself as "the show that beats Donohue," it landed syndication telecasts in seventeen other markets around the country.

In Baltimore, they were embraced as on-air sweethearts. For a while, rumors circulated that Oprah was having Richard's baby. In fact, they were pals. Oprah told everybody Richard was her "best girlfriend." She and Richard's wife, Annabelle, became close. When Oprah made out her will, she named Richard as her next of kin. The two of them were given to hypochondria, and spent hours analyzing each other's imaginary ailments. When Oprah went jogging, she'd head straight for Sher's house—where she always went to a junk-food drawer she kept there for herself. Wherever they appeared in public, they seemed the toast of the town.

"I eat out every meal," Oprah announced on the show one day. "I don't cook; I can't bake a roast." While the audience digested that little non sequitur, she went on, "I don't know my way around a grocery store. When I put things in my refrigerator, they go there to die. I have to call the fire department to come in and take them out."

She had two hobbies: reading and dieting. Sometimes she was bingeing, and sometimes she was starving. She couldn't locate a kitchen stove and didn't know what to do if she ever got there. It didn't matter. The *People Are Talking* plan was for Oprah to handle cooking demonstrations with guests. One day, a female chef from a local restaurant stood at the show's kitchen area preparing a turkey when Oprah picked something off the kitchen counter, looked into the cameras, and inquired, "What's this?"

"This?" the chef asked. "That's a meat thermometer."

The studio audience, mainly women, chuckled. "You never saw one?" the chef asked, her voice caught between incredulity and a desire not to make Oprah look dumb.

Behind the scenes, panic brewed. In the control room, an associate producer, Sandra Pinckney, muttered, "Lord, where has this child been?" Producer Sherry Burns frantically scribbled words on a pad and raced from the control room to the studio, trying to signal Oprah to move on. No chance. Oprah had locked into this meat thermometer and wouldn't let it go.

"Isn't this the best thing you ever heard of?" she asked the studio audience, her voice full of fascination. "Every kitchen should have one."

And with that, a remarkable thing happened: Oprah discovered TV honesty. You didn't have to be an expert. TV reporters are marketed as instant experts at everything they cover. It's the job requirement, even when it happens to be a sham. Sher still nurtured his career as a hard news reporter. Oprah was ready to kiss it off and be herself. She was liberated, while her sidekick was still working things out.

She wasn't afraid to say what she didn't know. She wasn't afraid to look naive or silly. She understood she was a proxy inquisitor for every viewer. She figured, if she didn't know something, neither did viewers. She wasn't afraid to ask the questions everybody else would be too self-conscious to ask. After a few days, she told Sherry Burns that the show felt as natural to her as breathing.

It wasn't so easy for Sher. Oprah yielded to him as the show's prime mover. She called herself "Richard's straight man." But he had to balance his two competing career images.

"Don't worry about it," station executives told him. "We've done the research. You're fine, viewers don't care about the different personalities."

Sher felt mollified. He seemed unaware that he was being overexposed, that viewers were seeing too much of him in too many different guises. Half the time he was the hard news reporter, and half the time he handled celebrity interviews and such piffle as *People Are Talking's* "Dialing for Dollars" segment.

One day they invited some friends of the general manager to help with the morning's "Dialing for Dollars." All it meant was calling a random number from the telephone book and asking if the person could name the day's winning number. It was designed to keep listeners hanging around until the last part of the show. And, for those who helped with the segment, it offered a few moments of TV glitter.

On this morning, though, Sher was told of a bulletin just as he broke for a final commercial before the show's end.

"We have a bulletin," he announced, "which we'll give you after the commercial break."

Now Sherry Burns, the tough, acerbic producer, told him, "When we get back, say your goodbyes, read the bulletin out of the TelePrompter, and thank these folks for helping with 'Dialing for Dollars.'"

"What's the bulletin?"

"Golda Meir's dead."

"What?"

Sher froze. Now came the floor manager's voice. "We're back in five seconds. Four, three..."

"That's it for this morning," Sher told viewers, the blood draining from his face. "We want to announced that Israeli Prime Minister Golda Meir has died, and thanks a lot to our guests for helping us with 'Dialing for Dollars.'"

When the show ended, he hollered at Sherry Burns, "How could you do that? How could you put Golda Meir's death next to 'Dialing for Dollars'?"

"Don't worry," Burns said drily. "Golda would have wanted it that way."

The black humor got them past the moment, but it reminded Sher of his dilemma.

He was not only mixing his morning chitchat with his evening hard news, he was tossing the two together in the same breath. The dilemma was his straitjacket—but Oprah's liberation.

One morning on *People Are Talking*, they had Siamese twins as guests, thirty-two-year old women attached at the tops of their heads. They talked about going through life sharing everything. Their mother said she'd been offered big money to put her girls in a carnival. She said no, she wanted them to hold onto their dignity. She said doctors had suggested surgery, but one of the girls probably wouldn't survive the operation. "I just couldn't kill one of my daughters," the mother said.

Then Oprah blithely asked, "When one of you has to go to the bathroom at night, does the other one have to go with her?" The question just popped into her head, and out it came.

One morning they hosted the famous chicken producer Frank Perdue. Oprah asked him, "Has anybody ever told you you look just like a chicken?"

Another morning the famous fashion model Beverly Johnson showed up and was asked about men. "I like handsome, sexy men," she said.

"What's your ideal first date?" Oprah asked.

"To be taken to a nice restaurant," Johnson said, "and to be wined and dined. And then have the man take me home..."

"Yes?"

"And give me an enema," Johnson declared.

Sher immediately broke for a commercial. He and Oprah hooted about the remark for years. But at that moment, it was another reminder for Sher: Could he talk to fashion models in the morning risking diarrhetic confessions, and maintain credibility in the evening?

The show lasted until late 1983 with Richard and Oprah. They interviewed Muhammad Ali and Arnold Schwartzenegger, Jesse Jackson and Barry Levinson and Ted Koppel. They interviewed Elvis impersonators and soap opera stars and charlatans who were just deep enough for twenty-minute TV interviews. They built one show around sexual orgasms. This was not the best of timing, because their studio audience that day happened to be comprised entirely of congregation members from a Baptist church. And they had Alan Funt show some *Candid Camera* film clips on a day when the audience was students from the National Federation for the Blind. They sat silently. But the folks at home loved it.

Those were heady days at WJZ. Judged by ratings alone, the station was one of the country's real powerhouses. It had *People Are Talking* dominating the mornings and the noon news with Richard and Oprah dominating mid-day. Jerry Turner and Al Sanders blew away all competition each dinner hour, followed by a half-hour feature show five nights a week called *Evening Magazine* that drew a strong audience and Sher's explosive weekly current events panel, *Square-Off.* Its eleven p.m. broadcast was among the highest-rated in the whole country.

And then came an early-morning program, with Marty Bass and Don Scott, which would dominate the market for years. The morning show started in 1982, when the idea of morning programming was just beginning to occur to most local stations.

It made sense on several levels. Studies showed that Americans were getting up earlier and earlier. Many of them instinctively turned on their sets. And the shows were natural lead-ins to national morning shows. At WJZ, the show was such a hit that it dominated the opposition by as much as seven-to-one margins.

The key to the show was Bass. On the air, he was an edgy, hyperactive court jester cum weatherman. Weather was important in these morning shows. At an hour of the day when people were showering, dressing, organizing their children, and eating breakfast, their listening habits were fractured. The weather grabbed them for a couple of seconds. So did verbal outbursts.

Bass seemed to wind himself up and race off in fourteen different directions at the same time. He had a Gatling-gun delivery in his native Kentucky drawl, and kept no opinions to himself. Off the air, he was only slightly less frenetic. One day in the newsroom, when Bass's wife Sharon was pregnant with their first child, and Marty seemed filled with anxiety, I tried to tell him about the joys of parenthood.

"Relax," I said, "you'll love being a father."

"Oh, yeah?" he shot back. "How'd you like to raise another Marty Bass?"

In the station's casting system, he was the wayward son to weatherman Bob Turk's easy-going kid brother persona. Did Marty once get into a little trouble (in his bachelor days) with an undercover cop posing as a hooker? Well, yeah, but he explained it away as a misunderstanding. Did he lose his temper and smash an old Babe Ruth baseball bat sent over to the station by the folks at the Bambino's birthplace? Well, as it turned out, the bat was only a Ruthian facsimile, so no serious harm was done. Did he call the news director a lot of bad names on the air one morning? Yeah, and he got hollered at afterwards, and then it was allowed to pass. For talent, you make allowances.

In the early years of the morning show, Bass continued to handle off-beat features for the evening news. For a while, he called the pieces "Catchin' Bass." Then, painting a new face on them, they were called "Mondo Basso." At their best, both the morning show and Bass's features were a smile and only occasionally to be confused with serious journalism. The other stations in town tried matching him and could not. It was Jerry Turner's essential rule: Be yourself. You couldn't concoct another Bass; his stuff depended as much on attitude as content. It was performance with a thin coating of journalism.

The morning show was a mix of headlines and community feel-good stuff. As the technology got better, they could put people inside neighborhood hangouts, on street corners and doughnut shops, and capture some of the town's off-beat characters.

Was that journalism? In the sense of covering government and politics, or serious neighborhood concerns, absolutely not. In the sense of capturing a city's quirky persona, though, it sometimes caught it better than anything else on television. One morning, reporter Brenda Carl might be chatting with customers at a bakery in working class Dundalk; other mornings, reporter Ron Matz would lead community sing-alongs on the cobble-stone streets of Fells Point.

It was a TV station holding up a mirror so a community could get a pleasing look at itself minus the usual shootings and stabbings. It wasn't McNeil-Lehrer, dolefully wrapping things up at day's end; it was an early jolt of caffeine to get everybody going, with basics such as weather and traffic reports and school lunch menus. For serious folks, there were news briefs each half hour.

Bass and his co-anchor, Don Scott, swam in a tricky sea. Their show mixed news and offbeat features in a way that tended to delight viewers, or make them turn up their noses. It started as a half-hour program and eventually went to three hours, from five to eight o'clock each morning. It was so strong, it pre-empted the CBS morning show after WJZ changed network affiliates from ABC.

Though it started out posing as a news show, straight news was not for Bass. He had a low boredom threshold and started ad-libbing. The ad libs became rants, sometimes comic and sometimes not. When the ratings kept improving, the show kept loosening up even more.

They'd do an upbeat piece, and Bass would say, "Give this

guy a big round of applause." So somebody in the control room would run canned applause. It was like radio. Eventually, they'd run all kinds of sound effects, including bodily functions. They ran pictures of children on their birthdays, but eventually had to give it up because they were getting too many pictures.

Bass was the powder keg and Scott was the guy who kept the noise from getting too loud. Scott never lost his composure. He'd been in Baltimore for more than a decade by the time he and Bass teamed, and covered all kinds of stories, and knew the turf pretty well. Also, he had the ability to read the TelePrompter, see a clunky sentence construction, and rewrite it on the air—as he was speaking.

And the two of them kept a sense of perspective about the show. One day during a commercial, a producer asked, "Can we say that on the air?" He was asking about a half-assed line of Bass's that bordered on a curse.

"Hell," Bass replied, "ten minutes to six on a Monday morning, it ain't gonna be Ed Murrow."

He'd gone to Southern Illinois University, where he knew right away that his motor mouth was perfect for broadcasting. But while still in school a TV consultant told him he'd have to wear a toupee if he wanted to have much of a career—so why not start wearing it now? It was Charles Kurault's complaint: TV news was all hair, all appearance, and content was an afterthought. Bass, still just a kid, figured the consultant knew what he was talking about, and he started wearing a rug even when he still had some hair left. Bass wore it until common sense prevailed: He was a grown man, enjoying lovely success, with an audience that embraced him for his skills and his personality.

He went to news director Natalea Brown and asked if he could ditch the toupee. Nobody knew this until Brown started calling staffers into her office, one by one, for a little man-in-the-street survey.

"I want to ask you something," Brown asked each staffer. Then she pointed to Bass, standing in a corner of the room, his head bare. "What do you think?" Brown asked.

This was television taking a step where no one had gone before—taking away some of its contrived artifice, instead of adding to it.

Bass went on vacation the morning after his private unveiling. When he returned, Don Scott was vacationing and a reporter named Don Williams sat in as co-anchor. Bass sat down bald for the first time. In the final moments before they went on the air, Williams suddenly looked up from some copy he'd been reading, noticed the new Marty for the first time, and said, "Haven't you forgotten something?"

Bass checked the zipper on his pants. "Nope," he said, "it's up."

The change to his natural state made headlines in newspapers and trade periodicals and broadcast stations around the world. Newspapers ran big feature stories, and television and radio stations called to interview him. The story had two elements: a well-known TV personality throwing off his toupee in a business where men are known for putting them on, and his employer thinking this was fine.

It defied every known dictum handed down by a TV consultant since the dawning of the medium. And a remarkable thing happened: Bass's popularity, already high, went higher. He was already known for his idiosyncratic nature. Now the response was: Look what that crazy Marty Bass has done this time.

And life went on.

But it went on in different forms. At WJZ, a woman named Debra DiMaio decided to look for a new job. In 1983, her job was producing *People Are Talking,* with Richard Sher and Oprah Winfrey. DiMaio sought employment in a larger market and tried Chicago. She sent TV station executives there a videotape of one of her Baltimore shows.

The executives, while impressed with DeMaio's production values, went absolutely nuts over the show's co-host, Oprah Winfrey. Thus is history written. Later, Sher would shrug his shoulders and joke, "Just my luck. Debbie sends a tape where

Oprah's having a hot day. If she sends her another tape, maybe it's a day where I'm the one who's hot."

That December, there was a farewell gathering for Oprah at Baltimore's Cafe des Artistes Restaurant, a bittersweet affair. Bill Baker, who'd picked Oprah for *People Are Talking*, was long gone. He was in New York, where he headed Public Broadcasting.

"I remember when I first came here," Oprah said, looking around the big gathering of her old colleagues. "I would drive around town just crying." She started to weep a little, but smiled through her tears, as though she saw clear sailing just ahead. She mentioned the city's historic rowhouses. "I didn't understand why they were all stuck together," she said. She was still the little country girl who had come to the big city.

Paul Yates, who had replaced Baker as general manager, put his arms around Oprah and then gave her a couple of gifts: a television set and a cuisinart.

And that was the end of it. Oprah went to Chicago, leaving Richard Sher in Baltimore with a television talk show and a new co-host. Her name was Beverly Burke. She'd been a radio disc jockey in Buffalo, New York, and then, as it happens in TV news, she was magically transformed into an anchor in Durham, North Carolina. In the *People Are Talking* format, she was okay. She just wasn't Oprah. In the shallow way television sometimes moves, station executives hired Burke because she looked like Oprah. Burke was black, she was big, and those qualities seemed sufficient. If nobody looked too closely, maybe they'd think she and Oprah were the same person.

Burke lasted a while. Then she was replaced by a woman named Linda Harriss. She was all right, too. But it was never the same. And the ensuing years would take their toll —not only on *People Are Talking*, and not only on talk shows across the country that turned tabloid and trashy—but on the career of Richard Sher, who tried to have it both ways and couldn't, and on TV news programs, which also try to have it both ways, and keep trying.

Small Screen Hero

Now comes the story of television's love affair with Ardern Hythe.

He was a hero precisely large enough to fill a small television screen. In the fullness of his moment in the public's eye, he gives us a lesson in the difference between television news and reality, and why so much of it comes down to having a legitimate staff of reporters, or faking it.

One winter evening Hythe rolled his wheelchair in front of a municipal bus in downtown Baltimore and refused to move. This won him an entire community's respect and admiration, which lasted for about forty-eight hours.

Hythe was paralyzed from the waist down. With the municipal bus traveling eastward on Saratoga Street, here was Hythe, twenty years old, striking a blow on behalf of all persons in wheelchairs. He said he was tired of drivers who passed him by instead of stopping to lower the wheelchair lift for him. Hythe told this to police when they arrived and ordered him to move on. Hythe said no. He wanted some attention. He wanted television cameras. Before the cops could pull him away, Hythe managed to back up ten buses and tie up traffic on two streets.

Oh, did television love him.

Oh, did Baltimore think this was a fine young man.

And this, in a nutshell, is our little cautionary tale.

For here we were, the day after the television stations of Baltimore were filled with the wondrous story of Arden Hythe, and as I walked through the city's Clarence M. Mitchell Courthouse, a voice called out my name. It was Milton Allen. He had been the state's attorney of Baltimore and was now a Juvenile Court judge. We knew each other pretty well, and for a simple reason: Over the years, I'd spent time in the courthouse looking for stories. Our lives had crossed. We knew each other well enough to trust each other. Allen motioned me into his chambers.

"Arden Hythe," he said.

"The kid on television last night."

"Right. Do you know why he's paralyzed?"

One of the TV reporters had asked Hythe the same question. The answer tore at everyone's heart. Hythe said he'd been paralyzed in a car accident fourteen years earlier, when he was six years old.

"If you check the records," Allen said, "I think you'll find a different story."

The records were available to anyone, including reporters, who might have bothered walking into the courthouse. The records said that Hythe, on the night of December 12, 1979, broke into a house, threatened to kill a thirteen-year-old girl, and then sexually assaulted her. He was not in a wheelchair then; he was, in fact, a fully robust sixteen-year-old boy.

Ten weeks later, February 28, 1980, Hythe shifted from house-breaking and sexual assault to car-breaking. But the owner of the car, Willie Crawford, looked through his front window, saw Hythe in action, and recognized him immediately. He had previously complained to police, and to juvenile authorities, that Hythe harassed him almost daily and had slashed his car tires. The authorities, filled with their customary vigor, did absolutely nothing.

Now Crawford had had enough. He grabbed a gun, and he

went out to his car. Hythe swung wildly at him; Crawford fired his gun. He severed Hythe's spinal cord and paralyzed him from the waist down.

Such was Hythe's character, and his full criminal record, that Crawford was given probation before judgment. But a sympathetic judge, looking at Hythe in his wheelchair, suspended all prison time in the sexual assault case—leaving Hythe free, a year later, to be charged with attacking a schoolgirl with a four-foot iron bar from his wheelchair.

None of this was reported on television about the hero Hythe.

In the world of those who get their news strictly from the tube, Hythe was a guy championing a worthy cause. It was a great and inspiring story, as far as it went, and I felt queasy disabusing everyone in town of his nobility. But I also thought his story should be told accurately.

When I reached Hythe later that day, I asked him the same question the TV reporters had asked him the previous night about the origin of his paralysis.

"It was a head-on car collision," he said.

"Was anybody else hurt?"

"My girl friend," he said. "She was killed."

"According to court records," I said, "you weren't in a car accident at all. You were paralyzed by being shot while trying to break into a man's car."

There was silence for a moment, and then Hythe said, "Oh, man, you been checking into my records?"

He wanted to be seen as a victim and hoped nobody would discover how he became one. He was almost an inspiration to a lot of people who knew nothing about his sexual assault, or his attack of a schoolgirl with an iron bar, or the rest of his criminal record. Rolling his wheelchair in front of a bus was a symbolic gesture of defiance for a lot of people in wheelchairs who are sometimes cruelly overlooked.

But it should not be the business of reporters to create heroes out of scoundrels.

And the story of Arden Hythe helps tell us some of the

fundamental flaws of local television news, as practiced across the entire country.

In the *Baltimore Sun* offices, where I worked, there were more than two hundred people gathering news. This is a business built on a foundation of journalism. Years ago, when I worked at the *News American*, there were about a hundred people on the news staff. When the *Sun's* sister newspaper, the *Evening Sun*, was still in business, that paper employed about a hundred news people.

On American newspapers, there is an old, unofficial rule of thumb: One reporter for every thousand readers. With this many people, specific reporters are assigned specific beats: this one the cops, that one the schools, someone else the mayor, and so on. It is the only sane way for honest coverage, for how else does a person get some kind of grip on the daily life of an institution, or a neighborhood, or the running of even a small portion of government?

Each of the television stations in Baltimore—and the same numbers are pretty comparable for big-city stations around the entire country—has about twenty reporters. It is therefore a business built on a foundation of shadows.

Twenty reporters to cover the basics: the governor and state legislature, the mayor and city council, the county executives and county councils, the various school systems, the neighborhoods, the police, the business community, the colleges—and the courts, where records are kept on heroes such as Arden Hythe.

Twenty reporters.

Well, not really twenty.

Each station has at least four anchor people (two at five o'clock, two at six o'clock). Their job entails arriving for work a few hours before air-time to write a few paragraphs to run with videos but, mainly, to look over copy already written for them—and then read that copy in front of a camera.

They do not, as a general rule, venture forth from the studio. That is a myth perpetrated by station promotional spots. It is a myth perpetrated to make these anchors look informed and authoritative and involved in actual journalism. In truth, almost all of them sit in a building all day and do not move except to get meals.

So there aren't really twenty reporters at each station—it's more like sixteen.

Well, not really sixteen.

Because each station has at least two sports reporters. They don't cover news, they cover ballgames. So it's not really sixteen reporters, it's more like fourteen.

Well...

It's not really fourteen, because each station has at least three weather people. Lots of people are interested in the weather. Every survey says so. This is why TV stations, which once had one weather person for weeknights and one more for weekends, now often have as many as four different weather people. They are checking all horizons for anything dramatic that might be headed our way, such as raindrops.

The weather people don't do news; they do weather. And, figuring a minimum of three weather people, that takes us down to eleven reporters.

Except there aren't really eleven. Because some people work weekends—generally, four or five on-air people—and this means they've got two days off during the week. Then there are people working the early hours of the day. They're hosts on the morning show, and handle the noon news, and then they go home. And maybe there's a reporter whose work appears on the evening news, but he specializes in the nightly kitten-caught-in-a-tree soft feature.

It is this way at local stations around the country.

In a 1999 *American Journalism Review* piece headlined "The Body Count," Deborah Potter related the story of Dan Rosenheim, who left his job as managing editor of the *San Francisco Chronicle* to become news director at the city's KPIX-TV. At the *Chronicle*, Rosenheim had a staff of 375, including 225 reporters. At KPIX, he had a staff of ninety, including just sixteen reporters—to cover the same territory.

"That statistic alone," Potter wrote, "explains more about the state of local television news than any diatribe about deregulation or media mergers. It's all you really need to know to understand why there is so little enterprise, so much cheap-to-cover crime and so little depth on the air. Most television reporters have a simple mission every day: Get out there and scratch the surface. How can they do anything more?"

Philip Balboni, president of New England Cable News in Boston, told Potter, "No TV station in America has enough reporters." Balboni's station had fourteen on-air people. Across town, ABC affiliate WBZ had the same number, but they were supplying stories for two different stations' newscasts—WBZ and the Boston UPN affiliate, WSBK. Both stations are owned by Viacom.

"Their news-sharing arrangement is becoming almost commonplace as the number of such duopolies expands," Potter wrote. "So while there's more news on the air, it's basically the same news, often produced by the same people."

Al Tompkins, a former news director at the Poynter Institute, created a formula to put the numbers into depressing perspective. Take the number of hours of news a station produces each weekday and divide it by the number of reporters. In Jacksonville, Florida, he found, a station had one reporter for every forty-five minutes of news on the air. In Kansas City, it was one for every fifty-three minutes.

Can there be a beat system with such a lack of reporters? Of course not. In the fall of 1985, such a subject arose at one of the occasional WJZ staff meetings held ostensibly to discuss issues of news-gathering. The ratings were high, but morale was not. Serious reporters were tired of simply following up on daily newspaper stories.

The next day, executive producer Ross Mason issued a memo for those who had missed the meeting. "Among the concerns raised was the need for some sort of limited beat system," Mason wrote. "The consensus was that such a beat system would enable us to develop more of our own stories and follow up on stories we've already done. As you well know, we are deficient in those two areas."

For a while, the station assigned one reporter to cover education and another (a retired school teacher, octogenarian Leona Morris) to cover senior citizens. But it quickly became clear that the very notion of a true beat system was absurd.

Across the country each day, a literal handful of people at local TV news operations actually goes about the business of reporting news. True, there are photographers and technicians who back up these reporters, but without the reporter going on the air with whatever information has been obtained, these backup people count for nothing. Their job is strictly to prop up the on-air folks.

A handful of news people—not a hundred, like the old *Evening Sun*, or the *News American*, or any of hundreds of daily newspapers around the country. Not several hundred, like the *New York Times* or the *Los Angeles Times* or a few hundred, like the *Baltimore Sun.*

A handful of reporters—and millions of people across America are tuning in to these local news operations each night, believing they are getting some semblance of life in their communities.

"Well, maybe that's not what they really want," said Paul Gluck in Philadelphia. "Television news and newspapers, it's a different experience. The TV audience demands a cute feature as part of their experience. A lot of them come to the set for the weather. They view that as valuable as anything they might read in a newspaper.

"Listen," said Gluck, "we dream of a world with two hundred reporters, but it's a different kind of news and a different kind of economics. Television stations are owned by large corporations that want higher profit margins each year. They believe in a world that's the opposite of the world journalists see. They say, 'I've already got the top-rated newscast in town with only ten reporters. Am I gonna be any more number one with twelve reporters?'

"I remember one station, which was running third in the ratings, wondering if they should renew their high-priced anchor's contract. One guy said, 'If we let him go, it will damage the station.' Somebody else said, 'We can still be number three without this guy.' Journalism has nothing to do with it. It's about deregulation, and companies buying twenty and thirty stations that now have to please Wall Street and stockholders. Corporate culture says, 'Give me the most for the least.'"

This gets us back to Arden Hythe.

He was beautiful for television, because his was a story waving its arms for attention. A paralyzed man faced down a municipal bus. As emotional viewers, this stirs us. As adults, it should trouble us in a secondary way: We're supposed to view the news as citizens, not merely as an audience in search of stirring drama.

The problem with Arden Hythe is that no television reporter went beyond the surface facts. Why didn't they check court records? Simple. Because almost no TV reporter has much connection with the courthouse. Why? Because, unlike newspaper reporters, there are no beats in television news, where a person goes every day to City Hall, or the police districts or the schools, and cultivates sources and knows where to look for records. There aren't enough TV reporters to allow time for such a thing.

And, not to be minimized, Baltimore, like many jurisdictions, does not allow cameras in courtrooms. Thus, television cannot capture the visual drama of the courtroom. Naturally, television reporters can enter the courtroom, and take notes, and come back outside and report the events of the day for the folks at home.

But television news is not interested in the news so much as it is interested in the look of news. It is a television program—given to all of the dramatic attributes of any program—and it's a program that happens, only incidentally, to be about news.

It is the look of things that counts.

With so few reporters, TV executives know they have to make choices. They have to send people where there is the absolute assurance of finding something resembling news. They don't have the luxury of sending a reporter to cover a story that might not pan out. For newspapers, this is called digging. For television, it is called empty air time. How do you sacrifice a reporter for digging when you only have a handful of reporters to begin with?

So TV goes for the look of things. If there's an empty warehouse burning, and there are flames—how high are they? High enough to grab people's attention at home, and hold it until the commercials? If there's a terrific car accident involving traffic backups and ambulances—can we get the station's Sky-Eye Chopper overhead?

If there's a kid in a wheelchair facing down a bus—well, that one's a no-brainer.

But, as television has made clear its need for easy little dramas, those wishing to get themselves on television have learned ways to stage those dramas. We used to say, "You can't fight City Hall." Now it turns out, you actually can, if only you contrive interesting ways to do it.

Politicians have long since figured this out, but so have ordinary citizens. In Baltimore, Anthony Griffin was one. He decided his life wasn't working out, so he decided to call a press conference. His rent was overdue, his gas and electric costs out of control, his kids without new clothes.

Disheveled, fumbling for authority, he marched into the Department of Social Services at the Mondawmin Shopping Mall. Since he needed a way to get his press conference, he brought along two guns and a machete, and he took thirty-five people hostage.

Reporters gathered en masse outside the social services office. A police spokesman, Dennis Hill, looked at all the cameras and microphones. "You guys know you're being used, don't you?" he said.

He was preaching the obvious to people who were way ahead of him. The real question was: Who was using whom?

Anthony Griffin's master plan was to fight City Hall through television, through a dramatic plea that would shake the heart of the coldest bureaucrats. Television's plan was to ride his outrage as far as possible.

It was the kind of confrontation that has repeatedly put television news on the defensive. Critics ask: Does TV cover the news, or create it by its mere presence? On the afternoon of Anthony Griffin's shopping mall hostage-taking, I stood there for a while with Jim Mustard, a reporter for WBAL-TV, the local NBC affiliate. Mustard was a local television rarity: He looked like a bag of bones. He had thick glasses and a broad forehead. And he had weird ideas about the news itself being important, not the TV reporter's intrusion into the news.

His heroes were the serious TV people. He worshipped at the shrine of Edward R. Murrow. Those who fluffed up the news lived in a different moral climate than Mustard's. I knew a little about him because I'd taught a few journalism courses at a local college, and Mustard would come by and talk to my students every semester.

They never got very far with him. He'd say a few words of introduction and then ask for questions. Let the kids guide the conversation. A hand would shoot into the air, but never a second one. Nobody got the chance. Fired with enthusiasm, he'd spend the entire hour answering the first question, free-associating from one point to another, trying to give these students not only the nuts and bolts of serious broadcast journalism but the beating of a ferocious heart.

"It's awful," I'd complain to him afterwards. They were journalism students, and they were bright and enthusiastic. But they seemed to have no feel for language, and certainly not for the written word. It was another gloomy reminder of television's ascendancy.

Over nearly a decade, I taught about five hundred of these kids. On the first day of class each semester, I handed them a questionnaire. I would ask: What publications do you read? In my own student days, it was important to read everything, to find out not only what writers were saying, but how they were saying it.

My students had no such concept. I never had a student who read any of the smart political-literary magazines. Maybe a dozen had ever read *Time* or *Newsweek*. They read *Mad* or *National Lampoon*. One fellow was still reading *Boys Life*, the scouting magazine. It didn't even occur to them to fake their answers for the teacher.

On this questionnaire, I also asked them what they wanted to do with a career in journalism. Almost none of them wanted to be newspaper reporters. They hadn't read a newspaper, so why would they want to write for one? Their big dreams? The most consistent answers were: To be TV weathermen or radio disc jockeys. This, at the height of their youthful energy and idealism.

"How does such a thing happen?" Mustard asked when I told him these stories. Every time he spoke to my classes, he tried to imbue them with his own passion, his sense of the importance of a strong press in a civilized nation. But they had grown up with television, and he seemed to have arrived too late. Their concept of news was merely a choreographed show seen on a picture tube. It was the reason, on that long-ago Watergate night, some of us from the *News American* had wondered aloud if our grandchildren would hear the word "newspaper" and wonder what it was.

So now we stood outside the social services offices waiting for the hostage taker Anthony Griffin, while the police spokesman Dennis Hill berated us for playing into Griffin's hands. Without reporters and cameras, Hill said, this man would not be jeopardizing people's lives. When nobody seemed to pay attention, Hill walked away.

"We have to fight this all the time," Mustard said.

"Hostage threats?"

"All kinds of situations like that," he said. "People stage events specifically for the cameras. If we don't show up, the thing doesn't happen. Or it happens, but nobody knows it."

We glanced toward the social services office, to see if Griffin was making any moves. It was now past four o'clock in the afternoon.

"I took a call one afternoon," Mustard said. "A labor official. He says, 'We're having a spontaneous demonstration at ten o'clock tomorrow morning.' 'Spontaneous,' right? He's being cute with me, he's showing me he knows how the business works. He says, 'Can you have a camera crew there?' Right away, you have a choice. You know it's not spontaneous, because he's already got a schedule set up. But you know you've got visuals if you show up, because it's all arranged ahead of time."

"So you're caught between your conscience and your needs," I said.

"Right. So I told him, 'We can't do it at ten, all our crews are tied up until eleven.' And the guy says, 'Great, we'll have our spontaneous demonstration at eleven.'"

Anthony Griffin took his social services hostages at about three in the afternoon. He took every local television station hostage shortly thereafter. When the stations learned of the drama, reporters were immediately dispatched.

When he saw cameras and microphones set up, Griffin tossed everybody a bone. He freed a hostage. Her name was Jean Dalton. As she rushed to her car, tight-lipped and trembling, she said, "He was nice. He didn't really bother us. He said he wanted to talk to reporters if they would come in."

The cops, of course, said no. But Griffin had whetted everyone's interest by sending out the one hostage. Finally, at seven minutes before six—seven minutes before the evening new—Griffin suddenly announced he would come out shortly. He stepped through the front doorway, and onto an escalator with an escort of many police, at precisely six o'clock—when local news programming commenced. He knew.

At the bottom of the escalator stood a reporter named Harry Martin, from WBAL-TV, Mustard's station. The hostage story was big enough for the station to double-team it. Martin, live on camera, declared, "It couldn't have happened at a better time."

For whom?

For Griffin, it was a moment of glory. As police led him away, a crowd gathered outside the mall cheered him. No longer was he just another guy with problems. Now he was a man who'd tied up the cops for a couple of hours. And he was a guy savvy enough to stage the dramatic visual moment precisely for television's lead story. He just wasn't smart enough to realize that TV wasn't interested in the problems that drove him to his crime; it only cared about dramatic pictures of the crime itself.

What happens routinely, all across America, is a complicity, a wink between mutual users. Television uses people who are driven enough to do something useful for its cameras, and the driven ones use television to express their cause.

The Political Dance

In the spring of 2003 the governor of Maryland, Robert L. Ehrlich, Jr., made a discovery that comes to all politicians who pay attention. He realized that television stations were not very serious about covering government or politics.

Ehrlich came to this conclusion after his first few months in office, a time during which both the *Baltimore Sun* and *Washington Post* sharply criticized his political programs, his sense of maturity, and his ethics. Ehrlich thereupon announced that he did not wish to deal with newspapers any longer, and declared "war" had commenced. He would now spend his time with television reporters, and with radio talk show hosts.

In Ehrlich's mind, the newspapers were nasty because he was a conservative Republican. In fact, this was the argument he would make in speeches across the state, where he spoke to cheering Republican audiences. The argument lacked only facts. For the previous sixteen years, the two newspapers (and columnists such as me) had been harshly critical of governors Parris Glendening and William Donald Schaefer, both of whom happened to be liberal Democrats and the *Sun,* (and columnists such as me) had been critical in that time of Baltimore mayors

Kurt L. Schmoke and Martin O'Malley and the entire city council—all of whom were also liberal Democrats.

Governor Ehrlich embraced the television and radio people because they were nice to him. When he said this out loud, he did not seem to understand he had indicted all broadcasters for not doing their jobs. It is not a reporter's business to be nice to public officials. It is their job to look at the work these public servants perform, analyze it as honestly as possible, and report it as fairly as possible.

For television reporters, there are special problems. One, that politicians understand the time constraints of television and manipulate them. Two, that local television executives aren't particularly interested in covering government, since they cannot figure out how to dramatize it visually.

Instead, they give lip service to the people's business. They cover press conferences and other staged events while completely ignoring the effects of government action.

Case in point: Ronald Reagan.

As all close observers knew, Reagan was the great role model for politicians wishing to slip one past television while the medium blinked its eyes. He was called the Great Communicator, though often this meant not communicating at all. In some empty affectation of open government, Reagan would allow television cameras to watch him as he strode from the White House to a waiting helicopter, where observers such as ABC-TV's Sam Donaldson could shout questions at him and Reagan could pretend not to hear.

One summer morning midway through Reagan's first term, he gave reporters in Baltimore a taste of such a practice. He arrived there to display his devotion to the cause of American cities. He went to an industrial park in a troubled part of town, where he spent precisely twelve minutes. Then he went downtown to deliver a quick speech to some conventioneers, and then he went back home. This made it just about perfect for the television news.

Presidents come to Baltimore pretty regularly. It's a short hop over from Washington, and it lets them stretch their legs a little. The TV cameras show the president smiling and waving, and this is reduced to a ninety-second dance intended to charm everyone in sight.

In Reagan's case, he was drawing criticism for neglecting big, decaying cities. It was part of the Republican Party's so-called Southern Strategy, dating back to the time of Richard Nixon. Southern Strategy was a euphemism for choosing up sides by race. Nixon, capitalizing on the Democrats' support of civil rights legislation, and assessing the deep resentment over it among many conservative whites, kissed off the big cities, many of which were heavily black. Baltimore was one of those places.

Under siege from the drug dealers, its schools leading the nation in dropouts and teen pregnancies, and its homicide rate among the country's worst, the city struggled for some sense of salvation. Reagan, accused of insensitivity and neglect toward such places, wanted to take a moment and show voters that he cared, and that cities were getting better under his "Morning in America" leadership.

On this steamy July morning, he showed up at an area known as Park Circle. In its heyday, the post-World War II years, Park Circle was the symbolic gateway to middle class life for thousands of the city's Jews. By Reagan's time, it was the industrial fringe of some awful poverty and crime for thousands of blacks.

The president was coming to the industrial park because, according to the White House, it stood for something: the grit and pluck of thousands of American businesses that were surviving without interference from Big Government.

Outside the park, police marksmen with high-powered rifles stood on rooftops, and Secret Service types moved around on the street. I stood in a little cordoned-off area for reporters and photographers, watching as two yellow school buses pulled up with sixty uniformed police officers.

"Forced busing," a police sergeant named Nick Caprolino joked as he got off the first bus. He said they were bused in because of the anticipated crowds. Ten thousand people were said to be coming. We looked around to see them. There were maybe a hundred people. Some were waiting for an overdue municipal bus.

The atmosphere was convivial. The local TV news crews understood the standard drill: a network reporter and photographer would accompany the president into the park, and the local guys would get a glimpse of Reagan when he came back out. If they were lucky. And from this they would attempt to create the bare bones of a story, as put forth by the White House to the American people: The president cared.

When Reagan's entourage finally showed up, his limousine took him straight into the industrial park. The network crew followed him in and trailed him as he walked around a book bindery. No reporters could ask questions. The idea was, Reagan was so busy soaking up knowledge and inspiration about the triumphant book bindery that he couldn't take time for reporters.

He soaked up this knowledge for the full twelve minutes. From his limo, emerging now from the industrial park, Reagan waved and waved, as though great throngs of people were cheering him. The hundred people waved back, not including those still looking for their overdue bus. Reagan didn't care. He understood the basic element of the dance between politics and television: the only people in the crowd who counted were those holding television cameras showing him waving to apparently huge, adoring throngs.

When Reagan left, I went for a little walk in search of a newspaper column for the next morning. Near the industrial park, I found Sherwin Jackson. He was walking home from his all-night stint at the local Amoco station. "Four years I've been here," he said, "and still making three-thirty-five an hour." A guy named Tim Johnson stood next to him, but Johnson wasn't coming from work.

"I been doing the same thing since I got out of the military," he said.

"What's that?"

"Nothing. You go for a job, they say you need experience. But how do you get experience without no job?"

Now came a woman who called herself Queen Mother Red, carrying photographs in her hand. She was a big woman with a voice that seemed to come out of her boots.

"Well, there's one thing that happened out of the president's visit," she said.

"What's that?" Tim Johnson asked.

"They got the city trucks out here," she said, "to sweep up the trash."

"Amen," Johnson said.

Then Queen Mother Red displayed her photos. They showed piles of trash on a street that had now been swept clean. The photos had been stapled to two big pieces of cardboard. "I wanted to show these to the president," she said. She wanted him to see the photos of a neighborhood so defeated that it habitually befouled itself, in a city so strapped for money that it sent cleanup crews only on special occasions. And she wanted him to contrast that with the staged, spiffy look given by city work crews the day before his arrival, so as not to offend Reagan's eyes or television viewers.

I walked along nearby Park Heights Avenue, with its rows of once-stately homes that were now boarded-up and abandoned, and stopped at a place called Robinson's Food and Variety Market. Clifton and Pettis Robinson had bought the place the previous year. Clifton had worked for Bethlehem Steel, and Pettis had worked for United Parcel. They saved their money over the years and sank it into the store.

"Is it working out?" I asked.

"Been broken into," Clifton Robinson said, "thirty-six times."

"Thirty-six?"

"That's just the break-ins," said his brother.

"Right, plus two stickups. One time the guy asked for a pint of Jack Daniels."

"I turned around, and he jumped the counter and put a gun at my head. Then you got people coming in here every day and just stealing. Not only kids. Working people. Or what used to be working people. They worked twenty years, and now they're laid off. And they come in here when it's busy, and they grab anything they can and slip on out."

"I wish the president had came up here," Clifton Robinson said. "I'd have told him that people need work. That's why we got people breaking in here. Just like the working man got to work to support himself, the criminal got to support himself. But what are we gonna do? Close up the store? If we leave this, where are we gonna find a job?"

I went back to the *Baltimore Sun* newspaper and wrote a column about all of this. It was a time of tight money, and joblessness and crime, and people trashing their own streets. The president had witnessed none of this while wishing to take great credit for sensitivity to it all. He saw a book bindery where they put on a show, and streets swept clean for his benefit, but he would not veer two blocks out of his way to listen to a few minutes of life as lived by ordinary, beaten citizens.

Of course, presidents are busy men. They cannot speak to every citizen in every troubled neighborhood in all deteriorating cities, but by going through the motions of caring, television allows them to in the most unquestioning way.

When I finished writing my newspaper column, I went home and turned on the evening television version of Ronald Reagan in my city. The coverage was beautiful. One of the local TV reporters stood outside the Park Circle industrial park and announced, as though it meant something important, that President Reagan wanted to get a close-up look at the book bindery. The bindery, he explained, was a sign of hope for a neighborhood in need of it. It was a symbol of American business sticking it out in a tough neighborhood in a difficult time. It was, the reporter said as Reagan's limousine drove past, a sign of better times to come.

The television story lasted less than ninety seconds. Then there was a follow-up. In the television studio, an anchor referred to this as "team coverage." When Reagan left Park Circle, he was taken to downtown Baltimore, where he delivered a speech at the city's convention center. He talked about the spirit of rejuvenation he saw in America. He said he'd been to the industrial park that morning, and it gave him hope. The station, having exhausted so much time and energy delivering its ninety-second piece about Park Circle, gave this story barely a minute.

Then Reagan went home, and nothing had changed even slightly except that the filthy streets around Park Circle had been temporarily cleaned.

So it goes when politics and local TV journalists wink at each other. Instead of news, we have mutual complicity. The politicians know what the local TV people can handle and what they will settle for. The local stations are content to have the visuals of the president because theirs is a medium based on sight instead of substance, in which the mother at home cooking her dinner glances up to see the president but does not look so long that the soup bubbles over. And reporters, with no other story line, are happy to buy the White House pitch that the visit symbolizes the president's deep concern.

This is the modern dance. The TV stations understand that viewers have limited attention spans and unlimited options. They can change the channel or simply turn off the set. It is why in television editing booths reporters sit with tape editors and cut great swaths of material out of raw video, leaving behind the politician's hearty wave at street corners full of emptiness. It looks as if action is taking place.

To television, the greatest sin is boredom. To fight boredom at WJZ, politics and government were generally avoided, as were the issues involved. Great election campaigns were waged, and these went unreported until the final week or two before voting day. Then, with great fanfare, anchors would announce, "Stay tuned to *Eyewitness News* for complete election coverage."

This meant for the week leading up to the election, the station would rouse itself to deliver one story a night, or perhaps two, totaling three minutes, tops. More than that was not to be risked, lest viewers change channels. And more than that was not to be risked between election campaigns, when the daily work of government was all but ignored.

It is this way around the country. In 1999, the Lear Center Local News Archive, a collaboration between the University of Southern California's Annenberg School for Communication and the University of Wisconsin's Department of Political Science, analyzed the early- and late-evening news programs in 122 stations in the top fifty markets.

Their report said only thirty-seven percent of 4,850 local newscasts included campaign coverage. But, during seventy-two percent of those broadcasts, a political commercial was aired. And in fifty-two percent of the newscasts, two political commercials were aired. On average, four ads ran for every election story—meaning, for those millions of voters who get their news strictly from television, they were four times as likely to hear political propagandizing as they were to hear legitimate coverage of such claims.

The reason is simple: Every news director fears that viewers will find political coverage boring and switch the channel. This threatens ratings, which in turn threatens the news director's job. But their terror is based less on politics than their own inability to cover politics in interesting ways.

In a 2002 *American Journalism Review* piece headlined "Local TV Eye-opener: Politics Aren't Poison," Dave Iverson and Tom Rosenstiel argued that viewers hungered for legitimate political news. Iverson was director of Best Practices in Journalism, and Rosenstiel was director of the Project for Excellence in Journalism.

"Much of the thinking about political coverage on local television is based on recommendations by TV consultants, who help steer newsrooms toward stories and story approaches they believe audiences want," Iverson and Rosenstiel wrote. "They generally base these recommendations on audience surveys, and therein lies the problems."

They obtained a standard consulting firm survey and found from other consultants that the questionnaire was typical. Questions about such topics as consumer news and health topics were worded quite specifically. But the question about politics was "How interested are you in news reports about issues and activities in government and politics?"

"Polling professionals told us," Iverson and Rosenstiel wrote, "that generally the less specific the question, the less useful the answer. In this case, the question was so general it was meaningless. The question probed interest in 'issues and activities in government'—not real-life problems that government confronts. They might as well have asked, 'Are you one of those political junkies who watches C-Span instead of *Survivor*?'"

So Iverson and Rosenstiel, working with the Pew Research Center for the People and the Press, conducted a little experiment. They compared the consultants' questions about politics with questions that asked about the same subject in a different way.

When asked the consultants' original question—"How interested are you in news reports on issues and activities in state government and politics?"—only twenty-nine percent said they'd be very interested in watching.

But when asked if they'd be interested in "news reports about what government can do to reduce health care costs," the percentage of "very interested" jumped to sixty-four percent. In "reports on what government can do to ensure that public places are safe from terrorism," sixty-seven percent said they were "very interested." In reports on "improving local schools," the percentage was similarly high.

As Iverson and Rosenstiel pointed out, "This doesn't just mean phrase survey questions differently. It means change the way you do political stories." In other words, focus on people's problems first—and find out what government is doing about it.

The problem is most TV stations have neither the available staff nor the inclination to do such reporting. Grabbing a few moments on camera with a well-known political figure is regarded as quite sufficient. Holding the politicians' words up to scrutiny is considered far beyond the scope of most reporting.

In the beginning of my television years, I was selfish and insecure enough to find this liberating. The less coverage the station offered, the more the field opened for me. Astonishingly, for months on end as these political campaigns were waged, my commentaries were the station's only mention of them.

Later, my delight over cornering the market changed to something else: embarrassment. How could any legitimate news organization so cavalierly kiss off the democratic process and then, in the final week, shamelessly declare it was offering "complete team coverage," as though viewers hadn't noticed the months of emptiness preceding this?

In the summer of 2000, the parent companies of all of Baltimore's television stations were called upon by a national advisory panel to devote at least five minutes a night to political coverage for thirty days before the election.

By this time, Jay Newman was the general manager at WJZ. "We will do what we always do, which is aggressively cover the candidates, the issues, and their impact on voters," Newman said. This was sheer baloney. The station had never done much election coverage, aggressive or otherwise, and the emptiness of Newman's remarks would subsequently be revealed.

In conjunction with the Alliance for Better Campaigns, the Annenberg School for Communications at the University of Southern California studied seventy-four TV stations' broadcasts from 5:00 p.m. to 11:35 p.m. nightly.

Of twenty-three stations that had pledged to devote at least five minutes a night to campaign coverage, WJZ finished twenty-first. During a hectic political season, the station had averaged forty-nine seconds a night—for all candidates, local and national.

Confronted about this by the *Sun's* David Folkenflik, Newman chose not to respond and would not let news director Gail Bending respond. But spokeswoman Liz Chuday declared the study "in error." She said, "Many days, we exceeded that five-minute coverage."

Big deal. By this time, the station was broadcasting several hours of news each night.

In Baltimore, TV news was interested in politics mainly as theater—particularly as comic theater. As the medium came of age, Baltimore had a comptroller named Hyman Pressman. His job was to balance the city's financial books, a job with utterly no allure for television since it involved nothing immediately visual. But Pressman, always hungry for attention, had two gimmicks. At his City Hall office, he installed TV lights in his ceiling to make it easier for camera crews. And he could make up poetry on the spur of the moment. About city finances, local TV stations reported almost nothing. But when it came to Pressman's poetry, he was a regular on the television news for years.

So was Dominic "Mimi" DiPietro. He was a city councilman who caused TV cameras to show up every Monday night at City Hall. He was five-feet-three, with a round face like a Cupid in a Renaissance painting and his hair was parted by his left ear and combed straight across. There were eighteen other council members, but Mimi was the one the TV people showed up to see.

He was a second grade dropout who fractured the language. When reporters showed up, other council members referred to "news media." Mimi thought the phrase was "news meteors."

"Here come them news meteors," he would say.

He thought the problem with the criminal courts was too much "flea bargaining." He said he loved the singing of his "church quarry." He thought the best coffee came from urinals. He meant urns. When his brother went through intestinal surgery, Mimi told reporters, "My God, they must have pulled four feet of testicle out of that man."

He was, strictly without intention, a colorful quote. He was so colorful that, when ABC's *Nightline* program devoted a show to Baltimore's spiritual renaissance, Mimi and Mayor William Donald Schaefer were invited to talk about the town's comeback. *Nightline* was serious television; it wasn't some local news catch-as-catch-can. But Mimi was too good even for Ted Koppel's producers to pass up. As it happened, the show aired the week that the Mt. St. Helen's volcano blew its top. On live national television, Koppel questioned Mimi.

"Councilman DiPietro," he asked, "what is it that makes Baltimore such a great city?"

"'Cause we ain't got no volcanoes," Mimi explained.

When Mimi died, so did television coverage of council meetings. Whereas every station in town had attended every week, waiting for DiPietro to erupt like a benign Mt. St. Helen's, now they came around only sporadically and then stopped completely. Never mind any important business the city might be conducting. Without Mimi, there wasn't a decent sound bite left in the bunch.

But the mayor of Baltimore, Schaefer, found other ways to coax television coverage. Schaefer was by nature a shy man. His strength was that he knew every brick and pot hole and alley in town, and he obsessed over all of them. His weakness, for television, was that so much of his strength wasn't photogenic.

Schaefer learned to adapt. He became the master of the funny hat, the comic expression, the strange bathing suit. He wore these to dedicate new buildings or to name new water fountains. It didn't matter. He was taking a city beaten down a few years earlier by the riots after Martin Luther King's assassination and teaching it to believe in itself again. He was chief cheerleader. The TV stations got behind it, and justified it by saying it was all about community welfare. The funny hats didn't hurt

Schaefer was mayor for fifteen years. He brought the city back to life. But the iconic image that remained, long after he moved on to become governor of Maryland, and long after he left the statehouse, was his picture on the day the city opened its new National Aquarium.

On that day, at the aquarium's outdoor seal pool, Schaefer

donned a straw hat and a nineteenth-century style bathing suit, and dipped himself in the water with the seals. It was beautiful. It was visual, it was funny, it was utterly empty of all meaning except the mayor of Baltimore having a little fun.

For television, it was like uncovering the very secrets of Watergate.

Here is the problem: Not only do politicians contrive ways to get themselves on television but the savviest also come prepared with script in hand. The job of any reporter, in television or print, is to get them to step beyond these prepared remarks, and thus find some semblance of spontaneity and maybe even truth.

This happened one special time in Maryland politics, and it was such a rarity that it caused political astonishment.

A reporter named Joan Gartlan, from WUSA-TV, in Washington, D.C., accompanied Thomas V. Mike Miller on a quick look at the city of Baltimore. Miller was the President of the Maryland Senate, the third highest political office in the state. He came from Prince George's County, a suburb of Washington. He showed up in Baltimore because he was thinking about running for governor and wanted to build some name recognition in the city.

Then he opened his mouth and made his name recognizable for all time, and for the wrong reasons. Gartlan told her cameraman to keep rolling no matter what. She asked Miller about Baltimore and asked it in a conversational way. Miller, looking around at certain slums and taking no notice of the camera at that moment, declared, "It's just shit; it's a goddamn ghetto."

That evening, the remark appeared on the television news. By the next day, as word spread, the town went ballistic. The words had the tone of an inside joke, a convivial slur among political snobs. Who was he calling shit? Naturally, Miller did what any politician in the fullness of his wisdom might do: He panicked and made it worse.

Instead of saying, "This is a city that clearly needs help,

and I was trying to show the seriousness of its problems," he dissembled. He went on Baltimore's WBAL-TV and said he was just a poor boy from Southern Maryland who was one of ten kids and really didn't know much about being interviewed on television. Never mind that he was a powerful elected official. Never mind that he'd been in politics for twenty years.

But there was one telling little insert between Miller's remarks and Gartlan's airing of them. Having said what he said, Miller suddenly realized the camera was running. "I hope you're not going to put this on tape," Miller said.

But Gartlan did. And she should have. Because television being what it is—a medium that is used each day by politicians who play it like a drum—this was that astonishing moment: Miller was speaking a truth as he saw it, and not merely issuing platitudes to appeal to the widest possible audience.

Such a moment was so rare, and so powerful, that it leveled the political career of Miller, and never again was he mentioned seriously as a candidate for governor.

Grand Theft

At TV news operations around the country, the day begins with grand theft of other people's work. At WJZ, it begins with an assignment editor who arrives in the newsroom early each morning and quite casually steals from the Baltimore newspapers. This is her specific assignment. It happens seven days a week, and the weeks and months become years, until no one in television even thinks twice about the underlying ethics of such a practice.

Local television news could not exist without this daily thievery from the newspapers. They steal from their home-town papers, and from *USA Today*, and from newspapers both grand and delinquent. Once, mainstream journalists sneered at the likes of the *National Enquirer*. Later, TV news operations came to lift such tabloid stories routinely—without ever mentioning precisely where they got them. The anchor delivers news of the latest movie star headed for drug rehab and shakes her head regretfully. We don't make the news, the gesture says. We just report it.

But first they steal it. From the local newspapers, TV steals stories about police and courtrooms and schools. It steals stories about highway problems and health departments and the environment. It steals stories about the city and the nearby counties and areas across the state where newspapers have daily beat reporters and TV stations do not.

And then, in the case of stations such as WJZ, it gives these stories a name. It calls them "eyewitness news." Eventually, in the era of general manager Jay Newman, WJZ would go even further. As it delivered these stories, reporters would be ordered to tell viewers, *"Eyewitness News* has learned..." What this often meant was simple: They learned it by reading the newspaper, but wished viewers to imagine their own reporters ferreted out the information, perhaps from mysterious sources who did not wish to be identified.

You eliminate the daily newspapers from any community in America and the result is the same. If there is no newspaper, then the people running television news do not know where to begin. They will have to take their handful of reporters and send them out to look for their own sources and their own stories instead of feeding off the material uncovered by scores and scores of newspapers reporters.

At WJZ, the process starts at about eight o'clock each morning with a conference call. The assignment editor, having arrived an hour or so earlier, has burrowed into the Baltimore papers and clipped out stories that might transfer easily to TV. This is her daily task, specifically handed to her in these strictures: See what you can steal. She has also scanned ideas left in the Futures file of her computer. These are, for the most part, stock stories, carefully choreographed for TV's particular benefit: The police commissioner has arrest statistics to brag about today, or Johns Hopkins Hospital is opening a new wing. The mayor is holding his weekly press conference, or a suburban county executive is dedicating a playground with facilities for the physically challenged. All TV has to do is show up, point a camera, and hold out a microphone to let the appropriate players have their say.

On this early-morning conference call with the assignment editor are several people: the news director, the assistant news director, a couple of executive producers, and a few producers.

All have prepared for this conversation in the same fashion: They have read the morning newspaper, and they have watched the early morning television shows, and they have larceny in their hearts but call it by some other name.

"Here's what I've got," the assignment editor will say.

Thus begins the daily sham. The conference call members will decide which of the station's reporters match up best with which newspaper stories. Sometimes, when reporters arrive for work, they are literally handed the clipping from the newspaper. Sometimes, these reporters have already read the morning paper themselves; often, they have not. At WJZ, there was one anchor who bragged that he never read a daily newspaper. So what? His job was to show up each day and read copy written for him to read on the air.

The better reporters have not only read the paper but might propose an idea of their own when they arrive in the morning. The lesser reporters are happy to be handed an assignment without having to think about it: Just follow the trail left by the newspaper clipping they've been handed.

Barbara Matusow addressed this in the *Washington Journalism Review*, in a piece titled, "Second-Hand News: How TV Feeds On Print." She wrote, "What's going on here? Do radio and TV originate any of the stories they air? The answer is yes when it comes to breaking news. For features, long-range trends and investigative stories, however, broadcasters remain woefully dependent on the print press for leads and story ideas."

There are other possibilities. Maybe an overnight telephone call from a viewer looks interesting. Usually some government public relations departments have checked in a day or two earlier with something they wish to stage. This is one hand scratching the other, the government outfit getting free publicity, and the station getting something to fill its air time. It is the way things work when sheer lack of manpower forces newsroom executives to grab the most easily available stories instead of digging for the best ones.

As Matusow, who was senior editor at the *Washington*

Journalism Review, wrote, in her March, 1987, piece: "For the most part, local stations rely on general-assignment reporters who never get a chance to develop sources or build up expertise. More often than not, producers and assignment editors originate the stories covered. But how can people sitting inside a radio or television station day after day come up with original ideas?"

Matusow brings us once again to the deeper problem: Only a few of these newsroom executives are attuned to actual news. They are, for the most part, individuals who studied TV production in college. Their skills are geared to arranging satellite trucks and helicopter coverage, not to the substance of community life.

In my time in newspapers, I worked for a series of editors who had one thing in common: they had worked their way through the ranks as journalists. In my nineteen years in television news, I never worked for any editors or news directors who had a background in news reporting. What I offered them they took unquestioningly. What they took I put on the air. While it was flattering that they trusted me, the complete lack of editorial give-and-take, of different people comparing observations and insights and institutional memory, was unsettling.

In local television, it works this way: All those who study broadcast journalism in college make a decision. They can gear their studies to on-air work, or they can study TV production, in which case they become writers (ironically, the lowest figures on the TV totem pole) and producers, executive producers who oversee the work of producers, and news directors.

In my time at WJZ, the woman who held the job of news director the longest was Gail Bending. As it happens, she was a student of mine when I taught college journalism. She had many strengths: intelligence, sensitivity, and knowledge of the Baltimore area that came from growing up in nearby Harford County.

She also had weaknesses common to almost all television news directors. In her thirties when she got the job, she had never worked as a reporter, had never left a building to cover a story, to interview a source, to find out how things work. And this was true of the assistant news director, the executive producers, and the producers below them. They knew the mechanics of putting together a news program—coordinating a small number of reporters and photographers with a large number of story possibilities—without the slightest idea how a story was uncovered. This doesn't mean they weren't smart people. Many of them were very bright. But they moved through the system with their heads under the hood of the car, while all the scenery outside passed them by.

At WJZ, Jerry Turner made it a point to sit in the newsroom, among the troops, while preparing for broadcasts. He liked the give and take, and the troops—the handful of young producers and writers working behind the scenes— loved the contact with this easy-going legend. When Turner retreated to his little office, though, he tended to shake his head in consternation.

"The children's brigade," he'd say, pointing toward the newsroom people who backed him up each night. He had affection for most of them, but he also saw himself as an adult surrounded by people his own children's age.

"They've just started to live," he said one evening, "and we're letting them run a durned newscast."

Sometimes I wanted to tell him about the newspaper where I worked and the layers of people putting together each day's editions. But it felt like pulling rank. Also, Turner couldn't complain too much. He was making six figures a year—and, considering the audience he pulled in, was probably underpaid. But in the traditional TV economics, his salary and the salaries of a few other on-air headliners were so high that it prevented management from spending more money on legitimate backup people.

And so he made do. There were producers only a few years out of college who decided which stories went into newscasts, in which order, and how much time each story would get. There were writers, most of them fresh out of school, whose TV-technical skills had been shaped but who had never reported a story in their lives—who were writing the shows' copy.

Turner did some of his own writing, and so did Al Sanders. Each had a reputation as a first-rate TV writer. In fact, though, their writing was essentially limited to a few paragraphs for each show. The rest of the early evening show was put together by a handful of people untrained in reporting, and the eleven o'clock show was handled by an executive producer, a producer, and perhaps one writer.

Night after night, thousands tuned in to watch these productions, presuming they were getting the news from the seasoned Turner and Sanders. But many of the stories they were reading had been written and produced by untrained kids.

In 2001, when Chris Tuohey of Syracuse University conducted a survey of local anchors and producers and news directors, he got back 368 responses. When anchors were asked whether they had considerably more experience than their producers—the ones putting together the broadcast—eighty-six percent said they did. One-third of them said the lack of experience made it difficult to trust producers. More than half the news directors said their anchors occasionally or frequently complained about inexperienced producers—"about poor writing skills (both accuracy and grammar), the high turnover of producers, lack of knowledge about current events and the community they were covering, more concern with TV production techniques than journalism, and a general lack of life experience," Tuohey wrote in the *American Journalism Review.*

The essentials of news, and special insights into the community it purports to cover, are a foreign subject to these producers and writers or, at best, an interesting afterthought. It stays this way through the years. Sitting in a hotel restaurant in the early winter of 2003 with a fellow named Samuel (Sandy) Rosenberg, I realized that nothing changes.

Rosenberg, by this time, was a veteran member of the Maryland House of Delegates. But, from 1976 to 1979, he was assistant to the program manager at WJZ.

From this hotel restaurant, Rosenberg pointed across a windy courtyard to a place once known as the Cross Keys Deli. This was where he would sometimes eat lunch when he worked at WJZ. It's where Richard and Oprah went to lunch, and everybody saw them as first-name royalty. Partly, it was their personal chemistry, and partly, it was television's. Everybody thought magic was happening. Television was going to replace newspapers. Who needed to pick up a paper and get ink stains on their fingers? TV was clean, it was instant, it was easy. And it created stars.

Almost nobody saw the future being squandered because an entire medium would refuse to take its mission seriously. If it claimed to give news, then surely it would deliver actual news.

"And it hasn't," Rosenberg said now. "What does it give you, the latest traffic accidents? I never learn anything from it. Which is why this thing has happened."

"Which thing?"

"That it's irrelevant," Rosenberg said. "I don't know anybody in the legislature who pays attention to it. We wonder what the newspapers are going to write, because they're down there every day. But the TV stations only drop in here and there. The state's business is being conducted, and they're generally oblivious to it. So, to the people running the state, television has ceased to matter. We don't even think about it."

But Rosenberg could see such a future from the late 1970s. In Rosenberg's time, he produced a Sunday morning talk show hosted by Jerry Turner. *Eyewitness Newsmakers*, it was called. The show was taped in the middle of the week, and then held for airing until Sunday. One week, Turner interviewed Ronald Reagan, one-on-one, for half an hour. Reagan was trekking across the country, hitting as many TV stations as he could, trying to capture his first Republican nomination for president.

On this occasion, he made a little news. He took a shot at Maryland's senior U.S. senator, Charles (Mac) Mathias, who happened to be a Republican like Reagan. But, unlike Reagan, he was a liberal. "Mathias," said Reagan to Turner, was "a Democrat in drag and ought to leave the Republican Party."

For a Maryland audience, this was a pretty significant story. Rosenberg knew this right away, and took it to the newsroom to pitch it. He went to the news director and to various producers. The story was a winner for everybody, a no-brainer. It gave the evening news a nice scoop on every other station. It beat the local papers. And it was an early plug for Turner's Sunday show.

But the newsroom geniuses shrugged their shoulders. "They didn't understand the significance," Rosenberg said, still amazed more than twenty years later, "and they had no sense of what a news story was." Having rarely covered the business of the U.S. Senate, they barely had any knowledge of Mathias's very existence.

Rosenberg had his lesson reinforced when he later auditioned for a job as an on-air reporter. Go out and get us a story, he was told. Take a cameraman along and do it just like you were packaging it for the show.

So he did. He telephoned a friend of his, Mark Sissman, an executive in the city's housing department. Sissman told Rosenberg about a rent-control initiative headed for public referendum. Nobody else had the story. Sissman said it could be the most important vote since the Harborplace initiative, the inner harbor development that was the heart of Baltimore's economic and spiritual renaissance.

Rosenberg put together a package saying all of this, and had a photographer shoot it beautifully, from lovely Druid Hill Park with the troubled Reservoir Hill neighborhood looming behind him. When he took it to the newsroom hotshots, they sloughed it off. If it was such a big story, they wondered, why hadn't there been anything in the newspaper?

The story was set aside and not aired. Several months later, the *Baltimore Sun* reported the story—at which point WJZ finally felt comfortable mentioning it. It did this in the traditional way, by lifting it directly from the paper.

Rosenberg stuck around for a while longer, producing Richard Sher's *Square-Off* program, and then left to run for a seat in the state's General Assembly. He had a law degree, and he'd worked for the city. It was time to get serious with his life.

Here, he got another perspective of TV news. Rosenberg went knocking on voters' doors every night, the familiar campaign ritual. "A cold night," he remembered years later, "and I get home and put on the TV news, and they've got an item about Governor Harry Hughes."

Hughes was holding a reception at the governor's mansion for some legislators and their spouses. Delegate David Shapiro was one of those invited. Shapiro was Rosenberg's electoral opponent. Shapiro had no spouse, so he decided to make a little political profit out of this. He issued a press release, which WJZ ran on the air. It said Shapiro was holding an essay contest: Whoever best expressed why they would like to join him at the governor's mansion could accompany him there.

"Damn," Rosenberg said as he watched the broadcast. "I'm thinking, 'I'm out all night in the cold, going door to door for votes, and this guy drums up this cheap little gimmick and gets all this free TV coverage.' Why? Because it was easier for the station to run a press release than to do any actual reporting."

As it happened, the gimmick backfired on Shapiro. The winner of the essay contest turned out to be a prison inmate serving a life sentence. The governor was infuriated that Shapiro wanted to bring such a person to the state mansion, and Shapiro's constituents, embarrassed at the gaffe, voted him out of office and elected Rosenberg to succeed him.

"But there's the secret," Rosenberg said twenty years later. "In politics, we talk about two kinds of people: show horses and work horses. The show horses are the ones who wind up on TV. They don't do anything except show off. The work horses are busy working. They're the ones you don't see on TV, because TV doesn't bother looking for them."

Here is the thing only hinted at by Rosenberg: Sometimes TV doesn't have to look for politicians. The politicians, understanding the nature of the beast, will come looking for them.

In the summer of 1992 when Ross Perot ran for president, a reporter asked him a question on television that Perot did not want to answer. And so, in front of America, Perot decided to undress that reporter.

"That's a sound-bite question," he said. Perot's voice dripped with ostentatious contempt. "You want an easy, six-second answer, and America needs more than six-second answers."

As I watched Perot, I found myself applauding without entirely knowing why. On one hand, I wanted him to answer the damned question, simplistic as it might have been. On the other hand, he was pulling a lid off of something important. He was exposing not only the reporter but the dangerous dance of television and politics. He was making us think about a nation whose collective attention span had been reduced to the length of sound bites, those little moments snipped and edited and then spliced into the body of some deeply superficial sixty-second story.

In the midst of the 1992 presidential campaign, new studies had been done on the sound bite. From the original Harvard TV study in 1968, when the average TV news bite was forty-two seconds, to the 1988 presidential campaign, when it had shrunk to nine-point-eight seconds, it had diminished even more. According to the Center for Media and Public Affairs, it was now seven-point-three seconds.

Why? Because television executives perceived this to be the collective attention span of viewers. And why was that? Because the TV executives had created that attention span with their nightly procession of quick-fix stories. And then they had shrunk it when remote controls arrived, and then they shrunk it even more when cable TV opened up so many more options for people with their trigger fingers on those remote controls.

So here was Perot, saying something pretty important on national television. He was saying he would not play that game. He was saying the issues were too complex, and too important, and he would not treat the American public like a bunch of idiots. And this made me applaud delightedly.

Then David Green called.

Green was Perot's Maryland media coordinator. Perot, he said, was coming to Annapolis, the state's capital, for a rally to announce he had gotten the required number of signatures to put him on Maryland's presidential ballot.

"It's going to be a spectacle," Green said.

"Oh, yeah?" I said. I looked for an opening to get off the phone. Spectacles were not my department. He mentioned boats in the harbor tooting their horns, and a brass band. Great television pictures, signifying nothing beyond the desire to grab attention. I looked for a way to say good bye. Then Green pulled me back.

"I can get you a one-on-one interview with Perot," he said.

I thought about Perot's television eruption from a few nights earlier, and his remark about sound-bites and the trivialization of the political process. I thought about Ronald Reagan that summer morning at Park Circle when no reporter could get near him, and all the times when politicians had spoken carefully rehearsed, perfectly constructed remarks and then danced away while pleading time constraints.

I thought: This man is serious about breaking the old system apart. He is giving us a chance to talk about real issues facing the country.

"An interview?" I said. "Great."

"Well, we think you're an important guy to tell the Perot story," Green said.

"Thank you," I said, already thinking about the myriad of questions I wanted to ask. "How much time can you give me with him?"

"Four minutes," said Green.

"Four minutes?" I said, imagining I had misunderstood him. "Isn't that a little brief?"

Green seemed stunned by my response, as though brevity hadn't crossed his mind. His man was running for the most important job in the world; who was I to ask for more than four minutes? The deal was implicit: Be happy with whatever I could get. Be happy with the look of actual news—and with the stature conferred upon me by getting an interview with a candidate for president.

"Look," Green said, "I've got four people I want to give one-on-one interviews, but I've got to divide up twelve minutes among you. I'm at the mercy of the schedulers from Dallas. See, I know what you really want. What you really want is, like, half an hour."

Fat chance. The man who decried sound bite journalism was also living by it. He was like every other politician finessing television and its time limits. You don't like the question? Then duck around it until the clock ticks you out of danger. Reporters press you? Turn on them, get feisty, decry the very thing you're practicing.

If you do the dance well enough, the folks at home don't notice the evasion so much as the pugnacious standing-up to all those nasty questions. That was Perot's game. It was just another aspect of performance, his way of marking himself as a bold outsider so tough he'd even take on the television boys. He was trying to win points for not answering questions, by appearing to do it on his own terms.

"What about all that baloney he mentioned about sound bites the other night?" I said to Green.

"He's trying to say that not all answers are black and white," Green replied.

He sure picked an interesting way to do it: giving sound-bite answers in which he decried those very sound bite answers to people whose medium lives off of sound-bite answers; and then offering four-minute one-on-one interviews to reporters—and knowing that the TV guys would understand. This will be good for your career. It's the look of things that counts. It's just the way the game is played.

Thus comes the march of cynicism across the political landscape: from the politicians manipulating coverage, to the TV reporters buying into it even as they decry its superficiality, to voters wondering why they feel duped by a process they never exactly get to witness.

13

A Death in the Family

Gazing across the city from the top of Baltimore's Television Hill, the world can look pretty magnificent. To walk outside of WJZ-TV after dark, and gaze across the landscape below, is to witness the city at its most twinkly. To the south, downtown's big office buildings appear majestic. To the east, the old neighborhood rowhouses nestle cozily. To the west, the ancient gnarled trees of Druid Hill Park stretch their arms heavenward.

From a distance, everything looks quite safe and manageable. To gaze upon such a scene, night after night the way Jerry Turner did, was to feel like some captain of the world. Turner seemed to steer the town through each day's rough seas, and then put everyone safely to bed each night. Yes, there was another murder on the west side, and, yes, the public schools were now havens of illiteracy and zip guns. But Turner wrapped up the news the same comforting way each night: with a light sign-off piece, occasionally accurate, occasionally made up, that let everyone turn out the lights with a smile. If Jerry was seeing us off with a chuckle, how bad could things really be?

Moments later as he departed for home, Turner could pause outside the station and look upon the city below with a sense of triumph. He was, in his late fifties, in ways that anchors across the country can only dream about, the unquestioned king of his little universe and the overwhelming ratings leader in a business that measured success strictly by numbers.

And yet, late one afternoon in the spring of 1986, there was Turner, furtively glancing up and down a little corridor at the station as though frightened someone might be watching. Then he motioned me into the men's room, the same one where he had dabbed makeup on my face my first night on the air. When I got inside, Al Sanders was standing there, silent and concerned.

"We're getting out of here," Turner said.

He made it sound like a prison break. He talked about the usual frustrations: the nightly bloodbath that passed for news, the absence of serious reporting on government and politics, the frivolousness of so many stories. I thought there was more to it, but I said nothing. I thought it had to do with money. For the ratings they were getting, these two men undoubtedly figured they were underpaid and could do better elsewhere.

But it went even further. In the midst of their very own legend, they felt the ground shifting all across the television landscape. Some of it was corporate buying and selling, and some of it was cable, which looked like the future of American television. Maybe this was the time to cash in a few chips.

One night the new general manager, Jonathan Klein, called a staff meeting. These meetings were always strange affairs. The on-air news staff would sit around a long conference room table, eating pizzas and salad from a local carry-out while the news director, Natalea Brown, a smart, energetic, sometimes frenetic woman, talked about the television business.

But it was never about the journalism part of it, about covering the people we said we were covering. Nobody ever mentioned inside dope from City Hall, or how to work a source in the police department. Unlike staff meetings at newspapers, there was never the slightest sense of mission in the air, other than the mission to seduce more viewers.

Instead, Brown might show videos: amusing commercial promos from stations in other cities. Or she would explain new electronic gizmos the station was purchasing. Or she'd give us a demographic breakdown of our viewers, to show how dominant we were and how important it was to hold onto the numbers.

On this night, though, a whole new world was being declared. Cable TV was about to come to Baltimore and, in an unusual move, Klein showed up to tell us what it might mean.

"In Boston," he said, "the network affiliates have lost one-third of their audience since the arrival of cable."

"This is big," Marty Bass whispered, putting down his salad fork.

Klein was tall, wavy-haired, and wore glasses, and he looked a little like the theater legend George S. Kaufman. He glanced around the table at familiar on-air faces, giving them a snapshot of the future of their profession.

"This is real big," Bass whispered again.

"We know that we're going to lose raw numbers," Klein said. "There's no getting around that. People will want to see what's on cable, and that means they won't be watching the usual stuff they watch. At least, for a while."

"This is like dropping the bomb on Hiroshima," said Bass, never given to understatement.

"But we hope some of the novelty will wear off after a while," Klein said, "and people will come back to us. And we certainly want to hold onto our percentage of the news market."

I walked out of the meeting that night with George Bauman, who had been with the station since its earliest news days.

"I feel like it's 1945," Bauman said, "and we're working at a big radio station, and the boss is telling us, 'Look, there's this new invention, which is called television. And we think it's just a fad, and we're gonna try to ride it out until the fad passes and people turn on their radios again.'"

"This is no fad," Marty Bass said. He seemed as if he wanted to race into the studio, break into the air with a bulletin, and shout frenzied warnings about the end of the world.

"I'm telling you," he said. "This is Hiroshima."

I disagreed. I thought cable would be a marvelous opportunity for WJZ, and for every local news operation around the country. The cable operations spread their reporters all over the world. If the Middle East exploded, they had somebody there. If there were earthquakes or floods, they had them covered.

But for day in, day out coverage of local news—they couldn't compete with local stations. Cable didn't care about falling math scores in the local public schools or a meat plant closing and hundreds of people losing their jobs. Cable didn't know the local cast of characters. This was a chance for the local stations to show off their strengths and solidify their markets, to say that nobody on the whole TV dial knows Baltimore the way we do.

The sports anchor John Buren thought the same thing. Cable meant the incursion of ESPN into the Baltimore airwaves—but ESPN wasn't interested in local high schools and colleges, or in local bowling or golf tournaments.

"Hey, babe," Buren said, delivering the words in his faux-Elvis accent. "ESPN's never even heard of Towson State. They couldn't care less about the Gilman-St. Paul's lacrosse score."

This was a time, he was saying, for local news operations to dig deeper into what should be their natural strengths: local news that the national folks did not care about.

But it didn't work that way.

Understanding the inherent superficiality of our own coverage, local news executives quickly reacted with a new sense of desperation. Panic was in the air. Instead of a handful of stations struggling over an audience, there were now dozens, and they were all angling for that same finite number of viewers. No one made the distinction between cable's strengths and our own. There was just a mad scramble to keep the numbers up. Old boundaries of civility vanished overnight.

Now there was a sense of many voices in the market place, and in order to be heard, everyone had to shout at the top of his or her lungs.

The news shows now carried items once seen strictly in the national tabloid newspapers. The talk shows were even worse. After Oprah Winfrey left for Chicago, and her replacements failed to catch on with viewers, WJZ decided to let Richard Sher host *People Are Talking* on his own.

When Sher finished his *People Are Talking* appearances each morning, he headed out to the street for his daily crime stories. Only now, he was hit regularly with questions about Oprah, who was becoming a national sensation. Strangers approached Sher to ask: Did he ever hear from her? Was it true that she'd given him a million dollars? Could he possibly get a message to her, or give out her telephone number? One afternoon, with the camera rolling, Sher interviewed the bereaved mother of a youngster killed in a gun battle.

"I can't believe they shot my baby," the woman sobbed. "I can't believe they shot my baby. I can't believe..." Suddenly she stopped, as though struck by an epiphany, and asked Sher, "Do you still talk to Oprah?"

After the station dropped Sher's *People Are Talking* partner, the decision was made to put Sher directly against Oprah each day. "We're sure you'll beat her in this market," Jonathan Klein said.

"You're out of your mind," Sher said. "This is a suicide mission."

In fact, there were two suicides in the works. *People Are Talking* would die an ugly death against Oprah's new show, and Sher, once perceived to be the next Jerry Turner, would watch the decay of his news career.

At the outset of the new Oprah competition, the station sent Sher to New York for promotional shoots with a top advertising agency. The promos showed Sher saying, "If you think you've heard it all on talk shows, you haven't heard anything yet. We're going to talk about..." As he mentioned each hot topic, a noise comically bleeped him out.

But it couldn't bleep out what was coming. It was right out of *National Enquirer*. One day the show was about sex maniacs. The next, "cosmic call girls." Then "androgenous male models," followed by "weird phobias." One day it was "transsexual mothers with brittle-bone disease."

For a while, they taped a few shows in advance. One Wednesday afternoon, Sher listened to a weather report predicting snow by that Friday. He approached an executive producer named Mike Easterling.

"Cancel Friday's show," Sher said.

"What do you mean?" Easterling said.

"They're calling for a major snowstorm," said Sher. "That means thousands of kids will be home from school. Let's do a live broadcast that day. Maybe something about the snow."

Easterling said no, they'd already taped Friday's show, and that's the one that would run. And so, when Friday arrived, and thousands of children stayed home from school for the snowstorm, those tuning to *People Are Talking* were treated to an entire show about "the thirty-minute orgasm."

Sher, who had wondered about his image as a newsman even when he and Oprah were doing the mildest features, now saw his news career crashing and burning. Station executives continued to assure him that surveys showed he could do both shows, the scuzzy *People Are Talking* and the evening news, without sacrificing his credibility or his image. They were lying. Sher worried about his career, but they worried only about the here and now.

Meanwhile, in the *People Are Talking* offices, his producers spent each day poring over the pages of the *National Enquirer*, the *Tattler*, the *Globe* and stacks of other gutter tabloids in search of material to steal for their daily shows. They giggled their way through it, but it was laughter to cover embarrassment.

One afternoon I bumped into Jonathan Klein in a hallway. He was a bright fellow, and I imagined he just wasn't paying close enough attention, or he didn't understand how offensive *People Are Talking* had become to so many people.

"It's like watching the *National Enquirer* every day," I said.

"You can't let it go on like this. It makes the station look bad."

Klein shot me a look that said, "That's your best shot?" So I threw in one more.

"And it's killing Richard's credibility," I said.

"You're wrong," Klein said, walking away. "It's not trashy enough. That's the problem with it."

If Sher dealt with the tabloidism close-up, it affected others, too. Jerry Turner and Al Sanders sat in the studio, watching the parade of blood and gore interspersed each night with trivialities. One night, Turner led into a commercial break with this tease: "Coming up—nightmare in a local school."

The story was about a gun—a toy gun that happened to look like a real gun. And nothing had actually happened—the "nightmare" of the tease was a fear that something could happen in a school.

When we broke for commercials, an infuriated Turner slammed his hand onto his desk.

"You ever complain about this stuff to the honchos upstairs?" I asked Turner.

"I should," he said. He said it as though the thought had never occurred to him. It had, of course. But such was the nature of television—of job insecurity, and of a system that was so spectacularly successful in spite (or because) of its journalistic shortcomings and excesses—that he'd never truly expressed his frustrations to the big bosses.

So he sat on his anger, or shared it with Sanders, and the two fed off of each other's anger.

But now Turner wanted to do something about it. Late on this spring afternoon in the men's lavatory, he said it was time to leave WJZ. He'd been talking with one of the other stations in town about switching. Hell, he was Jerry Turner; he'd had interest from around the country. He could go plenty of places. But he wanted to stay in Baltimore, where he had a secure following. And he wanted to take Al Sanders and me with him.

I was flattered, and I was leery. If these two men wanted

me to go along, it meant they valued my work. But, whatever its faults, this station had taken me in. I felt loyal.

"We don't have to put on this crap every night," he said. "Over there, we could have more say."

It was a strange thing to hear. I thought of all those nights in the studio when these two men bemoaned one story after another. If I implied they should complain to management about it, they usually withered me with stares that implied one of two things: Management wouldn't listen, or you didn't do such things in this business. It was too tricky, and nobody's job—not even Jerry Turner's or Al Sanders'—was safe.

In such a nervous atmosphere, this becomes one of the biggest problems in local TV news. Everyone knows that jobs are limited. While newspapers employ hundreds of people to report stories, television employs a few dozen. If you lose one job, who knows if there will ever be another one? Everyone is replaceable.

And now, finally, Turner was threatening to strike back. Even at his angriest, I had never seen him like this. He seemed to be trying to talk himself into the big move. His face was red and agitated.

"Look what they're doing next door," he said.

He meant WBAL, the NBC affiliate located just over the ridge on Television Hill. The big mover at WBAL was Ron Kershaw, who had brought in the news novices—Rudy Miller and the attorney Dick Gelfman.

They were doing interesting things at WBAL. Gelfman, especially, was setting a standard that was remarkable in television news. He was first snatched up by TV during the federal corruption trial of Marvin Mandel, the governor of Maryland. The station invited Gelfman on to analyze the trial, which he'd been attending out of professional curiosity.

He was a hit. He understood things in the courtroom that most reporters did not. WBAL's general manager, Malcolm Potter, offered him a fulltime job because he was smart enough to understand: You didn't have to look like a soap opera star to report actual news. Credibility came from the story, not just the star.

Gelfman reported unscrupulous real estate flipping. He revealed 70,000 warrants that the city sheriff's department had never gotten around to serving. He broke stories about the state's disastrous savings and loan scandal a month before the attorney general's office put it together. His station gave him days, and sometimes weeks, to do the meticulous investigating he needed. On WJZ's side of the hill, there was no one doing this kind of reporting.

"We're getting out of here," Turner said.

He said he'd been talking with the big shots at WMAR-TV, the CBS affiliate. They had some pretty good people there: Jack Bowden and his wife, Susan White Bowden, who had been around Baltimore all their lives and knew where to find stories; Andy Barth, whose father had written editorials for the *Washington Post* and had passed on a serious journalist's calling to his son; and George Collins, formerly of Baltimore's *Afro American* newspaper, who'd finally brought to the station a black person's perspective.

But getting Turner and Sanders would be an enormous coup.

"And you're coming with us," Turner kept saying to me.

A few moments later I walked out of the men's room, and the talk never went any further. There was a bigger problem than job dissatisfaction. It obscured all talk of jobs and all talk of journalism. Within months Turner was losing his voice until he was barely able to talk. On New Year's Eve the following year, as the seconds ticked off the final evening newscast of the year, he was gone.

The first sign of disaster arrived in November of 1986: a malignant tumor in Turner's esophagus. In the newsroom, Jerry kept his worries to himself, anchored the show whenever he could, and sloughed off all rumors of his demise in the grand manner.

He had laser surgery to keep his windpipe from being

blocked. Then he needed chemotherapy because the tumor had reached his trachea. Through it all, he kept smoking. He puffed away in his office, and in the studio when he got the five-minute break during sports. He and Sanders would slip off the set, light up, and stand there with wisps of smoke all around them while they dissected the show.

"You're still smoking those things?" people in the studio would ask incredulously.

"I'm trying to slow down," Turner would laugh. Nobody said the name of the thing he was fighting. Every time he failed to anchor the news, the station was bombarded with viewers' calls. This wasn't a face on a television set they worried about, it was someone who was with them every evening across many years.

That summer, the station threw a twenty-fifth anniversary celebration for him at the city's inner harbor. This was the power of television, and of Jerry Turner. The whole town wanted to get involved: the mayor, the governor, anchors from competing stations. When he finally talked to the big outdoor crowd, Turner said, "Most of you know I came that close to not being here." He held his thumb and forefinger close together. "But, obviously, I'm fine now."

He was being courageous, or deluding himself. That fall he went back for more treatments. He took off weeks at a time now. Around Baltimore, people talked as if a close relative was ill. Around the newsroom, people began to talk about him in the past tense. One afternoon, Richard Sher was called upstairs to the general manager's office. The context seemed clear: Turner's future was bleak. And Sher, the man who had been the only substitute whenever Turner or Al Sanders took time off for nearly a decade, was now going to be told to get ready for the inevitable. He would be the next Jerry Turner.

"We need to make a change," Jonathan Klein told him when he arrived upstairs.

"I understand," Sher said.

"From now on," said Klein, "we want you to focus on *People*

Are Talking exclusively. We want you to beat Oprah."

"What about news?" Sher said.

"No more news," Klein said.

Nobody mentioned Jerry Turner's name; it wasn't polite. Sher walked out of the general manager's office stunned and trying to keep his composure. All those years he thought he'd been groomed to be Turner's heir had counted for nothing. All those afternoons scrambling for homicide stories to lead the evening's broadcast, all those weeping mothers he'd convinced to come on camera when all they wanted to do was grieve for their murdered children, all those years anchoring the damned weekend show where it was just Sher and a bunch of raw kids scuffling to put together a broadcast—all of it counted for nothing. Now he was reduced to this insane suicide mission against Oprah. And one more thing: A few months later, he was back anchoring the dreaded weekends.

That October, Jerry Turner returned to the newsroom looking like a man whose blood had been drained from his body. His days were clearly running out, but he wanted to work. There were no more cigarettes. Now, if he had a break during the evening broadcast, he just sat there on the set, as though collecting his energy. He seemed barely able to make it through each broadcast.

Early in December, he finished an evening broadcast and walked with Sanders back into the newsroom. "I've got to get some more treatment," he said, "so I'll be out for the next week." The two of them shook hands, said nothing more, and then Jerry turned away and walked out of the building for the last time.

He died on December 31, 1987, right after the year's final early-evening newscast. As people dressed for New Year's Eve parties, Denise Koch appeared on television looking stricken. She was an occasional anchor during Turner's illness. Now she was here with the final bad news.

"We have to report something we hoped we'd never have to report," she said. Turner had died forty-five minutes earlier.

The station played a few old clips and then went back

to regular programming. A few minutes after Koch's announcement, the telephone rang in my kitchen. They were doing a farewell to Jerry on the eleven o'clock broadcast and wanted me to do a commentary on his life.

The broadcast was remarkable for what was said—and what was not—and so were the newspaper obituaries that followed. Sanders and Koch co-anchored the broadcast. In the final moment before we went on the air, Sanders reached over and gently touched Koch's arm, and she reached back and squeezed his hand.

The broadcast was almost entirely about Turner. We were a community of mourners, expressing grief within the parameters of journalism. Only one other news story was reported in the entire thirty-minute show. Two children were killed in a house fire in West Baltimore. Their deaths were reported, in a spirit somewhere between an obligation and an inconvenience, halfway through the show. Any strangers tuning in might have thought all other life in Baltimore had ceased that day.

When it was over, several of us trudged from the studio back into the newsroom as the clock ticked toward midnight. As Al Sanders turned toward his desk, Natalea Brown came out of her office. She and Sanders walked toward each other, and then Sanders collapsed in sobs. Then Jonathan Klein emerged from Brown's office, and the two of them grabbed Al, pulled him inside, and closed the door for several minutes.

"Jerry would have been proud," Brown said when she finally motioned us into her office.

Around the room, heads nodded assent.

"Very professional, but just enough emotion," Klein said. Heads nodded again. This kind of talk went on for a few moments more: how proud Jerry would have been, how comforting the newscast had been for a grieving city. There was one dissenting voice.

"I thought we handled the stuff on Jerry very nicely," said Al Sanders. "But I think we should have done more on those two kids who died in the fire."

Maybe he was the only one who could have said it. Maybe he was the only one who noticed. Everybody saw the "other" news that night as strictly incidental, as something to be gotten through as a self-conscious gesture of "journalism." He saw the tragedy in two children's deaths, even while mourning his friend's. He was saying: We lost the star of the television show, but the program is still supposed to be about news.

When they buried Turner, two days later, about 2,000 people stood on a raw morning in Baltimore County, outside the Towson Presbyterian Church to pay their respects. Maryland's U.S. senators were both there. The mayor of Baltimore was there, and so were former mayors. "We'll mourn him because we weren't ready to let Jerry go," Al Sanders said in his eulogy.

Coming out of the church, and seeing so many people still waiting in the street, many with tears in their eyes, I wondered what it was all about. Surely the sage of Baltimore himself, H.L. Mencken, hadn't had such a turnout. The daily newspapers were full of tributes, but even the people who covered Turner, and had watched him and interviewed him over the years, seemed unable to say what made him so special.

The *Sun's* TV critic, Bill Carter, mentioned Turner's "professionalism and dedication, his...clarity and pace." Clarity? Pace? He said Turner "expressed personality without sacrificing credibility. His style was smooth and utterly natural." Smooth? Natural?

The *Evening Sun's* critic, Michael Hill, described Turner's "concerned but calm manner, his self-effacing sense of humor." The newspaper's farewell editorial lauded his "comfortable rapport. He never strained, he never forced."

These were all fine, but they didn't express anything that explained his near-deification. In all the obituary tributes, there was nothing about his journalism skills—because, whatever they were, they were almost incidental. He was a pretty good writer, but he only wrote a few paragraphs a night. He could work a story when he had to—but he was called on to do it only occasionally. He had a deep voice. And he was a great guy.

All who wrote about his life intended praise. But all fell back on the language of television, of performance—for there was, ultimately, not much to say about journalism, about finding things out, and telling people what you've found, and why they should care about it.

It was the thing that Turner had discovered years ago, and it was his little secret. He was master of ceremonies for a television program that happened, by chance, to be about the news. He was a figure of comfort during the show's horror stories and a jovial uncle when it was time to cut up.

There were no memorable stories uncovered by Turner, because that wasn't his job. His job was to be Jerry Turner, to be himself, the pleasant, silver-haired fellow who showed up each evening the way a pal would, telling you what he'd heard since everybody got up that morning and dragged themselves through a long day. And then he saw you off to bed when day was done.

This was all television wanted from the man considered maybe the best local anchor in America.

A Woman's Work

Denise Koch is a smart and decent woman. But, like anchors all over America, she is propped up by a daily system consisting of fraud. She is thus an unintentional symbol of some of local television's troubles, as well as an example of how it sometimes does well in spite of itself.

Koch was like women in television news all over America, hired because they are telegenic and then forced to spend their careers worrying if they will be dumped when their visual charms start to wither. The problem is basic: When they get hired for their looks, they can lose it for the same wispy credentials.

In Koch's case, she was hired despite any trace of journalism in her entire history. In this, she was reminiscent of Maria Broom, Rudy Miller, and Oprah Winfrey.

Or Susan White (who later became Susan White-Bowden), the first woman reporter at Baltimore's WMAR-TV. In 1967, White was a professional model. In television commercials, she was the one pouring American beer. Also, the one eating Utz potato chips. She got a little part-time work at WBAL-TV and asked the news director, Jed Duvall, if there was any shot at a news job. It was a snowy day. Duvall sent White out to a local ski area, Oregon Ridge, where she followed a photographer around.

"When I got back to the station," she remembered thirty-five years later, "it took me four hours to write thirty seconds worth of script for Rolf Hertsgaard"—the anchorman—"to read over the film we'd shot."

That was her introduction to television news. By the time she finished, two decades later, she was forty-nine years old and considered an aging woman. This, in a time when Dan Rather, also forty-nine, was being considered as the *CBS News* successor to Walter Cronkite—except among those who said Rather wasn't an old enough man for the job.

When Susan White started in Baltimore, women were still considered oddities in the TV workplace. WBAL didn't know what to do with her after the ski story. But White had a connection at competitor WMAR and asked for a job there. They'd seen her potato chip and beer commercials. They told her to come out for an interview.

"I went out there that afternoon," White remembered, "and they told me, 'We've seen your stuff. We like you. You're a woman, you're soft, you're pretty.'" She smiled, not quite knowing what to say. "And then they said, 'Plus, you're married, and your husband supports you, so we won't have to pay you much.'"

White told them, "You're right. Whatever you offer me, I want it. I want to be in television."

She was paid fifteen dollars for every story that ran on the evening news. If she did another story for the late news, she got another ten dollars. It was the start of a twenty-two-year career that made her a Baltimore icon—but not without the same sexual conflicts dogging other women.

"That stuff about having a husband," she said years later, "if they said that today, they'd be sued. But I knew my place. The door had been opened. And it was opened because I had blonde hair and I was fairly attractive. I didn't know anything about news. I just figured, I'm a motivated person, and I'll learn how to do it."

She did women's stories. She covered the wives of politicians. She did fashion shows and flower marts. Then, in April of 1968, in the aftermath of the Martin Luther King assassination, the city of Baltimore raged and burned for four days and nights. When White arrived for work, she was humiliated to find her assignment for the day: Interview someone about dyeing baby chicks for Easter.

"You're kidding," White told the news director, Dave Stickle.

"No, I'm not," said Stickle, who doubled as the station's on-air anchor. "People have to see there's some normalcy, that life goes on."

"But the city's burning down," White said. "There are families torn apart. Let me talk to some mothers who have tried to keep their sons inside about what it's doing to their families."

"Do the baby chicks," said Stickle.

White went to the health department, where she and a department public relations person walked outside on a warm and sunny spring day in the midst of a riot-torn city to talk about the advisability of dyeing baby chicks.

"Humiliating," she remembered. "And then, as we're about to shoot the interview, we've got National Guard troops going past in the background to try to quell the rioting. So we had to wait for the troops to pass before we could do the shoot. God forbid anybody should get a dose of reality while we're dealing with chicks. The city's on fire, and we've got a limited number of people available to cover it, and this is what they've got me doing."

When she returned to the station, she begged Stickle not to make her go on the air with such piffle.

"I said, 'I'm gonna look like a fool,'" White recalled. "Stickle said, 'We've gotta have some balance in the show.' And there I went, with a big smile on my sunny little face, sitting on a stool to introduce the piece and vowing I would never let them humiliate me like that again."

The sense of embarrassment clung to her for years, reinforced by the thing that happened a few years later when White was sent to cover the city's annual Flower Mart, staged around the Washington Monument in the heart of downtown Baltimore.

"I knew my role," she remembered. "Get the story, and make myself a part of it. I wore some gaily flowered sun dress." Then, as she and her photographer made the rounds, getting snippets of action, she saw a horde of teenagers racing through the fair, upsetting booths, knocking down old people, and throwing rocks.

"A solid line, six to eight young people deep," she remembered, "and people screaming, booths going down, a wave smashing over everything. My cameraman was Bob Fleischer. He said, 'We've gotta get out of the way.' Then somebody smashes his camera. And I'm trying to crawl away, under one of these booths, and a man gets hit with a rock and there's blood all over me. I mean, I'm crawling, my stockings are torn, I'm a mess."

When they reached their car and called the station, they were ordered to report back. Dave Stickle told her, "We're sending another crew down." The reporter was a man, Jack Bowden, whom White would marry years later, after her first husband's death. Bowden reached the Flower Mart an hour after White and her photographer left. When she got back to the station, the news director told her to go home.

"You've got to put me on the air," White said. "Let me tell people what it was like down there."

"No," said Stickle, "I don't want you to do that. Our viewers wouldn't be comfortable knowing you were in harm's way. And they wouldn't like it if they knew we had put you in that position."

"But I was there to cover the Flower Mart," White said. "And this is what it turned into."

"Go home to your family," Stickle said. "And be safe."

Years later, as women reporters went off to cover the

Persian Gulf War, White-Bowden still wasn't certain why it happened this way. Maybe, she suggested, Stickle came from a generation where women were to be protected and would stay in their protected place. Maybe, several years after White's hiring, he was still uncomfortable with the notion of a woman reporter.

Or maybe Stickle understood her history and had never gotten past it: She was a potato chip and beer model who was hired because she was pretty and blonde.

"Maybe that was it," White-Bowden said. "I know the thinking was they've got all these white men on the air, and it just looks like a corporate boardroom, so let's put a blonde on with them to shake it up a little. I mean, the blonde thing mattered."

The station had a general manager, Don Campbell, who showed up one day and ordered changes in the studio lighting. He'd watched the news from home the previous night, he told the production crew, and didn't like what he saw. White, sitting in the studio as she always did to introduce the day's filmed report, didn't look right.

"Susan White didn't look as blonde as I want," Campbell told the studio crew. "I hired a blonde; I want to see a blonde. You make it happen. I don't want to go home and see a dark blonde. I want a blonde."

The crew spent an entire day re-lighting the studio. White sat under the lights as they made their adjustments. She was a blonde. When the riots of 1968 arrived, the blonde would cover baby chicks getting a dye job; when the Flower Mart riot of 1971 arrived, the blonde would be sent home. It was television's perplexing dilemma: When you've hired a woman for her looks and not her news skills, do you keep her away from the big stories or let her anchor the entire production?

In Denise Koch's case, she was an actress who needed a fallback job and wound up, in no time, as a news anchor.

Around Baltimore, Jerry Turner's demise seemed like some planetary convulsion, after which life would never be the same.

But it was. In a day or two came the usual human reaction: tragedy translated to commerce and gossip. The newspapers carried stories questioning the future of WJZ's ratings, and viewers wondered who would take Turner's place. Everybody said it was unseemly to talk about such things when poor Jerry was newly gone, and everybody did it anyway. To talk about the local newscast was to talk about people you knew, people in whom you had some investment, emotional or financial. Jonathan Klein, WJZ's general manager, did it in the newsroom the day after the funeral.

"It's terrible that Jerry died," Klein said, drumming his fingers atop a wire service machine and scanning the room to make sure nobody heard him being insensitive. "But, you know, it does make it kind of interesting now. I mean, with Jerry here, there was no challenge. We were gonna be number one no matter what we did. Now..." He let it hang in the air for a moment. "Now it's interesting again." He walked away with an ironic little smile on his face.

Klein's first big decision was replacing Turner, whose run had lasted a quarter-century. In Turner's last year, his primary substitute was Koch. For all her intelligence and poise, her most noticeable strength, in the nature of such things, was that she was a white woman who looked right sitting next to Al Sanders.

In television, everybody talks about news "talent" but feels uncomfortable mentioning the obvious; it is "talent" within certain balances of race and gender. This is not necessarily a bad thing. Those who report the news should be sensitive to issues not fully understood by, say, a cast comprised entirely of white men. And in television the cast of characters should mirror its audience. But the hiring should be based on substance, too, and on history. Koch is a woman of substance; as for her puny history, WJZ got marvelously lucky in spite of it.

She'd studied acting at California Institute for the Arts and the University of Michigan, acted in theaters around the country, and came to Baltimore because her husband, Jackson Phippin, directed plays at the city's Center Stage, where Koch sometimes performed.

She took an offer to do tips for *Evening Magazine*, the daily feature program WJZ ran when the news was over. The station offered her a two-year contract. Koch told them, "Two years? No way will I be two years in the same place." She was accustomed to spending half the year on the road. Now, for the first time in her career, she had a little stability.

The station billed her as "Daring Denise." In what ultimately became her entree to anchor the news, she performed escapist stuff in front of a camera: snorkeling and rock climbing and sky diving. After a few years of this, the station's news department needed someone for movie and theater reviews. Koch, as a trained actress with a husband who directed legitimate theater, was a natural.

A little too natural, actually. Once, she reviewed one of her husband's plays and did not mention that she was the director's wife. A gross conflict of interest, the *Sun's* Bill Carter stormed the next day. Remarkably, though, no one in WJZ's news department seemed to understand it. They knew she was the director's wife, and they knew she was doing the review, and the obvious conflict of interest did not seem to occur to anyone, or to bother anyone if it did.

To those running the newsroom, a critic was just another face to take up a little time on the show. A little culture was a nice change of pace after the nightly homicides, and it offered interesting visuals to hold viewers' attention. The newsroom bosses' daily jobs were generally consumed by technology—by the mechanics of getting the program on the air each day, by making sure there were enough reporters to deliver the most easily available stories, by making sure it had the right mix of hard news and soft features, and by making sure there was enough time for anchor chit-chat.

In such an atmosphere, any nuances of serious journalism, or of ethics, are a kind of intellectual luxury. The ethos: Just get the damned thing on the air. In the case of Koch's review, nobody stopped to think about the unique role that a critic plays: being the only independent voice letting people know if a performance is worthy of their time and money. In the modern media flood tide, all else is advertising. And Koch, however innocent her intentions might have been, was posturing herself as an objective voice about a play that happened to be directed by her spouse.

As such things go in television, the conflict was seen as negligible. The station thought the *Sun's* Bill Carter was being unfair, and saw his piece as an example of a modern newspaper, gasping to be noticed along the darkening edges of television's glare, just being hissy. Station executives appreciated Koch's on-air manner. She was classy. In no time, they jumped her to weekend anchor. Now, instead of snorkeling or rock-climbing, or reviewing plays, she was the centerpiece for the station's weekend coverage of all news.

When the inevitable criticism quickly arose that TV was now showing its true colors—letting an actress play the role of a news person—Koch faced it directly. Was the charge true? Of course. She told the *Evening Sun's* Michael Hill, "Everything I've done—acting, teaching, and now this—is about communicating information, each telling stories in its own language."

She told the paper's Steve McKerrow that TV news "is a whole new language of ways to tell a story, which is what I wanted to do all along anyway. Like an actress, you still are essentially telling viewers a story."

She was right, but she was also short-changing her new profession. At its best, journalism is not only about story-telling. It's about finding stories in the first place—some of them stories that certain people want to keep hidden. It's about knowing where to look for those stories, and knowing whom to question, and having some grip on a community's history and the workings of its government and law enforcement and business. It's about trying to piece things together.

It is, in fact, the very thing lacking in so much of local television—and one that Koch did not yet grasp, though she was about to be tossed into the heart of it. One night, years after she'd begun anchoring the news, we prepared for an eleven o'clock broadcast of that day's election for governor of Maryland.

Moments before we went on the air, Koch leaned over to me and whispered, "Now, how often is it that they have to run for governor?"

She was, by this time, the grand matriarch of Baltimore news, having outlasted all other anchors in the market. She was sophisticated, smart, worldly, and curious about many things. But she had been deposited onto a television set and told to play the role of a news person. And, as she said when she took the job, everything she had done as an actress had prepared her.

It was the same way across the country, and across the TV landscape of Baltimore. Women sometimes became anchors for reasons quite unrelated to journalism, and then both they and their audiences had to live with the consequences. Men, too, frequently had little training in being reporters. But the women had to live with an extra unsettling knowledge: Since they were hired for essentially frivolous reasons, they could be fired—or short-changed—for frivolous reasons. Men were allowed to age; women were required to hold onto their glow.

Rudy Miller joined WBAL-TV after her discovery doing the mattress commercial in a nightgown. She left because of sexual discrimination –in her wallet. Carol Costello, later a CNN anchor, followed Miller at WBAL. One day Costello talked about the more traditional sexual discrimination.

"My first job," she told the *Baltimore's Sun's* Mary Corey, "I was a reporter and I wanted to become a weekend anchor. I took my tape up to the general manager's office and I said, 'I made this tape and I'm really proud of it. I think I can do a great job at being the weekend anchor.'

"There was one chair in the room. I took my tape, put it in the videotape machine, and went to stand beside him. He was sitting in the chair. He said, 'You don't have to stand.' I said, 'No, that's OK.' And he said, 'No, no, no, you can sit down.'

Then he put his hands on my hips and sat me on his lap."

The story plays both ways. Costello was twenty-three at the time. She was young and blonde and pretty, and the general manager found her attractive and, at that moment, especially vulnerable. He was, without debate, a creep. But go beyond that. Costello was a year out of college—and already imagining that the job of an anchor was nothing more than a television performance requiring poise and grooming and an ability to read well.

As the general manager pulled Costello to his lap, she thought, "Oh, my God, what would my mother say? I didn't want to make him mad because I wanted the job. And I didn't want to get fired. I thought he was going to blackmail me. I said, 'I don't want to insult you, but this isn't right for me.' He said, 'Are you sure?' I said, 'I'm positive.' I went out and thought, 'My God, what did I do? Did I come on to him? Was I showing my cleavage?' I went downstairs and thought I would never get the job."

Three weeks later, she learned otherwise. She was given a weekend anchor job. Who knows the reasoning? Was the Neanderthal general manager worried Costello might file suit? Did he imagine that, at twenty-three, she really was seasoned enough to anchor?

In either case, the job didn't last. Never mind that Costello found herself in a position that some reporters work decades to get—she didn't like the work shift. So she soon left for another station. By the time she reached Baltimore and was interviewed by the *Sun*, Costello happily predicted a bright new day in local TV news—by her standards.

"I think the younger people coming up view news way differently than the old guard did," Costello said. "The old guard was very stuffy, very journalistic." Gosh, what a concept: journalism, as practiced by journalists. "I think the new generation coming up realizes that TV news has to be more than that. Unfortunately, it's part of prime time. And people expect a certain look because they've been watching Northern Exposure. They expect us to be just a little tiny bit

Hollywood."

Costello was being conservative. At Baltimore's WMAR-TV, the anchor woman Sally Thorner became one of the reigning queens of television news for reasons relating to her soap opera star good looks, and endless promotional advertising by the station. They ran commercials showing Thorner hugging terminally ill children at Johns Hopkins Hospital. They showed her helping students at the city's School for the Arts. They sent her off to lead high-profile marches for charity.

Journalism was a subsidiary product. At Smith College, Thorner took theater courses before starting a broadcast career. When she was twenty-seven, WMAR found her in Wichita, Kansas, and brought her east to be weekend anchor. It quickly became clear that she was merely a lady in waiting.

The station's main anchors were Jack Bowden and Nelson Benton. Bowden had grown up in Baltimore and spent years as a reporter for local radio and television. He'd covered politics and crime, and sometimes the connections between the two. He knew neighborhoods, community leaders. He was, in short, what a local anchor was supposed to be: someone who had paid dues over the years, had learned the trade, and understood the texture of the community whose news he was now anchoring.

His partner, Nelson Benton, was a former CBS reporter who had spent his career jetting around the world for stories. Benton was solid, seasoned, journalistically respected and, as a local news anchor, an absolute dud. He had no pizzazz. Whatever insights he had were buried in a hesitating, ponderous delivery. When he arrived, the station promoted him as the man who'd been in Dallas when Kennedy was shot, the man who'd been at Cape Kennedy when the astronauts took off, the man who'd been to Russia while Khrushchev was frightening the world.

The idea was to show a person who was serious about news and had covered it long enough to understand it. That's what a news anchor was: a seasoned hand who could bring experience and insight to bear on the events of the day. But, while Benton had been around the world, the local critics asked: Has he ever been to City Hall? Would he know the mayor of Baltimore if he bumped into him? Benton was seen as an interloper, a man of the world instead of a man about town.

The pairing of Bowden and Benton didn't work. The problem was, having spent a fortune promoting Benton as its great new addition, the station found itself in an awkward position. How could they dump a man whose arrival they had trumpeted so unceasingly? So they did the only thing they thought they could do: bumped Bowden, sending him back to street reporting, and brought in the young, sprightly, sexy Sally Thorner to co-anchor with Benton.

With Thorner, the station made no promotional claims to a great news background the way they had with Benton. She was what she was: a doll. She had the perfect orthodontic smile. When she delivered an upbeat story, she sold it with a little upturn of the mouth that set off dimpled cheeks. When she delivered a sad story, the smile turned upside down. If the story had a little sex to it, she flirted with the camera. A news director told her, "You just go out there and smile and bat those eyes." Subtle it was not. Successful it was. Nelson Benton was let go, and Thorner became the station's centerpiece.

When she married, it was news; when she divorced, it was news. When she remarried and had a child, it was news again. After Benton left, the station brought in another out-of-towner, Ken Matz, to co-anchor with Thorner. By now, she was becoming local television royalty.

In 1987, the nation was stunned by the death of University of Maryland basketball star Len Bias, killed by a cocaine overdose the night after he was professional basketball's top draft choice. That week, WMAR opened its late news with co-anchor Matz declaring, "Good evening, this is Ken Matz. Sally Thorner isn't here this evening. Today is Sally's birthday, and her husband has whisked her off to dinner. They're not saying where. And Sally's not saying how old she is.

"And now, the news," Matz finally declared. "Len Bias is

dead."

Oh, that news. When a magazine reporter asked about her success, it didn't even occur to Thorner to fake an answer.

"Let's face it," she told *Baltimore Magazine* in 1990, "when you flip around the dial, you're going to see pretty much the same stories at the same time. So why do people watch different stations? A great deal of the answer has to be the personalities."

Newsroom critics described her spending her days on the telephone—not with sources, but with family, friends, and hairdressers. One night reporter Randy Paige prepared a special report on the twentieth anniversary of the Vietnam War's Tet Offensive.

"How long does your piece run?" Thorner asked Paige as he sat next to her during a commercial break.

"Five minutes," Paige said.

"Good," Thorner said.

In Paige's mind, Thorner was happy that an important story was getting an extraordinarily long amount of time. He was flattered that the newsroom doyenne took such an interest, and surprised that she had this kind of previously unnoticed sensitivity. When they came back from the commercial break, Thorner introduced the piece with the full operatics. Then, the instant tape began to roll and the tragedy of the Vietnam experience was recalled for viewers, she picked up a telephone and began checking on a clothing order she'd made at Saks Fifth Avenue.

Asked, years later, about the incident, Thorner said she couldn't remember it happening. But several reporters spread the story, and it became part of the *Baltimore Magazine* piece—and part of the baggage Thorner would carry as someone not precisely devoted to the work of real reporting.

By the late 1980s, local newscasts had been around long enough for their first generation of women to begin to show some age. Around the country, visions of Christine Craft—

fired in Kansas City when deemed not young enough, not attractive enough, and not deferential enough to her male co-anchor—continued to linger.

In 1988, two Baltimore cases sent shock waves through the industry. By this time, Rudy Miller spent a decade anchoring WBAL's newscasts, and Susan White spent two decades at WMAR. White was the noon news anchor but was best known for her warm, heartfelt profiles of ordinary citizens, called "Susan's People."

But she wondered about her security. She was forty-nine years old and the glamour girl in the building was clearly Sally Thorner. After Susan's first husband died, she and Jack Bowden had married and later co-anchored the noon news.

When Susan's contract came up for renewal, she decided to let Jack handle the negotiations. The station's response stunned them both: a five-year contract, at six figures a year, with none of the usual windows along the way for termination.

"They said, 'We know how popular you are,'" Susan recalled, "'and we just want to lock you in so we can be secure with promotional stuff and programming.' The only qualm I had was, not only couldn't they get rid of me—I couldn't get rid of them, either. There was no out for either of us, for five years. It just seemed very strange for this business."

But the deal offered too much security to quibble over. She signed. And, in short order, station executives approached Jack Bowden and told him they were cutting his salary by fifty percent.

"What are you talking about?" Bowden said. "I've been here twenty years, I'm a good reporter. Is it my work?" They assured him it was not. They said he was making too much money. They said his wife was a personality, but he was just a reporter. And they said he had no choice.

Bowden quit. "I was so miserable," his wife said. "It felt like they had stabbed my husband in the back." So she did what she felt she had to do. She found a lawyer to get her out of her contract.

"I said I needed to be with my husband," she said. "So they

let me go."

Jack Bowden never worked in Baltimore television again, and Susan White-Bowden never worked anywhere in television again.

That same year, Rudy Miller came up against her own crossroads. Miller settled in as the WBAL-TV co-anchor for a run that lasted through much of the 1980s. Nobody ever accused her of being Walter Cronkite—nor was she supposed to be. She was perky. She had non-threatening good looks. She was a kind of little sister counterpart to her male co-anchors. She was comfortable with stories that tugged at the heartstrings. Co-anchors came and went, as was often the nature of television news. But Miller stayed—at a price.

As time went on, though she clearly had more experience than her male co-anchors, and more audience recognition, she nevertheless continued to make less money than the men.

In August 1988, when she began negotiations for a new contract, Miller was ready to do something about it. It wasn't easy. When she looked back at her career, she knew the thing that most people did not know: She had slipped into news through a side door and crashed the party. She got lucky because she looked good in a nightgown, and then she got lucky again because a news director liked her perkiness. Those things had gotten her started, but they also contributed to a sense of something Jerry Turner had understood: the impostor syndrome.

Turner felt it because his great success was based on reading other people's copy for a living. Miller felt it because she'd slipped into the party and then pretended to belong. And it took a decade of proving herself, night after night anchoring the news, to feel strong enough to say she did it as well as her male counterparts.

But in 1988, she was making $141,000 a year. And the men were making nearly $200,000 a year.

"This is sexual discrimination," Miller said. She pointed to the Equal Pay Act of 1963, and she pointed to Title VII of the 1964 Civil Rights Act. She said she wanted the same pay as the male anchors. WBAL said no. They offered a $4,000 raise. Miller refused. She was fired.

Now she was in trouble. She was pushing forty, an age where perkiness wasn't so much in season. She was in a profession where jobs were scarce, and anchor positions even scarcer. Fighting back panic, Miller went to the U.S. Equal Employment Opportunity Commission and filed suit against the station. She claimed she did "substantially equal work" as her male co-anchors but was subjected to "different assignments" because she was a woman. She said the station fired her because she had asked for equal pay. The station said they had simply hit a wall in negotiations. She also said she was refused choice news assignments and "subjected to increased scrutiny of clothes and hairstyle" because she was a woman.

David J. Barrett, WBAL's vice president and general manager, said he disagreed "strongly and emphatically" with the contents of the lawsuit. He was defending his station. Miller was defending her livelihood and, not coincidentally, her gender.

"I never had any plans to be a symbol," she told reporters. "But if it helps other women, God, that's great."

By the time she said it, though, several things had happened. She was out of a job. She was hosting a daily radio talk show in a dreary studio on the outskirts of town on a station with a small audience. And she had taken a huge cut in pay.

And, in a crossroads moment, she wondered which direction women in television were taking. It wasn't particularly clear. In private, they cheered her. In public interviews about Miller's case, women with anchor jobs seemed tentative, as if thinking of their own precarious positions. They mentioned audience research and ratings. They said the politically correct thing—that maybe this would cause all industries to look at gender bias.

But they knew something else: There weren't many anchor jobs around. There weren't many jobs around for anyone, men or women, paying the kind of salary from which Miller had walked away. And many in the business knew the other piece of the truth: a generation of women had been hired for reasons unrelated to their alleged job—covering the news—and would therefore always be vulnerable to corporate short-changing.

More than two years after she first filed her lawsuit, Miller and WBAL settled out of court. WBAL painted its best possible face on it. "All claims have been dismissed," said a terse statement from the station.

It had the odd sound of victory, as though a judge had thrown the case out. In fact, WBAL paid Miller about half a million dollars. And by the time of settlement, Miller had found new work.

She was now co-host of the morning show on WMAR-TV, where Susan White-Bowden and Jack Bowden had worked for years, and where Sally Thorner was now the evening anchor, the younger version of the perky centerpiece Rudy Miller had once been.

She's Not Family

You never know about people. When Al Sanders arrived at WJZ-TV in 1972, a nervous Baltimore still suffered the emotional after-effects of the race riots four years earlier. Every summer the city held its breath and wondered if more trouble was coming. Sanders came out of St. Louis, where he was known for playing late-night jazz on the radio. Then he got into news, where he was known, somewhat comically, as Scoop Sanders. When he got to Baltimore, he was known in some circles as "the colored guy," because there were still so few people of color to be seen anywhere on television news.

By the time he left, he was the man who had helped sustain a television station's dominance, and helped a community feel more comfortable in its variety of skins.

The television stations never say a lot about it, but race is always there. The white female anchor is paired with the black male anchor, or the white guy with the black guy (though rarely two women together, in any color combination.) Each pairing is a signal to viewers, many of whom are people of color, some of whom are old enough to remember when they were utterly ignored by television (and by newspapers) and are sensitive about such a thing happening again.

In Baltimore, the greater metropolitan community is about twenty-eight percent African-American. The city itself is about sixty percent African-American. To present a nightly television program not reflecting such numbers would be an act of social insensitivity and, not incidentally, economic suicide. But television stations are also watched by white people, who have comfort zones of their own. Thus we have one more matter faced by television as it pertains to journalism: not merely staffing a news organization, but also casting for purposes of drama and of social sensitivity.

One night at a small gathering in the news director's office at WJZ, the sports anchor John Buren looked around and muttered, half aloud, "This station has to be the only one in the country with four white anchors."

He was thinking about the configuration since Jerry Turner's death: Al Sanders and Denise Koch, the weatherman Bob Turk, and Buren himself. And then it slowly dawned on him: Sanders, who was sitting right there in the room, wasn't white. He wasn't passing for white, either. For a brief while, as a new street reporter in town doubling as weekend anchor, Sanders sported an Afro haircut that seemed as much political gesture as fashion statement. He was fully African-American, and comfortable with it—and able to make others comfortable with it. And Buren, a man finely attuned to the racial dynamics of television, had unconsciously counted Al Sanders as white.

Some of this was attributable to Sanders, and some of it to his TV role. He was sensitive about stories involving racial politics in a volatile time and comfortable letting Jerry Turner deliver them. It kept Sanders out of the line of fire in a time when race was particularly hot.

On the air, he found stories that showed a common humanity. Off the air, he was kind and courtly. He had a wife and three children at home. He was a television star but still saw himself as the rotund kid he had been. He was quick to make strangers comfortable and quick to poke fun at himself in order to raise everyone else's self-confidence.

When female reporters sat next to him in the studio to deliver live reports, he knew which ones were nervous and reached over to pat their hands reassuringly before the camera went on. He had James Earl Jones's voice of God when the story called for it and a comic's sense of timing when it was right. He wrote with grace and delivered the words with velvet sensitivity. He also did a slow comic take that fell somewhere between Jack Benny and Oliver Hardy, and he could dance a light fandango across the newsroom when the spirit moved him.

But he was a worrier. He became WJZ's lead anchor during a time of great change in American broadcasting. Cable television was snatching away large portions of local news audiences. Now the audience ratings were measured a new way. In the old method, the Nielsen and Arbitron companies asked families to keep diaries. In the new system, there were meters, little black boxes attached to television sets.

They would deliver near-instant measurements of audience preferences. Instead of only six times a year, ratings would now arrive at the station five mornings each week, with the audience numbers from each of the previous night's shows broken down into fifteen-minutes increments. Copies were passed around the building each day, and pored over like stock market reports.

One day I telephoned the station from the State House in Annapolis, where Maryland's governor, Parris Glendening, was giving his inauguration speech that noon.

"I figured I'd do Glendening's speech tonight," I told my producer, an intelligent young woman named Mindy Bloom.

Across the telephone lines, I heard her sigh resignedly, clearly reflecting orders from higher up. "We had a couple of political stories yesterday," she said, "and the ratings weren't very good. So they'd rather you do something on the Ravens.

The Ravens are a professional football team. Governments come and go, but the people will always want football. And now that we had our daily ratings, we could more carefully calculate what viewers might want—rather than offer actual news.

"We'll have to act accordingly," Marcellus Alexander had said the week the meters arrived. Alexander had replaced Jonathan Klein as general manager. He was thirty-six years old, the second African-American general manager the station ever had.

"What do you mean?" he was asked.

"Well," he said, "you know about Dallas?"

Dallas was already using the new meters. One station there had run a three-part series of "special reports" on killer bees on the last three nights of a key ratings period. Each one was increasingly stupid, and each drew bigger audiences. The station won the ratings battle, and the general manager there hailed the killer bee series. Alexander was telling us he paid attention to such things.

"This is not good," the stage manager Skip Ball declared one day in the newsroom. Ball was the one who usually kept everyone else cool. "Have you talked to this guy?"

He said he had gone to Alexander's office about some union business. He noticed a plastic figurine Alexander kept near his desk: a "typical television viewer" watching the news. The viewer was an unshaven, beer-bellied slob in a sleeveless undershirt, slurping a brew with his feet propped up.

"That's how he sees our audience," Ball said. "He thinks they're idiots, and we should put on news for idiots."

In fact, Alexander was like almost all television general managers. He had come up through the ranks as a salesman, and judged a station's success strictly on its revenues. What he thought about journalism he generally kept to himself. His strength, as it turned out, was that he allowed the newsroom (with one awful exception) to run itself.

When he arrived, the station was still fat and cocky. It was already producing the nightly *Evening Magazine*, part of a nationally syndicated operation, plus *People Are Talking* and *Square-Off*, and there was talk of more local programming.

Instead, all would get the ax—and, with that, jobs would be eliminated. In the early 1990s, Baltimore-area television revenues declined ten percent. It was this way at network affiliates across the country. In large part, it was cable's incursion.

Another sea change was the ratings meters. These were changing the approach to ratings around the country. For one thing, the Nielsen and Arbitron families could no longer lie. Instead of watching *Family Feud* but claiming they had watched a public television program on the crisis in Somalia, the meters captured actual viewing habits.

Many of the traditional ratings leaders now found they were losing ground. Viewers had marked down *Eyewitness News*, for example, simply because they had been loyal to it since Jerry Turner first started building an audience. They filled out diaries by habit, or by memory. But the memories weren't as accurate as the meters. If you watched something else—or didn't watch at all—the new meters recorded the new truth.

Then there was the network switch. For forty-six years, WJZ had been affiliated with ABC and reaped the benefits. Coming out of WJZ's powerhouse audience, *ABC News with Peter Jennings* ranked first in Baltimore for years. NBC and Tom Brokaw, linked with Baltimore's WBAL, ranked second. CBS and Dan Rather, with WMAR, ran third.

Now ABC and CBS would switch affiliates. Why? Rupert Murdoch.

As Murdoch expanded his Fox network, he snatched CBS stations in Detroit and Cleveland. Left without an affiliate in those two cities, CBS tried to woo the ABC stations there, which were owned by Scripps-Howard—as was Baltimore's WMAR. CBS offered millions to Scripps-Howard to switch; ABC asked Scripps, what would it take to stay with us? That's when WMAR's name came up.

Scripps told ABC that, in order to keep Cleveland and Detroit away from CBS, they had to dump powerful WJZ in Baltimore and take on its struggling WMAR station there. ABC took the plunge.

CBS would no longer run third in Baltimore. Behind WJZ's lead-in, CBS became the number one network news show. The network was so grateful, it dispatched its morning anchors, Paula Zahn and Harry Smith, down from New York, to walk around the WJZ newsroom and thank everyone personally. Then, having expressed such thanks, the money-counters at the network would later reach down to Baltimore and pluck every piece of loose change they could find.

In the face of so many industry changes, WJZ made changes of its own: first, it expanded the early-morning feature and news program, which would dominate the market for years to come. And, around the same time, the thing that television does best: The station began to steal.

Only this time, instead of merely stealing stories from the daily newspapers, they stole on-air people from other television stations. Stunning everyone, they started by snatching away WBAL's Dick Gelfman, the attorney who had turned his legal background and investigative skills into one of the dominant forces in local news.

One day in the WJZ newsroom, Natalea Brown, the news director, cautioned about a new day dawning.

"My feeling," she said, "is that most markets won't be able to support three local news operations. Not with cable around. Maybe they'll spread out enough to support two stations, but that's it. And we want to be one of those two."

Her words signaled an unspoken and quite unanticipated change in the media landscape. For years, newspapers had been giving ground to television news. By the mid-1980s, Baltimore had lost both of its afternoon daily newspapers. Only the *Sun* remained, with its morning circulation bolstered by snatching the remaining readership of the afternoon papers.

Meanwhile, TV news operations around the country now struggled to hold onto the exodus of viewers discovering the new cable landscape. The effects would be dramatic. WJZ and WBAL would each struggle for about 100,000 households each night, while WMAR would reach fewer than 30,000 households a night. Its evening ratings would be topped by competing stations' cartoon reruns.

By grabbing Dick Gelfman, WJZ seemed to push his old station, WBAL, toward serious trouble. Gelfman brought reporting skills, and he brought a built-in audience that would follow him over the hill from WBAL. At his old station, he had gone after everybody: real estate frauds, savings and loan thieves, unscrupulous home improvement people. He had passion tempered by an adult sensibility, not a standard combination for television.

Also, he didn't look like television was supposed to look. He was big and beefy and wore thick glasses. He wore cowboy boots and sometimes rode a motorbike to work. In his thirties, he already looked fifty. His thinning hair tended to fly off in different directions when he wasn't paying attention, which was often, and his clothes seemed pulled out of a storage trunk from somebody's attic. Neckties ran halfway down his belly and then stopped.

"Thank goodness you're here," I told him. "As long as you're around, it means I'm no longer the worst-dressed guy in the building."

When he sat down with news director Natalea Brown, she asked him, "What do you need from us to do the kind of work you were doing over there?"

"Two producers and some volunteers," he told them. "And time enough to do the work."

All were crucial—and all would eventually be taken away when the new general manager, Jay Newman, arrived. For years, though, Gelfman was one of the pillars holding up WJZ. First, he pulled in a team of volunteers. These were mostly retirees, a different handful of bright people each day of the week whose working careers were done but who still had too much energy to spend all day sitting in the house. With Gelfman, they felt they were working with the angels. They had late-in-life television stature to tell their families about, and they gave the station something that resembled an actual staff.

The Gelfman gang handled letters and phone calls and e-mails, more than 2,000 each month. Huge amounts of story possibilities poured in. Most of it wasn't exactly toppling a government, but it was useful, resolvable—and visual. Once a week, as a change of pace, the station ran a consumer feature: "Let Dick Buy It." He'd check out products that promised miracles and expose the rip-off.

But he also had legal insights and connections that no one else had. When the state was hit with a savings and loan industry scandal, Gelfman was far ahead of other television reporters. When the Baltimore Ravens' linebacker Ray Lewis was involved in a murder case, Gelfman had legal contacts no one else had.

But Gelfman wasn't alone. Years earlier, the station had hired Suzanne Collins away from WBAL and put her on the air. For Baltimore television, Collins was another odd type: a serious reporter who seemed somewhat oblivious to the usual sense of broadcast style and the usual attention to visual dramatics. She combed records to uncover illegal gun sales. She investigated abuse of the handicapped. Once, she checked handicapped tags on cars parked downtown—and found that huge numbers of all the handicapped tags were fakes.

The 1990s were transitional years for local news operations, in which many passed from immature childhood into pretentious adolescence. But adulthood was a different story.

A lot of the early excesses were gone now. No more five-part series on the secret fantasies of anchors, no more hand-puppets delivering the weather. The people running the business got a little tired of the public ridicule and realized it was time for their medium to grow up—or at least give the appearance of growing up. Their concept of news, or public service, had almost nothing to do with it. It was strictly economics. The novelty was gone. Cable had arrived, and so had the Internet. Television had to do things it had previously never done or watch its audience drift away.

So the industry developed better technical equipment. They could put a reporter on any street corner, from where the reporter could offer the appearance of delivering actual news. In fact, though, they put the technology to absurd use. In the afternoon, a teenage boy is struck by a hit-and-run driver while leaving school. The reporter puts together videotape of interviews with police and school officials. And then sits in the Eyewitness News van for hours, with his cameraman, while the station runs teases declaring, "Nightmare at an elementary school. Story at eleven."

At eleven, the studio anchor opens the show by announcing, "Our reporter is at the scene of the hit-and-run accident, and files this live report." Whereupon, maybe eight hours after the accident, the reporter, shivering in the cold, offers a live, ten-second introduction to a sixty-second videotaped piece put together hours ago, and then delivers a live, ten-second close.

"Thank you for that live report," the anchor declares when the piece ends.

It was strictly about appearance. In this era, the old half-hour early-evening shows, having expanded to an hour, expanded once more. Much of the reason was cost: It was simply cheaper to produce a news program than to pay outrageous fees for situation comedy reruns, such as *The Cosby Show*, that had been running as news-hour lead-ins.

Now, seeing what some of the cable news stations offered—not only journalism, but sobriety—the local operations had a new role model to copy. Operations like CNN showed it was okay to look for actual news, and to deliver it without waving your arms for attention.

The problem was, the locals didn't have staff to imitate that role model. Around the country, they were still sending out a handful of reporters each day to cover entire states. Only now, as the shows expanded to two hours, the same handful of reporters had to fill the extra sixty minutes. At WJZ, for example, no new reporters were hired to fill the extra hour.

"We'll have to work a little harder," said Gail Bending, when the five o'clock announcement was made.

"What do you mean?" I said. "This is like starting a newspaper without any reporters."

"We'll have reporters," she said. "The same ones we have now."

"But they're reporting for the six o'clock."

"They can do the same stuff for the five o'clock," she said. "It's just repackaging."

"But we're telling people it's two different shows. How dumb do we think they are?"

Bending turned away. This was out of her hands, a matter strictly for the money managers. But among the station's newsroom people—reporters, photographers, producers, the technicians and tape editors stringing everything together— there was generalized outrage. They were already scrambling to make legitimate stories out of flimsy material. Once pressed to fill an hour each evening with a handful of reporters, they were now pressed to fill two hours. And so there were strategies.

For big civic events, the station would flood the area. Opening day of the Orioles baseball season, for example, or the annual running of the Preakness Stakes. But, for all the bodies thrown at such events, the coverage remained stupefyingly simplistic.

One year the Reverend Jesse Jackson showed up for the baseball opener at Oriole Park at Camden Yards. In the midst of about 45,000 people milling outside the stadium before game-time, Jackson led a picket line to protest the lack of front-office integration of baseball.

In the newsroom at WJZ, management sang hosannas when they heard this would happen. It meant they had a hard-news story to attach to their baseball coverage. They were already planning to devote much of the show to the opening game festivities, but the demonstration—and a live interview with Jackson, who never met a camera he didn't like—would give it a patina of seriousness.

"I'm a social justice fighter," Jackson said when TV photographers managed to get themselves in place. "Baseball has taken an arrogant posture. It is a dying art in urban America."

He was talking about the sport's old-boy network that kept the management of ballclubs overwhelmingly white. There was no argument with that. The argument was with television's coverage of it and its sense of perspective.

For here was Jackson, who had stood over Martin Luther King's lifeless body on that hotel balcony in Memphis, and was still considered King's spiritual heir, and he was making a case that on this day, here was the most important problem facing black America.

If Jackson had glanced, for even a moment, in a westerly direction, he would have noticed a street perhaps two blocks away. It is called Martin Luther King Boulevard. At this time, April of 1993, the average major league baseball player made $1.2 million per year—while, in the vast public housing projects on Martin Luther King Boulevard, there lived thousands of African-American families. Their median income was not only far below what the average major leaguer earned—per day— but far below the government's official poverty line.

The blame here was not only Jackson's. He understood the system of Opening Day news coverage and was merely trying to exploit it. The fault was of the people who sent the cameras to the ballpark but never any further.

At WJZ that evening, several people gathered in news director Gail Bending's office, sitting in an air of self-congratulation. They thought Jackson's demonstration had lent an air of drama to the broadcast.

"What about those projects two blocks away?" I said.

Nobody answered. Nobody seemed to know what I was talking about. I mentioned the irony of Martin Luther King's successor worrying about major league baseball issues when people living on a boulevard named for King were scraping by on poverty money. Didn't that lend itself to a story? Wasn't the irony ripe for reporting?

Nobody felt the need to reply, so I shrugged and walked out of the room. The housing projects were only good for the dramatic moments, such as drug squabbles that led to homicides. They were not noteworthy for any conditions that led to such deaths.

What's more, to argue the point was to mark yourself as a trouble maker, no less than any reporters who might have argued about having to double their work output when the five o'clock broadcast was launched. To complain was to be perceived as difficult to handle. Since everyone lived with personal service contracts, and renewals were always just around the corner, no one wanted to be seen this way.

In fact, plans for the new five o'clock show would bend the old reporting techniques in a number of ways. For one thing, management now insisted that certain stories could be covered without any actual reporters. Send a cameraman. Let the cameraman ask any questions that needed to be asked.

Thus, at a City Hall press conference, the mayor might be queried by a photographer who had never ventured a thought about city issues—because there were no reporters available.

At WJZ and elsewhere, the notion of sending out photographers to do reporters' work was infuriating. Reporters saw themselves as trained journalists. Management, feeling otherwise, did not care. They knew that certain stories called for expertise, but such stories could be avoided. The medium had been living off this distinction for years.

One balmy night in 1995, the station's AFTRA—American Federation of Television and Radio Artists—union members met to thrash out the changes. The union sent two of its attorneys to talk to us.

"Changes are coming," one of them said darkly, "and you'd better get used to them."

I looked around the long conference table where the most familiar faces in town had the same reaction: They looked, in that moment, utterly vulnerable.

"Everybody's cutting back on money," the second attorney said, "and there are no jobs around. You want to give management a tough time, you aren't going to win." The room was silent. "All over the country, they're looking to hire kids now. Kids come cheap."

"This is bullshit," a voice muttered. Then another voice said photographers couldn't possibly do the same quality job that trained reporters could do. Somebody else said it was insulting, that viewers would see they weren't getting a full story.

I listened to the arguments, and I commiserated because these people were my friends. But I knew the game was up. The way television covered news, there really were lots of stories that anybody could cover. Day after day, the show was always filled with one-dimensional stories absent of all texture.

Everybody in television complained about this all the time, and then cashed large checks at the bank. The stations had invested in them not as reporters, but as personalities. Getting the look of a story was the thing that kept people from switching channels.

The reporters felt themselves getting phased out. If photographers could do the work of reporters, then what would keep the station from sending out a college kid, an unpaid intern? How smart did you have to be to get a couple of sound bites? In a medium that valued the look of things, and not the content, what did it matter what question was asked or, for that matter, what answer was given?

Feeling threatened, the reporters wanted to claim expertise—but, in what, exactly? The very system that had created them, and promoted them, had also kept them from gaining any real insights into the world they allegedly covered. Their expertise was in TV skills, which are not always the same as reporting skills.

"They send a photographer on a story," the AFTRA lawyer told us that night, "it means they got more work for less money. The attitude is, the hell with the product. Just get us cheap."

The real expenditures went for more hardware. Many stations brought in helicopters, which could cost the equivalent of two or three reporters. The copters were great at getting pictures, such as traffic backups and house fires. Sometimes the shots were dramatic, but rarely were they very meaningful. It's rush hour, so there's a traffic tie-up. Big deal. But the sheer expense of the helicopters meant that management had to cut editorial costs somewhere else.

Through all the changes, WJZ continued winning the numbers game. The new anchor combination—Al Sanders and Denise Koch—had the look of maturity, and they were comfortable with each other. Those things still mattered. Ratings didn't dominate the way they had in Jerry Turner's time, but they were still high. To those running the station, this meant more than anything.

In the newsroom, where ratings pervaded the culture, there was also a sense of some pretty good journalism being conducted—by Gelfman and Collins, for example, and by Alex DeMetrick covering environmental issues and Pat Warren and Mike Schuh on general assignment. They took their work seriously. Then there were two more additions. The *People Are Talking* show, having gotten nowhere in its mad competition with Oprah Winfrey, finally folded, and Richard Sher came back to news, where he brought energy and home-town insight. And so did Ron Matz.

Matz was a veteran radio reporter. He'd spent his whole life in Baltimore and knew its biggest players and its neighborhood characters. Years earlier, when a gunman walked into City Hall and started killing people, Matz was on the air, broadcasting the horror while it was still going on. Hiring him at WJZ was a coup for a station that had always understood: familiarity counts. Reporters have to be familiar with their surroundings, and viewers like to be familiar with reporters.

But the most stunning news arrived in the fall of 1992, when Marcellus Alexander announced that the station was adding the five p.m. broadcast—and had hired Sally Thorner away from WMAR to anchor it.

If getting Gelfman from WBAL pushed that station to the edge of a cliff, taking away Thorner would push WMAR into the abyss. Thorner had no reporting skills at all, but she was the sexy centerpiece anchor around whom almost all the station's promotions had been constructed. The good news was Thorner was the competition's biggest star, and now she belonged to WJZ. The bad news was almost everything else.

Thorner was a kind of punch line in Baltimore television, a symbol of the medium's reach for glamour at the expense of substance. At WMAR, her co-workers described her as a dilettante who almost never left the studio to pursue a story, or even lifted a phone for one. She knew her role: playing the princess. She was seen as the embodiment of everything for which television news was accustomed to being mocked: its superficiality, its pretty faces masking its inner emptiness.

When the news hit WJZ, it was met with open anger. There were people who had been there for years—Richard Sher, Sandra Pinckney, Deborah Stone, Don Scott, Pat Warren—who had imagined an anchor spot might be theirs with the new show.

On the set that night, Al Sanders and Denise Koch seemed like two clenched fists, barely able to keep from pounding out their rage. The anger seemed out of proportion. I knew Thorner's reputation, but I saw her hiring as one in a series of empty-headed moves by local stations.

"What's the big deal?" I asked Sanders.

He turned to me, this gentlest of men, with absolute fire in his eyes. "She's not family," he snapped.

He meant two things: her hiring showed that the station's own in-house people were being passed over after years of loyalty; and, she wasn't like us. At this station, anchors worked in the newsroom with the rest of the staff, wrote their own copy, paid some attention to the program beyond their own roles. Thorner's reputation said she wasn't like that.

She was in trouble before she even arrived at WJZ. In Baltimore, as in many television markets, on-air people have a no-compete clause in their contracts. If they leave one station, they can't join another station within a certain geographical radius without a year's layoff. It is management's way of keeping reporters from jumping from station to station and running up the pay.

But WJZ was paying for Thorner's layoff. They were

paying her $250,000 to sit out a year. At the station, it was seen as $250,000 that might have gone toward hiring some reporters to staff the newly-created five o'clock show—instead of the ludicrous act of starting a news program by simply doubling the existing work load of everyone in the building.

Around Baltimore, which sees itself as a working-class town, the news did not sit well. WJZ was the home-town station, the voice of the ordinary working stiff. What was this all about? Thorner was seen, fairly or not, as taking money that didn't belong to her. The money seemed to capture every snide remark ever made about her.

When the new five o'clock show opened in January of 1994, the response was pretty rough. The *Baltimore Sun's* TV critic, David Zurawik, called it "a curious mix of Thorner perkiness, semi-weird tabloid stories and 'live' remotes—from an editing booth. It's hard to say which was the lower low last night. Maybe it was when Thorner and John Buren talked live on the telephone with a guy in Scotland about the Loch Ness monster. Or, maybe when Buren delayed his sports report to search the floor for a button that fell off his coat."

That was Buren, trying to play the court jester on a show on which he wasn't just the sports guy—he was a co-anchor. The show had been billed as somewhat less formal than the six o'clock show. Thus, there were features on the actress Loni Anderson, and some fellow in Denver getting his nose bitten off in a bar fight. Neither story had a local angle, or an ounce of significance. For local news, the show opened with Ron Matz reporting from a grocery store, wondering if there would be a run on food since weather forecasters were predicting snow.

But moments after Matz's story, weather man Bob Turk reported, "I don't think there'll be much snow."

The solution to staffing problems was simple. Having decided not to spend money for any new reporters for the new, hour-long program, the station would have to find other news to report. They would use network feeds, syndicated stories, all manner of packaged fluff. Loch Ness monster, indeed. Skip Ball had been right; we were treating viewers as if they were real-life versions of Marcellus Alexander's little statue of the TV-watching slob.

After a few weeks' watching, even the slobs looked elsewhere. The ratings plunged, and the criticism around town was general.

At WJZ, nobody was accustomed to such things happening. This was a station that had spent twenty years marching from triumph to triumph. Now it was losing viewers. Now there was newsroom tension around the outsider Thorner.

And then came the death of Al Sanders.

Dear Albert

The end of a life begins with the mundane. In the newsroom, an old friend tells Al Sanders, "You've got to do something about your shirts; they're hanging on your neck."

"I can't get the right size," says Sanders.

"Well, you've got to do something; they're hanging."

It didn't look good on the evening news. Sanders was losing weight and wondering why, and refusing to see any doctors about it. He had the flu, and then he blamed everything that followed on the effects of the flu. His weight dropped, and then his voice started to go. A different face began to emerge on the television screen. No longer the round, slightly cherubic features that reminded him of his overweight boyhood self, they were now distinguished, contoured. Nobody connected it yet with dying.

He showed up at work every night and sat with a series of co-anchors. Denise Koch, pregnant with twins, was home on precarious bed rest. Sanders's work didn't seem to suffer, and neither did the ratings. He was still writing gracefully, still anchoring the top-rated shows at six and eleven and still, during the commercial breaks, moaning about the dreadful story selection that aired every night.

The work took his mind off his health. It was now seven years since Jerry Turner's death, and nobody wanted to imagine such a thing happening again or even mutter the comparison.

"What?" Sanders said one winter night in the newsroom. "What are you looking at?"

He was losing weight ever more noticeably, and his clothes were hanging ever more loosely. On the air, he looked so tired that viewers were calling the station to inquire about his health.

"Why don't you see a doctor?" he was asked.

"Will you stop?" he said. His voice would have sounded exasperated, except he understood the concern behind the questions

"Everybody thinks I'm dying," he said. "I had the flu and I'm having a hard time getting over it, that's all. But I'm not dying."

"Nobody says you're dying."

"Then don't say anything."

He'd gone to doctors, who turned up nothing indicating cancer. But the checkups were cursory. The station was locked in a ratings battle that February, and with Denise Koch on maternity leave, Sanders's presence was more important than ever. It wasn't like the old days, where WJZ marched triumphantly through one ratings period after another and then celebrated with parties in the newsroom.

By the winter of 1995, the competition was tighter than it had been in years. So Sanders showed up every afternoon. And every evening he looked a little weaker by the time he went on the air. When I sat next to him on the set one night, he was obviously straining when he spoke. When I finished my commentary and we broke for a commercial, I stayed in my chair for a moment.

"Your voice," I said.

"What about it?"

"Kind of weak, isn't it?"

"Don't start with me."

"Why don't you go to a hospital?" I asked

He looked down at the stack of papers in front of him as if too busy to respond. When I saw his eyes start to fill, I stood up to walk away. I was embarrassed that I'd pressed him when it wasn't any of my business.

"Because of Jerry," he finally said, choking out the words.

That was all. He was still haunted by Turner's death and still performing the escape artist's self-delusion: Ignore the trouble, and maybe it will go away. When it did not, in early March he finally went to a hospital. When he didn't come back for a few days, and viewers kept calling, the station announced that he'd had the flu and it had turned to pneumonia.

But it was cancer, and it was inoperable. In early May, Sanders lay in a bed at Johns Hopkins Hospital with his wife, Ruth, and his three children nearby, and he died. He was fifty-four. Denise Koch, having given birth to twin girls, came back to work and anchored a show announcing his death. Then, in ceremonies at Wilde Lake Interfaith Center, in the suburban city of Columbia where Sanders had lived, Koch delivered a magnificent eulogy.

"My dear Albert," she said.

As she stood before the big crowd, she thought about all the evenings she'd sat next to him on the air, and all the late nights after the eleven o'clock news was finished when she' d driven her car next to his through the tough parts of town on her way home. She tried to keep her composure. Around the big hall, some had begun to cry. "In a vain and shallow world, he was neither," Koch said. "Albert was a humble man, and he didn't like a lot of fuss."

But there was one last bit of fuss: a special hour-long show devoted to Al, in which several of his colleagues remembered how much he'd meant. I thought a lot about his personal decency. But I also remembered the professional broadcaster who'd sat there night after night bemoaning what local television news had become.

A lot of it was the crime coverage. Some of it was bloody, but plenty of it was trivial, oddball, quirky, made to seem important merely by television's coverage of it. Sanders thought the worst of it was veiled racism: the blood in the streets, followed by the most hysterical people, out of their minds with grief and anger, some of them drug-dependent and most of them utterly inarticulate. They were the modern urban stereotypes. Implicitly, Sanders thought, such incessant coverage said this is how black people are, this is what the city of Baltimore has become, this is why you must leave now.

It wasn't that crime should be ignored. In a city with thousands of criminal acts each year, to minimize this was to ignore reality. But there was so much more going on that was utterly ignored—merely because it wasn't visually dramatic.

Sanders was an African-American man with lofty anchor stature, working for an African-American general manager, Marcellus Alexander. Both men were sensitive to racial stereotyping. But Sanders, like Turner before him, was leery of confronting management in any profound way. And Alexander was a salesman whose sense of successful journalism was computed in the traditional TV measure: High ratings translated to high advertising dollars, while low costs were maintained by keeping a small newsroom staff, scratching each day to get the easiest available stories. Thus, the nightly crime in the streets, the look of drama—all of it the classic model for stations around the country.

As always, all coverage was slapdash. Reporters had no beats, and therefore no sources or special insights. There was coverage, but no un-coverage. If a politician held a press conference, television could cover it. But there was never any sense of the texture behind the press conference. Television covered staged events; it was, in fact, part of the staging, but it had no concept (and no curiosity) about the things happening beyond the lights.

And, sometimes appallingly, there were reporters who covered such public events and seemed utterly oblivious to the basics of journalism.

One night, Khalid Muhammad came to Baltimore. He had been Louis Farrakhan's Nation of Islam henchman but was disciplined after referring to Jews as "bloodsuckers."

In one speech he declared, "Who's pimping the world? The hairy hands of the Zionist in the world." Then: "Don't let no hooked-nose, bagel-eating, lox-eating, perpetrating-a-fraud so-called Jew who just crawled out of the ghettoes of Europe just a few days ago..." Another time: "Look at it, so-called Jew. Look at it, impostor Jew. Somebody must call you what you are. Somebody must look you in your cold lying blue eyes and pull the cover off of you today. I don't give a damn about you and I will give you hell from the cradle to the grave."

With this language as background, Muhammad arrived in Baltimore for a speech one Saturday night. It was the usual business, blaming Jews, blaming whites in general. WJZ sent reporter Dennis Edwards to cover the speech, and then Edwards came back to the studio to sit next to Richard Sher to deliver his report. Sher was anchoring that night.

"I don't think he's really anti-semitic," Edwards declared on the air, launching into an editorial defense of Muhammad.

Sher shot him a look that said, "Excuse me?"

He didn't know where to take it next. He didn't want to show his audience that he had a rogue reporter sitting next to him who didn't know the difference between covering a story and pontificating, but he didn't want to let the moment get further out of hand, so he quickly moved on.

Nobody had checked Edwards's copy before he went on the air. Nobody had ever told him the difference between fact and opinion. And nobody had told him his job was dealing with facts, since so much of television's job was primarily dealing with image.

In the early 1990s while many American cities began to return to life in a booming economy, Baltimore lagged behind. Formerly besieged by heroin traffic, the city was additionally inundated with crack cocaine now, and a new generation of crack-addicted babies was born and began to act out in schoolrooms. The city's housing stock was aging badly and, in thousands of cases, was now deserted. A suburban exodus of families that had started twenty years earlier now picked up steam; a thousand families a month were leaving, on average.

And the numbers of homeless went up and up.

Now more than ever, there was additional work to be done. Now, instead of merely producing a story for the six o'clock show there was also the five o'clock show to be fed. The same taped press conference had to be packaged twice. And at WJZ the five o'clock was starting out as a distinct clunker.

In the newsroom, griping was general. Reporters who had traditionally filed one story a day now often found they had to stretch the material, or present it twice and try to make it look fresh when it wasn't. Those with real talent for story telling, such as Alex DeMetrick and Mike Schuh, found themselves rushing about to grab what they could and get it on the air twice.

The station had always scored heavily with anchor personalities, but this time the personalities weren't working out. The Sally Thorner–John Buren anchor duo was disastrous. Buren was fast and edgy but out of his element, and Thorner didn't know what to make of him. They clearly hated each other, and management had to take them aside and issue formal instructions: Whatever your anger, you'd better fake some warmth on the air. The chill was making people at home feel uncomfortable. Off the air, Buren issued written instructions that in the event of his sudden death, Thorner should not be invited to the funeral. The instructions were passed around the newsroom.

Meanwhile, viewership tumbled disastrously. WMAR, the station Thorner had deserted, now led the five o'clock ratings, pulling in some 38,000 homes more than WJZ. Nobody could remember such a thing happening. At her old station, Thorner's birthday had gotten higher billing than the basketball player Len Bias's death. Here, she seemed to fumble for some sense of presence. This was a station, WJZ, that had been a luxury liner, that still saw itself floating triumphantly above the drowning competition. What was going on?

In public, news director Gail Bending denied any trouble. It was her move that had brought Thorner on board. In the newsroom, though, you could smell the panic. Jobs were at stake. People still muttered darkly about the $250,000 Thorner had gotten for her year off, and imagined new reporters who might have been hired with such money.

"You bring in five kids for that kind of money," Al Sanders had said one night, not long before his health began to fail. "And then you've got coverage where no other station in town would have coverage." But he was talking about news. He knew that management's chief concern was the impression of news.

There was another concern: If the five o'clock tumbled, could it bring down the six o'clock with it? A viewer at rest tended to stay at rest, sticking with the same news channel. Scrambling for answers, Marcellus Alexander called Richard Sher into his office late in the summer of 1994.

Sher was fifty-three now. He was lean and energetic. His hair, long since gray, had now turned white. He looked the way a traditional anchor was supposed to look, as though he had a little experience on him. After all that time in the cold—covering murders, anchoring weekends, fronting for *People Are Talking* as the station fruitlessly pursued Oprah, and then coming back to news to cover more murders—his hour had finally arrived.

"I think we're gonna try you out on the five," Alexander said.

"What do you mean, 'try out'?" Sher said.

"Well, a test," Alexander said. He wasn't sure how to parse his language. "See how it works out."

"A test sounds like school," Sher said. "For Christ's sake, I've been in this market for twenty years, how much of a test do you need!'"

"Let's try it for a week," Alexander said. "You and Sally. We need to do a little more research."

He knew what Sher represented. He was a symbol of the station's continuity. He was a Baltimore native who had come of age in his home town and then stuck around. He was a solid presence, and quick-thinking, and he knew the local turf.

"We know what your strengths are," Alexander told him.

"If you don't get the job, it's not you; it's a diversity issue. I mean, we have four whites."

He meant Sher and Thorner, Buren on sports and Bob Turk on the weather. He was talking to Sher as one friend to another, and crossing color lines to do it. But this was extremely sensitive territory, and Sher wanted to make certain he understood what Alexander was saying.

"You mean, if I don't get it, it's because I'm white?" Sher asked.

"Let's just say it's diversity," Alexander said.

Sher walked out of the room figuring the tryout was worth the shot. But he went to his agent, Ron Shapiro, and told him what had happened, just to get it on the record. Shapiro told him two obvious facts of life: This was a clear admission of discrimination by Alexander. But if Sher wanted to file suit over it, his career at WJZ would soon be over—and, perhaps, his career anywhere in television. Race was too uncomfortable to bring up in public, except in the most benign, feel-good ways. The public was tired of it, and so were TV sponsors.

Shapiro and Sher agreed to let it go. The "test" went well. In October the station announced Sher's appointment as Thorner's "permanent co-anchor." Thorner said it would be nice having Sher sit next to her. Nobody mentioned how it might affect news coverage, since everybody knew that news had nothing to do with it. This was about personality. You give up the veteran reporter, because reporting is secondary. You add the personality, because personality covers up the lack of reporting. Nobody replaced Sher on the street.

The ratings climbed steadily. The early 38,000 gap in viewers vanished. Now on most nights the station took the lead at five o'clock. Sher was authoritative and energized and funny in all the right moments. But he was too fast for Thorner. She responded to his ad libs with a schoolmarm "boys will be boys" shake of the head as she looked into the camera. It made her look helpless, overmatched, slightly disapproving. This was supposed to be her show, but Sher had quickly become the dominant figure.

For a while, attempting to add a familiar face to the program, they brought Maryland's newly retired governor, William Donald Schaefer, on board as a weekly commentator. Schaefer was perceived as a natural, a mix of politics and personality who had been mayor of Baltimore for fifteen years and governor of Maryland for eight years.

As mayor, he was famous for driving around town and looking for alleys to clean, potholes to fill. He wore funny hats. Once, he went to the city's aquarium and waded into the seal pool wearing a straw hat and a turn-of-the-century bathing suit. As governor, if somebody ticked him off, he ticked back at them. He wrote them angry letters and called them names. He knew more about the city and the state than any twenty people in the rest of the building.

Having watched years of local news, Schaefer figured he knew the drill. Wait for the introduction, say a few words back to the anchor, turn to your camera and launch into the commentary. The night after the catastrophic bombing of the Oklahoma City federal building that took scores of lives, Schaefer veered off course.

"And here with a commentary about the tragedy in Oklahoma City," Richard Sher declared that night, "is William Donald Schaefer."

Schaefer, sliding into what he imagined was a charming little bit of TV cross talk, said, "Before I start, let me just say that that's a beautiful necktie you're wearing, Richard."

"Uh, thank you," said Sher. He waited for Schaefer to turn to his camera and start the commentary. Schaefer did no such thing. He was gone now, past Sher, past Oklahoma City, past all reasonable sense of the seriousness of the moment. Looking beyond Sher to Thorner and the medical reporter Kellye Lynn sitting next to her, Schaefer waxed rhapsodic.

"And let me also say," he went on, "how nice it is to be on this set with two beautiful women." He grandly gestured their way. "And what a beautiful day it is here in Baltimore."

"Yeah, well, it wasn't such a beautiful day in Oklahoma

City," Sher finally said, pulling everyone back to reality

Schaefer only lasted a few months. For all of his insights and all of his quirky character, the thinkers at the station never figured out how to harness all that he knew and how to market it to juice the ratings. Never mind the untapped history in his head. You were a hit, or you were not.

So the panic at WJZ deepened. Now WBAL was getting closer. They were emphasizing hard news instead of personalities. They didn't attempt to be anybody's personality kids. Such a concept was still foreign to the thinkers at WJZ. They didn't understand, this was the first glimmering of a new era in local TV news.

In Baltimore, it was hastened by the thing happening to Al Sanders. His passing would symbolize the end of a time when a few likable anchors could disguise the emptiness behind them. But the change happened, too, because viewers wanted something more from news than simply another television program. First they had been charmed by TV news's very existence, by its mere mention of local personalities and landmarks. Then they were indulgent when it came to TV's adolescent excesses. Now they were asking for something resembling adult substance, and television would respond by offering something close: a new kind of appearance of substance.

WBAL had begun to figure out the change a few years earlier, when the station had nothing to lose. They were running such a pitiful third in the three-station ratings fight that they canceled the five o'clock broadcast and then trimmed the six o'clock back to half an hour. This, while billing themselves as "Baltimore's twenty-four-hour news source." But then they got lucky.

They brought in a general manager, Phil Stoltz, who benefited from NBC's prime time ratings, which lifted local affiliates all over the country. They acquired rights to Oprah Winfrey. Then they brought back their five o'clock news and ran "Oprah" directly in front of it. The ratings jumped remarkably. Then Stoltz started a morning news program for weekends. Nobody else in town had one. And he hired Dave Roberts as his news director.

Roberts was the journalistic heart of it. He was smart and tough and driven. He had a sense of mission rare among television news directors. When he first walked into the WBAL newsroom he beheld a defeated outfit. Losing in the ratings meant pointing fingers of blame, and promulgating an old assumption that WJZ could not be beaten.

Roberts wouldn't hear of it. The station kept pounding out the message: Live, local, late-breaking. It was a cliché being used around the country, but in Baltimore it made WJZ looked a little old, a little tired, a little lazy. Roberts drove people; and those who didn't need driving he let strut their stuff. One was Jayne Miller, who was their best reporter and thrived under Roberts. Miller was full of herself, but she also loved the chase of a good story and had a true believer's faith that journalism could do big, important things.

She'd grown up in a small Pennsylvania town, the daughter of an attorney who taught her that girls could be as smart and as tough as boys. He also taught her how to research land records and court documents. She went to Penn State University to study journalism. When she graduated in 1976, she worked for a local newspaper and then hooked on with a TV news operation.

This was something new for television. It wasn't Rudy Miller being discovered in a mattress commercial or Susan White leaping from potato chip and beer commercials to news. Jayne Miller was not only serious but also seriously trained. She wanted to be a reporter, not a talking head.

At Pittsburgh's public television station, WQED, she covered the Three Mile Island nuclear reactor breakdown. When state prison inmates escaped, she jumped on the story. By the time she arrived at WBAL in 1979, she had the beginnings of a legend forming around her. Once, it was said, she walked across the newsroom in Pittsburgh and demanded a colleague turn over his files on three different stories.

"These are my stories now," she declared.

When the *Sun's* David Folkenflik asked her if the story was true, Miller laughed but didn't refute it. What the hell, it added to her legend. In newspapers, such characters were part of a historic tapestry; in local television, they were like nothing previously witnessed.

After three years at WBAL, CBS News in Washington offered her a job. It was too good to turn down—but too boring to keep. She hated the pack reporting, hated not getting the top assignments. She came back to Baltimore a year later. As the station made its move on WJZ, Miller—not the anchors, who were traditionally the heart of promotional ads—and her reporting skills became the center of the station's identity. And still WJZ did not react, imagining it could coast on its old reputation.

But it could not—and when Al Sanders died, the handwriting on the wall was now etched in stone.

In the newspaper the day after Sanders's funeral, the *Sun's* David Zurawik called him a "trusted, avuncular, and reassuring presence." A local business newspaper, *Warfield's Business Record*, noted, "He exuded an easy air of authority and confidence in front of the camera. His persona was warm, friendly and trusting, character traits he exhibited in real life as well. His presence on the air was reassuring in times of trouble, comforting in times of tragedy and welcome in times of celebration."

Again, as when Jerry Turner died, there was a sense of reaching for something that wasn't entirely definable. Like Turner, Sanders could be described easily, and honestly, in human terms: He was one of God's gentlemen. But defining him professionally wasn't so easy. He was a good writer, but the writing was limited to a few paragraphs a night. He was a good reporter, but he hadn't reported in years. I thought about that moment, years earlier, when the city's police commissioner's men had followed Al and said they'd only been interested in his sources, and Al had blurted out the painful truth about his work: "I haven't got any sources."

He understood what he was. He was a local news anchor, which is television's branch office of entertainment, a job consisting of remedial reading and giving viewers some sense of your actual personality when they let you into their homes each night.

But Al Sanders's era was the last one in which personality would be enough to carry an entire operation. The local news was not yet ready to get serious, but it would eventually learn to go through serious pretense. At WJZ, this would begin with the search for Sanders's successor.

Rodney King Redux

The tip-off on the immediate future of WJZ-TV came the day Frank Bond showed up for a job interview. Bond was a big, handsome African-American man who had worked for WBAL-TV for several years, then moved to Washington TV but still lived in Baltimore. He knew the town, and he knew television. He was smart and serious. He was a natural to take Al Sanders's place. He had no chance at all.

His job interview lasted for about an hour one afternoon, and when he left the building, the assistant news director, Pat Costello, strode into the newsroom laughing caustically.

"He came in wearing a great big 'J' on his shirt," Costello said.

"What do you mean?" I asked.

"A big 'J,' for 'Journalist,'" Costello said.

"And that's a bad thing?"

"Come on," Costello said.

He meant Bond had been too serious for WJZ's taste. Bond was interested in the pursuit of news. WJZ still marketed chemistry between personalities, with news as a byproduct. The station had always dominated the market by tempering all seriousness. Sometimes we had to show a little friskiness on the air. Bond made the mistake of thinking he was a newsman instead of a showman.

For several weeks, the station went through the motions of trying out some of its own people to replace Al Sanders. But nobody took these auditions very seriously, since the people trying out were white. In Baltimore's majority African-American community, the station needed a black-white balance; thus, Denise Koch would need a black male as her co-anchor. But in the modern context, in which lawsuits are always possible, it was also understood that the charade of auditions must be held.

To say such a thing does not imply a stacked deck—far from it. Television needs more minority news people. At century's turn, the Radio-Television News Directors Association and Foundation reported only ten percent of television news professionals are African American. But it raises the question about hiring blacks who have the best professional credentials. At WJZ, for example, the veteran Pat Warren had established her abilities as a reporter and weekend anchor. But she had two strikes against her: the station wasn't ready to have two women anchoring the show; and Warren, despite her news skills, was not considered warm and fuzzy.

WJZ eventually brought in Vic Carter, who had professional credentials but at least two major drawbacks. He'd been named Journalist of the Year by the School of Journalism at the University of Georgia and gone on to television reporting in Atlanta. He was a morning and noon anchor there when hired by WJZ. His problems were philosophical and practical.

Philosophically, the anchor of a local news program is supposed to be a kind of wise man (or woman), a person who knows the community intimately and can place the day's myriad stories into some kind of context. Carter, or any outsider stepping into such a job, clearly knew nothing about Baltimore, and the station made no effort to educate him— such as by handling some basic reporting assignments—before putting him into the anchor chair.

His second problem, noticeable to all from the first sentence he uttered on the air in Baltimore, was that he could not read very well, even when furnished the right information. He spoke faster than he knew how. Words ran together, or tripped over each other. They seemed to tumble out of his mouth and onto the desk in front of him, where they piled atop each other. Later, TV people in Atlanta would call friends at WJZ to let on that they had nicknamed him "Bryant Stumble."

The fundamental job of a television news anchor is remedial reading. This is not a difficult thing, even when reading from a TelePrompter. It involves looking into the camera, situated perhaps six feet in front of the anchor desk, and pronouncing words as they are scrolled directly in front of you.

The biggest trick is making sure you know pronunciations, such as street names and the names of well-known local personalities, and to know them before air-time. This, too, does not involve much hard work. It means inquiring of a veteran colleague, seated perhaps three feet away, "How is this pronounced?"

Between the reading problems and the lack of inquisitiveness, Carter had many problems. Whenever he stumbled over copy, he looked for someone to blame, as though his script had been typed poorly or gremlins had rearranged syllables while he wasn't looking. It was the tip-off of someone who hadn't bothered to look over copy that had been written for him before he went on the air.

One night, he announced the death of Mark Belanger, who had played shortstop for the Baltimore Orioles for more than a decade. But Carter kept calling him "Mark Bah-lenger." To a generation that had watched Belanger play ball, the mispronunciation not only felt insulting but clearly marked Carter as an outsider who'd been jarringly inserted into the hometown lineup.

The next night, he announced that Ordell Braase was organizing a reunion of the Baltimore Colts. Braase—pronounced "Bray-see"—had played for a decade for the legendary football team, and everyone in town knew him.

Except Carter. He kept pronouncing Braase as "Bra-see." Again, viewers found it jarring; it marked the station as uncaring and lazy and unauthoritative.

By the third day, someone must have gotten to Carter and told him to check pronunciations. That afternoon, he approached my desk.

"I have to read your intro," he said. "How do you pronounce this name?"

He pointed to one of the most famous names in American journalism.

"It's pronounced, 'Men-kin,'" I said. "H.L. Mencken."

"Oh," Carter said. He shot me a look that said, "Like, I'm supposed to know who that is?" Then he turned and walked quickly away.

One night, reading the introduction to a story about musical instruments, he mentioned the composer Chopin—but pronounced his name "Chop-in." Another night, when the copy said, "U.S. fishermen need a break," Carter read it this way: "Us fishermen need a break." Suddenly, he was a fisherman!

In the newsroom, such blunders first provoked laughs but then added to a growing unease. WBAL, with its new seriousness and energy, was gaining in the ratings. WJZ was dropping. WBAL continued to stress its mantra: Live, local, late-breaking. No matter that it was a marketing cliché echoed in TV newsrooms around the country, in Baltimore it seemed to resonate.

When the big February ratings book arrived that winter of 1996, WJZ hyped its newscasts with "special reports" on soap opera stars and interviews with talk-show hosts. The station spent a fortune on advertising and promotion. When the month ended, the Nielsen ratings service said 126,000 homes had watched WBAL's broadcasts each night—and 105,000 had watched WJZ.

No one could remember such a thing happening—but no one, at WJZ, connected it yet with a need for harder news coverage. The station was still sending out reporters to do silly fluff pieces in which the heart of the story, too often, was the reporter's own involvement. "Look at us," we seemed to be saying. "We're your extended family. You love us for who we are, remember?" Serious news was strictly secondary. If there was the hint of nasty weather in the air, the station led with weather reports. Maybe it wasn't real news, but it was easy.

It sent the weatherman, Bob Turk, into rage. "What do they want me to do?" Turk would say, in a kind of stage whisper lest management overhear him. "Lie about the weather? I'm not gonna say snow's on the way when it just isn't true."

No one suggested he lie. But by leading the newscast with a weather report—snow possibilities in winter, heat waves in summer—it suggested drama. There were two reasons: Viewer surveys indicated a desire for weather news; and it was easier to do than actual reporting. No expertise, outside the weatherman's own ability to read a weather report, was needed.

It was part of a continuing downward spiral for the station, in which no one in newsroom management seemed even slightly sophisticated—or caring—about events of the day. The city itself was a mess. There were now thousands of vacant and decaying homes marring scores of neighborhoods, and there was crack cocaine traffic that sparked homicides beyond any previous counting. There was a racially-heated race for mayor.

The station's response? As usual, there was virtually no political coverage at all until the last two weeks before Election Day. But then (as if to cover its collective ass), the station promoted itself with great flourishes as the city's prime source for campaign news, incessantly reminding viewers in those last two weeks to turn to WJZ for what it called "full coverage" of the campaign.

There was also the disturbing news out of the public schools, where academic scores continued to drop and violence—particularly at one school—was so bad that WJZ's general manager, Marcellus Alexander, decided to involve the station. He did this not as a news operation, but as a pal.

It was the sort of problem with which many stations around the country flirt. They want to show involvement in civic life. Thus, some stations' anchors will wear the home team's jerseys on the opening day of the baseball season, or cheer on some local kid who's done well. In its place, this can be innocent enough. But purists dislike any kind of cheering because of the places where it can lead.

In this case, it led to Northern High School, where a principal named Alice Morgan Brown looked over her 1,800 students and, astonishingly, decided to suspend 1,200 of them. The story made news around the country. The school was known for drug and alcohol problems and violent fights. Students roamed the halls when they should have been in class. The suspended kids, Brown said, were disruptive, chronically truant, indifferent about their work. She called the suspensions a cry for help.

She got it from WJZ. Marcellus Alexander decided the station would "adopt" Northern High. He pledged to be "partners" with the school. He said WJZ would "help generate enthusiasm and momentum by encouraging students, parents, and other business leaders to become more involved," and that WJZ would "tell the positive stories of things that are happening across the state" in education.

This was seen—by Alexander, at least—as a coup for the station. He saw it as a public sign of what television stations like to call "community commitment." The station would score points for caring about school kids. It did not occur to him that such a gesture would compromise the station's coverage of actual events at Northern High or any other schools. But that's what happened.

Now, instead of running news stories about Northern's troubles, WJZ began manufacturing good news and ignoring the bad. "Feel good" pieces were assigned. In the newsroom, reporters huddled in little groups to air their gripes—and then did what they were told. But the station was bucking a tide of reality. Within days after the mass suspensions, news from the public schools got worse. In a nationwide math test, ninety-one percent of the city's eighth graders flunked. Then figures were released showing two-thirds of all city students disappeared before graduation.

It was worse at Northern High. The school's ninth and eleventh graders failed to pass a single section of the annual Maryland Functional Test designed to measure academic skills. Its SAT scores were announced as the second lowest in the city. And then came the shooting of a teenage boy named Wayne Martin Rabb, Jr., killed outside the school in the same week his mother was trying desperately to transfer him to another school.

That was the final straw. On the night of February 10, 1998, hundreds gathered at the school auditorium to talk about all of these problems. But it wasn't the picture seen on WJZ. We were, after all, a "sponsor" of the school, trying to show the bright side amid the rubble.

The actor Charles Dutton, a Baltimore native, showed up and said a few words from the stage. So did Marcellus Alexander. On the late news that night, viewers saw residents gather to hear words of hope about Northern High. They did not see angry parents or reminders of disastrous school conditions. What they saw were Dutton and Alexander talk about great hopes for plucky Northern High.

So I wrote a commentary for the next night, laying out some of the unreported (by WJZ) recent history at Northern and expressing considerable criticism. As usual, nobody in management read it before it went on the air. But the next afternoon, for the first time ever, I was summoned to the general manager's office.

Alexander did not like what I had said on the air. This is not a bad thing, in an ideal world. In fact over the fifteen years I had been at the station, there were many nights when I knew in my bones that certain management hated what I was broadcasting.

But this is part of the deal in any journalistic enterprise: A commentator, no different than a newspaper columnist, is an independent voice within the context of the overall package. Democracy emerges out of a clang of many voices. At the *Baltimore Sun*, for example, I disagreed many times with editorial policy. It didn't matter. Management understood the beauty of the disagreement itself.

This time, at WJZ, Alexander did not. He never raised his voice, and he never questioned the importance of my voice being independent—in the general sense. But when it came to Northern High, he said, it was time to put aside negativity and cynicism.

"But there was a kid shot to death there," I said.

"We had that on the air," Alexander said.

"There were twelve hundred kids suspended there," I said.

"We have to move on," he said.

"There were teachers outside the school the other night with bullhorns, saying they wanted to work in a civilized place."

"You're not listening to me," Alexander said. "We have to move on. We can't always be negative. This is a school where they're trying to turn things around, and we have to support that kind of an effort."

He was very nice through the whole conversation. There was no explicit threat of losing my job, and Alexander's pleasant demeanor never changed. But he left it clear: This kind of commentary will not happen again concerning Northern High; and, in a more general way, he said negativity was frowned upon.

We were still a station counting on viewers' good will toward its on-air people, and still imagining that such good will came primarily from superficial stories and the glossing over of uncomfortable truths.

Except for street crime—in which case, we offered sledge-hammer coverage. Case in point: James Quarles, a man in a horrible police confrontation that was captured on videotape.

When seen in his moment of immortality, Quarles has a knife in his hand and stares into a gun held by a uniformed Baltimore police officer named Charles Smothers. The scene is a crowded downtown corridor, with street merchants hawking their wares. Quarles, according to his defenders, was a man helping out a buddy. He was opening a few packs of socks to be sold on the street. How did he open the packs? With a knife.

Officer Smothers saw it differently. The knife was a potential weapon, carried on a public street, and so the policeman ordered Quarles to put it down. Quarles refused. Now, as seen on the videotape, a crowd gathers and a standoff commences with the two men several yards apart.

Though neither Quarles nor Officer Smothers seems to move more than a few muscles, the crowd grows increasingly restive and begins to holler. Voices can be heard: "Don't shoot that man." Then Officer Smothers looks to the crowd at his right and shouts angrily. Quarles does not appear to turn aggressive. The policeman, turning back to Quarles, fires anyway.

Then, standing over the prostrate Quarles, Smothers shouts at his limp form, "Go ahead. Go ahead." It sounds like a man saying plaintively, "See what you've done? See what you made me do? See what's happened to you now?"

In Baltimore, the television stations lost their minds. For here was not only a story about crime, around which they built their nightly news programs, but the actual thing, happening before everyone's eyes. The first question in every news director's mind was: How can we get a copy of this before anybody else?

WBAL found a way. The station bought the video, and then they showed it on the air. They showed it on the early news, and then they showed it on the late news. They showed it several times per broadcast. Then they showed it, through the days and nights, as promotional ads for what they trumpeted as their hard-hitting news with their exclusive news footage.

The syndicated tabloid show *Hard Copy* then purchased the video, interviewed the fellow who shot it on national TV and trumpeted it as their own exclusive. The man who shot the video knew what he had. In the final moments of Quarles's life, you can hear the voice of someone standing next to the cameraman saying, "When this shit hits the fan, you're gonna make a lot of money from television." Once *Hard Copy* bought it, the show's local outlet, WJZ, now had access to it. Then WMAR wound up with it through its own syndication outlets.

Every station now had a copy of the tape, and every station ran with it for days and days—in WBAL's case, at least a hundred times—as news and promotional shots.

Quarles had become Baltimore's Rodney King, his dreadful moment with the police captured for the whole country to witness. He was public property, not just a shooting victim but also a marketing tool. Rodney King survived his Los Angeles police clubbing, but Baltimore's James Quarles did not, and this meant nothing at all. In death, Quarles took on a stature he never had in his anonymous little life. In the great American way, he was sandwiched somewhere between an Oprah fashion shoot and a lottery commercial leading into the news. In such surroundings, Baltimoreans began to ask: Do we feel haunted by this incident, or hustled?

Viewers watched Quarle's final seconds because many had never seen anybody die before, at least not so repeatedly. But they also gathered because it was television, the community meeting room. All became experts on what happened. Baltimore was a jury of TV viewers, ready to deliver a verdict before the commercial break.

Eventually, like so many things seen on a television screen, the shooting became just another piece of filler for an audience eventually numbed by its repetition—and the repetition of so many nights of nightly television crime.

In the summer of 1998, crime coverage in Baltimore was at last quantified and local TV news operations were vilified.

A study called "It's a Crime: The Economic Impact of Local TV News in Baltimore" was conducted by the Project on Media Ownership, a research center affiliated with New York University. It blasted Baltimore television news for excessive coverage of serious crime, and for excessive coverage of crimes "just too trivial to be mentioned, much less solemnly reported—and with visuals—by the news teams of a major city." Among its findings:

• Newscasts devoted far more time to isolated acts of violence than to any other kind of story. "The average Baltimore commercial newscast," it said, devoted thirty-nine percent of its news hole on local crime, another nine percent on accidents and natural disasters, and only eight percent to government and politics, four percent to education, four percent to health, less than one percent to business and labor, and point-two percent to the environment.

• Because of the TV stations' "broad neglect of important stories," this imbalance is "a civic wrong...that in the long run, threatens this community and our democracy."

• The newscasts' vision of the city is "not only uninformative but automatically alarmist, yet most viewers take what they see at face value...Most area residents are very frightened of the city."

Mark Crispin Miller, director of the Project on Media Ownership and author of the report, declared, "Through their routine over-emphasis on local crime...the commercial TV stations in Baltimore have helped make the city poorer by affecting how the viewers perceive the city." He accused stations of "anti-urban propaganda motivated not by any malice toward the city but by the drive for higher ratings and advertising revenues. The same invidious and repetitious sort of 'coverage' is widespread throughout this country—an everyday bombardment that we all long since have come to take for granted."

In the newsroom at WJZ, the study was met with a chorus of yawns. If the country took such coverage for granted, so did television stations take such criticism for granted. It would pass. The academic snobs would blow off some steam, but viewers would do what they always did: Tune in every night and let themselves be conned.

The station gave the study brief mention on the air, as a way to dodge any criticism that they'd completely ignored it. But probably only Mike Schuh took it personally. One of poor Schuh's stories—a story he hadn't wanted to cover in the first place—was singled out as an example of trivial moments hyped into the stuff of headlines.

"The story of a flasher in Howard County," the report said, "or the peeping tom annoying female students at the University of Maryland, or WJZ's long piece—'Student Attacked'—about the pair of sneakers stolen in Glen Burnie, are just a few examples of the newscasts' frequent hyperbolic scrutiny of minor crimes, which are reported with the same air of intense concern with which the anchors and reporters also tell of rapes and homicides."

The sneaker story was a thing of beauty. In a metro area with plenty of legitimate crime, the station decided this sneaker theft, just over the city line, was the stuff of high seriousness. Anchor Vic Carter introduced it this way: "A sixth-grader in Anne Arundel County is attacked at school by other students, and his shoes are stolen. And tonight the children accused of doing it are facing charges. Mike Schuh joins us now, live from Glen Burnie, to tell us what happened."

On the right side of the screen, Schuh appeared, standing in front of a house. Carter was on the left, seated at his anchor desk. Below Schuh there appeared, in bold capitals, "STUDENT ATTACKED."

Schuh: "Vic, for the past three years the middle school kid who lives in this house has dreamed of owning a really cool pair of sneakers. Well, a couple of days ago he got those sneakers. But for a brief time today, he probably wished that he was wearing another pair. Sixth-grader Ken Pursely spent much of today roaming the halls of his middle school..."

(cut to Pursely's shoeless feet)

"...in his stockinged feet."

Pursely (close-up): "It was just a lousy day. Kids stealin' shoes."

(extreme close-up of shoes)

Schuh (voice-over): "Yesterday, for the first time, he wore these $140 Nike Air Maxes to school. And they attracted attention."

(tight shot of boy's face)

Pursely: "I got jumped. My shoes got stolen."

Schuh (voice-over): "Ken says that three seventh graders tripped him and went for his Nikes."

Pursely: "I pulled my shoes on once with my feet, but then they got 'em off anyways. Then once they got 'em off, they started runnin'."

Schuh (voice-over): "Later the three were rounded up, and in the principal's office they met with police."

Pursely: "And the cops showed up, and we went into a room, all of us, and the three that did it said they did it."

(close-up of official's face)

Principal Bill Callaghan: "It is being investigated, it has been turned over to police—it is a police matter—and the school will conduct a parallel investigation, and suitable action will be taken when we finish the investigation."

(close-up of boy's face)

Pursely: "I'm kinda happy that they got what they deserved because, if they woulda known what the consequences were they woulda never did it."

(tight shot of shoes)

Schuh (voice-over): "As for the shoes, you'll see them tomorrow—on Ken's feet, at school."

(close-up of dad's face)

Terry Carroll: "I think schools need to do something about it I think it's absurd, that he's gotta be intimidated to walk around school in something he likes to wear."

Schuh: "Even though Ken had a lesson in social studies today, he obviously learned his lessons in economics earlier, because while those were $140 shoes, he waited for them to go on sale, and he purchased them for $70. He views this whole incident as ridiculous. Vic?"

Carter: "Well, Mike, what happens to the kids who were arrested?"

Schuh: "Well, the thirteen-year-old seventh graders will not be in school tomorrow while this matter is being investigated by the school officials. But the police are continuing their investigation, and all three are charged with second degree assault, and as such they will go before a Juvenile Master, who will decide if any punishment will be handed out."

Carter: "Okay, Mike. Thank you for the live report from Glen Burnie."

For all those who read the above transcript and imagine it to be "News from Mayberry," the first question to be asked is: Why run the story at all? Answer: It was a phoned-in tip, easily verifiable. It was easy to interview the major players, who were eager to talk. It involved kids.

For his part, Mike Schuh had argued against doing the story. He thought it was small and stupid and beneath a metropolitan news operation. But it was a slow news day, he said, and he was given an order and did the best with it that he could.

Without minimizing any aggravation suffered by young Ken Pursely or his family, the question lingers: With a staff of perhaps half-a-dozen street reporters, was this one of the half-dozen most important stories that day in the metropolitan Baltimore area?

Of course not.

It was just one of the half-dozen easiest.

Hello

In one of his final acts as general manager of WJZ, Marcellus Alexander called Richard Sher into his office and relieved him of his anchor duties on the five o'clock news. The decision sent shock waves through the newsroom. When Sher took the job as Sally Thorner's co-anchor, the show was near death and trailing miserably in the ratings. With him at Thorner's side, the program was more authoritative and lively and usually topped the ratings.

"You've done a great job," Alexander said, smiling in apparent appreciation as Sher sat down in his office, "and we're taking you off."

"What do you mean?" Sher said.

"We need Kai in there for this market," Alexander said.

He meant Kai Jackson, a pleasant young man whose reporting skills were just beginning to be developed and who was known, on occasion, for remarking to colleagues that he made it a habit not to read a daily newspaper, a strange declaration for any journalist but particularly one wishing to anchor a news program.

"'This market,'" Sher repeated numbly.

Alexander meant having at least one black anchor for a significantly black audience. It was the big question surrounding Sher when he'd first taken the five o'clock job. He had imagined, over the course of four years, that he'd answered the question on every level and that his performance on the job transcended all questions about his appeal crossing racial lines. Now Alexander was telling him he was wrong. But he had to explain it with language that didn't invite lawsuits.

"Our research indicates people see you as hard," Alexander said.

"Hard," Sher repeated.

"We need warm," Alexander said. "Kai is warm."

This is the language of television general managers. It is insulting but moves the blame around. It is only research, the boss is saying. It's those faceless viewers out there, so if you want to blame someone, blame them; blame those beer-guzzling slobs in their undershirts who don't understand what a marvelous talent you are.

As Sher digested the news, Alexander tried to soften the blow. He said the station was putting Sher on special assignment, to be called "A Hard Look." It was a sop. Sher would be allowed to issue a public statement saying the choice had been his, that he'd grown weary of anchor duties and wished to devote his time to "special" reporting. This was intended to assuage any wounded ego. He would be given free reign to develop a story of his own choosing each day.

"Plus," Alexander assured him, "you'll be the fill-in anchor."

Sher glared back at him. "I will never, ever anchor at this station again," he said, "unless one of your anchors drops dead half a minute before show time. I'll step in and read a script, because I'm a professional. Otherwise, don't ever ask me to anchor again. If I'm not good enough to stay on at five, then I'm not good enough to substitute."

It was the end of his anchoring days. Moreover, his leaving was the end of an era during which the station drew any of its anchors from its pool of veteran reporters who had a combination of experience, street savvy, and a particular knowledge of Baltimore.

Now the five o'clock anchors would be Jackson, the pleasant young man with limited news background, and Sally Thorner, the Annette Funicello of local news. The six o'clock and eleven o'clock anchors would be the former actress Denise Koch and the pronunciation-challenged Vic Carter, formerly of Atlanta.

All would soon find themselves at the heart of a new WJZ, molded in the hands of a new general manager named Jay Newman.

Newman arrived in Baltimore in the autumn of 1998 after TV stints in Miami, Chicago, Pittsburgh, and Detroit. He grandly informed everyone at WJZ that he was a journalist at heart and not some traditional general manager whose world was defined by profit margins alone. He informed no one that he intended to take over the newsroom like a one-man army of occupation. But this became clear within days of his arrival.

He did not so much enter a room as take possession of it. Newsroom cynics would come to refer to him as "Osama bin Newman." Those who saw him nearby learned to avoid eye contact. They were caught between fear and disdain. Newman wore a hangdog expression and walked with his arms at his sides and his body bent slightly forward, as if he might tip over.

"This is a guy," I said, not very kindly, the first time I saw him in the newsroom, "who spent a lot of time as a kid getting beat up on the playground."

"Yeah," said another voice. "By the teachers."

"And the rest of his life," I added, not kindly but perhaps with prescience, "playing Operation Get-Even with the world."

The station was still top-rated when Newman arrived. But he perceived, quite correctly, that it needed change. For years, the bright aura around Jerry Turner and Al Sanders had blinded viewers to the flimsiness of news coverage behind them. But the viewers were starting to catch on, and ratings reflected it.

No one in station management had a combination of news-gathering smarts and a feel for the community itself. Therefore, those running the newsroom went for the easiest stories: dramatic crime and traffic accidents easily spotted from the station's expensive new helicopter. The new five o'clock show sapped the energies of the half-dozen or so reporters who actually left the building each day. The news director, Gail Bending, had surrounded herself mainly with assistants whose strength was the soft, off-beat feature story but who had no sense whatsoever of hard-core news. When Baltimore was hit by threatening weather, there seemed a sense of relief among management: "Oh, good, we've got a built-in lead story." Without snowstorms, a sense of aimlessness prevailed.

In the face of this, Newman initially seemed a sign of hope. He sent Kai Jackson to the site of the Republican National Convention in Philadelphia. But this became an early tip-off of Newman's real instincts. Jackson was never even sent inside the convention hall. Instead, he did features on such "political" items as the Philly cheesesteak, available outside the convention hall. Why send him at all? Because it allowed the station to loudly trumpet its "live convention coverage" and showcase its new five o'clock anchor.

Newman had a clear sense of editorial direction but a malleable sense of integrity. Though he believed the time had arrived for local television to get more serious, he knew he didn't have many reporters, and he knew corporate money was tight. This, in Newman's mind, meant one thing: If his station could not deliver real news, he would at least give the impression that it was. Cosmetics were the key.

In one of his first moves, he shifted on-air reporters out of the studio. This seemed reasonable enough, but it started a direct path to some insidious practices. No longer would reporters sit next to one of the anchors to deliver live introductions to their taped packages. Now, more than ever before, they would report from the location of their story, as though live coverage was vital to some ongoing drama. Anchors would introduce them by saying, "Reporting live from...,"even if all actual news at the scene had ended hours ago and all those involved had long since gone home.

One night anchor Vic Carter introduced a story about a University of Maryland student who was stabbed to death after a football game. *"Eyewitness News* is live in College Park, Prince George's County, right now," Carter said, "where reporter Derek Valcourt has more on the story."

In fact, Valcourt was not standing in College Park, Prince George's County. He was standing outside Dulaney High School, in Baltimore County. But, questions of location screw-ups aside, why was it necessary for Valcourt to be at either spot? In the newsroom, where I sat across from reporter Katie Leahan, we looked up at a monitor that evening and watched Valcourt's story.

"There was a time," Leahan said, "when that kind of reporting was considered heresy. They throw it to us and make a big deal that we're live—but we shot the story five hours ago. They act as if viewers are too stupid to figure it out."

In this case, the murder had been committed a day or two earlier. On this dark November evening outside the school, not a soul was around but Valcourt, whose actual reporting had been completed early in the day. He looked lonely standing there in the cold. But Newman, like generations of real estate agents, thought location was everything. It gave us a look. It was the kind of thing TV stations around the country were doing more and more, but for the most skewed reasons: they had the technical equipment, so why not use it? Adapt the coverage to fit the technology, just as a generation of reporters had been taught to adapt their story lines to fit the video that was available. Shooting "live" gave the broadcast a greater sense of immediacy, even if it was based on emptiness.

At WJZ, some reporters were still dispatched to the so-called "Outback"—the exotic-sounding name given to the station's parking lot "out back." In the dark, these reporters might have been anywhere, even some place important to the story. Sitting in their living rooms, viewers wouldn't know the difference.

Still other reporters were assigned to stand in the newsroom itself, located about twenty yards down a hallway from the studio. All, so that the anchors could declare, "Pat Warren [or anyone else] reports now from the Eyewitness Newsroom."

"What's the point in throwing it down a hallway?" I asked Gail Bending.

"Jay thinks it gives us more sense of action," she said. "People are moving around in the newsroom."

"What's that got to do with actual coverage?"

"It's like the story's breaking right now," Bending said.

"But it isn't," I said.

"But it looks like it," she said.

In shots from the newsroom, people strode about, talked on telephones, worked on late-breaking stories—or appeared to be. Moving the television pictures into the newsroom would not improve our coverage, but it would improve the coverage of the coverage, the image of a bustling news operation that we wished to show the world. As background atmosphere, it was a slightly less obvious version of the rows of desks WMAR-TV had tried twenty years earlier, when reporters were reduced to telephoning their families in order to appear busy while they sat idly behind their station's anchors. Instead of improving our coverage, Newman was still assuming viewers would be charmed by the thought of witnessing what appeared to be the news-gathering process itself.

When it was explained that I would now deliver my commentaries in the newsroom instead of the studio as I had for the previous fifteen years, I shrugged it off. I understood it was strictly cosmetic, and I didn't care one way or the other as long as nobody changed what I said. Then came Newman's next moves. On a wall behind the spot from where we would now broadcast our standups, he erected a large neon "13," for Channel 13, in case viewers forgot what they were watching. It had all the charm of a sign above a strip tease joint.

Then Newman introduced choreography, the Eyewitness Shuffle. Instead of merely standing in front of the newsroom camera, all reporters were ordered to stride three steps to the left as they delivered their opening words, finishing their little trek when they had the neon 13 directly behind them.

"More sense of action," Newman explained.

"More bullshit," I told Bending when she told me about Newman's new choreography. "You want to have reporters do their little walk while they're talking about a traffic jam, go ahead. But I'm supposed to be explaining things that are a little more subtle, and if I'm walking while I'm doing it, and people are moving around behind me, I think that's a distraction from what I'm trying to say."

Bending nodded her head but said nothing. She had already come to understand that her days as the real news director were over, and I felt guilty talking this way to her when she was only the bearer of someone else's orders. Newman camped out in her office every day. Usually he sat at her desk, used her telephone, and left her standing about wondering where to situate herself. If he wasn't sitting in her office, he telephoned her from his own second-floor office. He called repeatedly through the day, in particular during the news hours, demanding changes, sending dozens of e-mail critiques, issuing new sets of instructions over-ruling some previous set of instructions issued only a few days earlier. Sometimes he sent questions for reporters to ask when they interviewed people, as though they were novices who had never worked their way around a story. Other times he told them how to walk, how to talk, how to hold up props, how to dress, or he ordered them to change the color of their hair.

In the newsroom, all questions were answered in sardonic code: WWJD, a variation on the religious question "What would Jesus do?" At WJZ, it stood for, "What would Jay do?"

The day after I balked at Newman's three-step on-camera choreography, Bending came back to me and said I didn't have to walk. Sanity had prevailed. Then she added, by the way, that Newman had decided I would no longer be given ninety seconds for my commentary. It would now be seventy-five seconds.

"Seventy-five seconds to talk about tax legislation?" I asked.

"Jay just thinks we need to tighten things up," she said apologetically.

The seventy-five seconds would include the time it took one of the anchors to introduce my piece each night. It was, in fact, part of what would become a general contraction of all story lengths. There would be no more flexibility on the old ninety-second limits, no matter how important the story. I walked away from Bending, figuring Newman would never keep precise tabs. In a little while, I thought, I can edge my way back toward the full minute and a half.

"The son of a bitch is treating our viewers like they're watching MTV," John Buren said one day outside his sports office. "It's all quick bites for short attention spans. The problem is the people who watch news aren't MTV viewers, they're folks in their fifties. Their attention span's longer than a twelve-year-old kid's."

But the neon "13" sign and the newsroom three-step dance and the cut in story length were just the smallest overtures to much larger orchestrations. While insisting that the news itself was at the heart of all decisions, Newman added a series of new cosmetic elements.

Now, he insisted, all reference to coverage must include the phrase "absolute latest" news. Simply saying "the latest news" would not suffice—even if the "absolute latest" news had occurred hours earlier. Now the phrase "useful information" would be drummed repeatedly. The words "live" and "team coverage" were to be dropped into copy at every opportunity. Now, instead of saying, "As we reported yesterday," or "As we told you earlier," all references would declare, "As *Eyewitness News* told you..." or "As *Eyewitness News* reported yesterday..." or "*Eyewitness News* has learned." Sometimes those references came in successive paragraphs. Sometimes, in successive sentences.

Many of these buzz words were becoming standard practice in local television operations around the country. But under Newman they became obsessions. The "Eyewitness News" phrase was injected like a mantra. In television, it is known as "branding," a shorthand phrase for "brand-naming." But it was employed at WJZ with all the finesse of a cowboy branding it into the side of a calf, each mention a yelping reminder to viewers of the program they were watching.

One night I started counting the number of times the station's anchors mentioned "Eyewitness News" during the course of the broadcast. The first came moments into the show, with Denise Koch declaring, "Check in with *Eyewitness News* for complete team coverage on the showdown with Iraq. Count on *Eyewitness News* to update you on all breaking developments." Seconds later, Vic Carter intoned, "*Eyewitness News* is live with team coverage on this story, beginning with Alex DeMetrick with the absolute latest details." Then Carter announced, "*Eyewitness News* is live in Northern Virginia, where Katie Leahan continues our team coverage." When Leahan's report ended, Carter said, "Stay right here with *Eyewitness News* for live team coverage of the sniper case. We'll bring you the absolute latest developments." And on and on, sounding like an old Top Forty radio station shouting its call letters across the ether, brandishing one set of buzz words after another.

I stopped counting the "Eyewitness News" references that night before we broke for the first commercials. There had already been seven. We were barely twelve minutes into the program. A few minutes later, when my nightly commentary arrived, the introduction was delivered this way: "As *Eyewitness News* reported earlier, Mayor O'Malley is talking about higher taxes. In his *Eyewitness News* commentary tonight, Michael Olesker says..."

What everyone in the newsroom said—amongst ourselves, anyway—was that we were drowning in preposterous heapings of self-reference.

Then Newman went beyond cosmetics to questions

of ethics. He injected another echo into the broadcasts: "Eyewitness News Investigates." It was an empty catch-phrase designed to signal viewers that we offered serious, hard-working, no-nonsense journalism. In reality, it stood for nothing. The phrase was dropped into stories because station research indicated viewers liked investigative pieces. In Newman's mind, the poor saps who were watching wouldn't know a real one from a phony. Labeling would suffice.

One day, a producer found a truck drivers' magazine that purported to name some of the toughest states in which to drive. One unnamed truck driver mentioned Maryland. At WJZ, a reporter was quickly dispatched to find a couple of truck drivers for quick sound-bite comment. One of them said Maryland had pretty rough traffic, while the other said it was no different than any other state. That was the entire WJZ piece. But the station teased it as an "Eyewitness News Investigation." This kind of branding, night after night, particularly infuriated Dick Gelfman and Suzanne Collins, whose serious investigative pieces were cheapened when given the same empty label as the phony investigations.

"What is that?" I asked Gail Bending when the truck drivers story ran. "How can we call that an investigation?"

Bending looked up from her desk—temporarily unoccupied by Newman—and shrugged her shoulders. It was all out of her hands now.

One afternoon, Bending and Dick Gelfman talked over an investigative piece he would broadcast that evening.

"In the intro," Bending said, "we're gonna say, 'After months of investigation...'"

"What are you talking about?" Gelfman said. He thought she was kidding. "This thing didn't take months."

"He wants it," Bending said. She didn't have to explain that "he" meant "Newman." The exaggeration would give the story a little boost out of the ordinary. Gelfman thought the piece spoke for itself. Why was it necessary to lie about it?

"It's not true," he said.

"Jay wants it," Bending said.

"Then have him record the damned thing," Gelfman said. "I'm not gonna say something when it isn't true."

One night, Katie Leahan declared that *Eyewitness News* had "learned" of a diversion of raw sewage into Jones Falls. Where did the station learn such a thing? Actually, from a story in that morning's *Sun*, headlined, "Sewage Spilled in July Mishap." The mishap was two months earlier. The newspaper broke the story after a beat reporter worked to obtain city and state records. WJZ "learned" about it from picking up the newspaper that day. Leahan was ordered to use the new phrasing.

Another night, Vic Carter introduced a story about more than a hundred fatal accidents involving Ford Explorers with Firestone tires. He said, "*Eyewitness News* investigates a new report that says it may be the vehicle itself that is the problem."

Reporter YaKenda McGahee then recounted details lifted from that morning's *Washington Post*, analyzing crash statistics contradicting Ford's claims that the tire manufacturer was to blame. McGahee, reporting "live" from the side of a highway, essentially recited a few paragraphs aloud from the *Post* story. Two days later, in another front-page story, the *Post* partially retreated from its first story when Ford provided new data. For its part, WJZ did not bother with the update.

The *Sun's* David Folkenflik related some of these stories, declaring, "When it comes to investigative reporting in this region, no channel appears more willing to sound off about less than WJZ," and then confronted Newman about falsely labeling them "investigations."

Newman's defense? "It helps the station form a brand and an image with the viewers," he said. "That's part of defining your station in the viewers' minds."

It did not matter to Newman that it was empty phrasing, implying we had made serious reporting efforts when we had not. Nor did it matter that he was sending out reporters who had no say over the stories they were covering—and no control over the phony labeling of the pieces once they went on the air.

Sitting at her desk, Katie Leahan shook her head mournfully one evening. Newman had already ordered her to change her wardrobe and the shade of her blonde hair. He wanted a more authoritative look, since Leahan was now anchoring on weekends. But the more fundamental issue of telling the truth about ourselves—this was something that seemed not to trouble him.

"I tell my kids, 'Find something worthwhile to do with your life,'" Leahan said. "I went to Chicago to see a friend who's doing great things with his career. He said, 'You're a reporter, but you never brag about your work.' I said, 'Brag? I'm embarrassed by it.'" Leahan later left WJZ to become spokesperson for the Maryland Transportation Police.

The embarrassment was spreading in the newsroom. Every day, small groups of people gathered to complain about Newman's changes. The station had always put on songs and dances to distract viewers from its shortcomings. But the truth was now being bent and hyped in previously unknown and dangerous ways. For all of the intramural griping, though, nobody wanted to confront Newman himself. It was clear that he was a man on a mission, and part of that mission was removing people from their jobs.

In May of 2000, the station reached a new level of deception when the Baltimore Ravens' fabulous linebacker, Ray Lewis, stood trial for his involvement in two murders at a Super Bowl gathering. The trial was held in Atlanta, where two young men had been beaten, stabbed, and left in the street during a 4 a.m. brawl.

"You will be able to follow a blood trail from the scene of the crime all of the way back to Ray Lewis' hotel room," Fulton County District Attorney Paul Howard declared in his opening statement before a packed courtroom and a national television audience.

As part of that courtroom gathering, there were reporters from newspapers around the country, and from all of Baltimore's television stations—except WJZ. Newman felt it was not necessary for the station to send anyone to cover it live.

But he didn't want viewers to know this.

"What do you mean, we're not sending anybody there?" Dick Gelfman said when he heard the news. Gelfman assumed he would be sent to cover the proceedings. He was an attorney, he had already broken several exclusive stories on the case, and he had well-placed sources.

"Not necessary to travel," Newman said.

"Let me ask you this," Gelfman said. "If we don't travel on a story like this, then when do we travel?"

"There's no justification to go," Newman said.

"What are you talking about?" Gelfman said. "Are we reporters or not? Any reporter knows, you get a better story when you're there."

"Nah," Newman said, waving him off. "How many exclusives have you broken already?"

"Three," Gelfman said.

"See?" Newman said. "And you haven't left Baltimore."

"If I was in Atlanta, I'd have given you ten," Gelfman said.

Newman had other ideas. He wouldn't tell viewers we had no one in Atlanta. In fact, he would present the distinct impression that we were there. The station got itself a shot of the empty courtroom in Atlanta, and on-air people such as Vic Carter and Christa Delcamp, using wire copy, would deliver reports standing in front of the backdrop, as though they were there. The courtroom backdrop would also be used for incessant promotional spots implying WJZ had reporters on the scene.

Each day, anchors would introduce Ray Lewis trial updates from a so-called Trial Update Center. The title had a nice ring. It didn't say we were there, but it didn't say we weren't there. It sounded important. It had the word "trial" in it. It had the word "center," which made it sound official. In fact, it was just a reporter in Baltimore, in a television studio, standing in front of the courtroom photograph.

It was one more manipulation of the truth, setting off veiled rage in the newsroom. Everyone hated the duplicity, but no one wanted to buck Newman. He was now known for screaming at employees who challenged him and for firing so many others that in the newsroom there was now a list, circulating surreptitiously, of a few dozen people who had already left the building—fired, or quit in disgust—in the first two years of Newman's reign.

One evening, though, Gelfman decided he had had enough. It wasn't just the Lewis story. It was a whole philosophy of pretending we were doing things that we were not, and of assuming viewers were too dumb to figure it out. For months Gelfman had bumped around the newsroom fuming about Newman.

"When I came here," Gelfman muttered, "I told them good stories always take time. That was the understanding. I'm aggressive, but you still have to take enough time to get it right. Now I've got Newman telling me, 'We can't spare time. We'll have you retrack a network piece, we need you on the air.'"

As Gelfman knew, "retracking" a network piece meant taking someone else's work and calling it his own. In other fields of endeavor, this is referred to as plagiarism. For Newman, it would mask our lack of reporting. But it would translate as our lack of integrity.

"It's completely dishonest," I said, stating what was obvious to all but Newman and a few blinded sycophants.

"Of course, of course," Gelfman said. "What bothers me is that they don't even see it as an issue." He was fuming. Gelfman was a man of professional substance, and of conscience. He had given up practicing law because he felt genuine passion for his adopted profession. He reveled in the public exposure of fraud, but now he was being asked to take part in it himself.

"When I was at WBAL," he said, "I'd take stories to the general manager and he'd say, 'How much time you need?' When I take them to Newman, he says, 'How much trouble is this gonna be? If there's risk, I don't want to do the piece.' He never, ever talks about the quality of journalism."

The phony labeling, the constant cheap "investigative" reference to pieces in which no investigative work had been done by WJZ, finally sent Gelfman where I had never seen anyone in television go. When Newman walked into the newsroom one evening, Gelfman confronted him.

"How can you call this 'investigative'?" Gelfman asked, referring to some trifling story we aired that evening. "When I do an investigation, it doesn't mean anything anymore because we've cheapened the term so much."

Newman seemed taken aback, and then a defensive little grin spread across his face.

"Maybe your concept of 'investigates' has been wrong all along," he said.

"No, it hasn't," Gelfman said. "We don't investigate shit any more. We just have somebody rip something off the wires. 'Investigative' means doing our own research. It doesn't mean fronting for somebody else's and calling it our own."

Newman glanced around the room, as though hoping no one within hearing distance would notice his bluff being called.

"It's branding," he said. "It's promotional."

"Aw, bullshit, Jay," Gelfman said.

The moment was astonishing, because it bucked years of history in which no one—not Jerry Turner or Al Sanders at the top of their games, nor anyone since—had unloaded on a general manager quite like this. Gelfman was only a reporter. This was his boss he was dressing down. He knew the perils of television employment. He knew he had a contract that could be terminated. But he was throwing all of that aside now, because he knew he had every rule of ethics and morality behind him.

"And what about all the times we say, '*Eyewitness News* has learned'?" Gelfman said now. "Where did we learn it? We learned it from the goddamned morning paper, or the wires."

"Well?" Newman said. He still had the sickly grin on his

face, as if he imagined he was putting something over on someone. "There's nothing incorrect in saying we learned it. We did learn it, didn't we?"

"No," Gelfman said, "we're just copying it. The implication is that we uncovered something."

"I don't think it does mean that," Newman said.

"It cheapens what I do," Gelfman said. "And it cheapens the station. Christ, Jay, if they don't trust us on the small stuff, why should they trust us on the big stuff?"

Newman turned away. Gelfman had won the argument but lost the war. The phony labeling stayed, night after night.

One morning I interviewed Casper Taylor, Maryland's House Speaker, the fourth most powerful politician in the state. Taylor told me, off the record, that he expected to be picked to run for lieutenant governor on the Democratic Party ticket. That evening on WJZ, though, we reported, "*Eyewitness News* has learned" that Taylor might replace the retiring state treasurer. This story made no sense, since the treasurer's job was a step down from House Speaker—and Taylor had given me precisely the opposite story that morning. The reporter who did the story ended her piece by saying, "Sources tell *Eyewitness News* that Taylor is the leading candidate for the treasurer's job."

"Where did you get that story?" I asked the reporter, moments after it aired.

"I think I heard it on the radio," she said. "WTOP or WBAL."

The radio? I let pass the business about "sources tell *Eyewitness News*." Since when were we calling radio reports our "sources"? I told her what Taylor had told me about running for lieutenant governor. I said it made no sense for him to take a lower government job.

"Oh, well," this reporter said. "You go find the story for us."

It was a defensive, embarrassed, patronizing response. I walked away, not wanting to seem high and mighty because I had done some reporting on the story while she had only played at being a reporter. This woman had a track record for integrity. But it felt like one more piece of fallout from Newman: claim to be a reporter, claim to have sources, claim to have investigated—even when it wasn't so. Grab your material wherever you can, and then claim "Eyewitness News has learned."

One winter afternoon, a producer sent a camera crew to the Baltimore Zoo to shoot thirty seconds of some easy, traditional footage of polar bears cavorting in a snowfall. When the piece appeared on newsroom monitors that evening, I was sitting with Alex DeMetrick.

"Ah, our traditional polar bears in the snow shot," someone said.

"No," said DeMetrick, "that'd be our *Eyewitness News* Investigates polar bears in the snow."

For WJZ, weather coverage took on ever more increased importance as surveys indicated viewers' desire for reports— and as Newman realized how heavily snow could be promoted. Where the station once employed two weather reporters, they now increased it to four—only one was a meteorologist. On hot summer days, the weather was automatically the lead story. On winter days when snow was in the air—or in the air somewhere nearby—the station incessantly promoted the possibility of a downfall to lure viewers to the broadcast.

"I am not going to lie about the weather," Bob Turk, the veteran weatherman, fumed to Gail Bending one evening. "I will not."

"We're not asking you to lie," Bending said.

"Then what's all this hype?" Turk said. "We're doing it all the time." This time, the station had opened the broadcast with shots of a heavy snowfall. The snowfall was in Cincinnati, a fact conveniently unmentioned by *Eyewitness News*. Instead, against a backdrop of Cincinnati's snow, an anchor's voice opening the program in Baltimore declared, "There's snow in the air. Is it headed our way?" It might have been approaching from western Maryland, instead of some city in the nation's midwest.

Newman reached for any excuse to play up the possibility of dramatic weather. One day when forecasters indicated the possibility of snow, he wandered over to Alex DeMetrick's desk. If there was snow on the way, Newman wanted reporters splayed across the metro area for a series of breathless reports.

"Ready for the traditional *Eyewitness News* snow coverage?" Newman said, attempting a little small talk.

"Sure, Jay," DeMetrick deadpanned. "The usual three flakes of snow covered by six inches of bullshit."

As Newman turned away, Richard Sher looked up from his desk and declared, in mock Voice-of-Doom tones, "Tonight, a frightened city braces itself for possible snow flurries."

For a while, Newman insisted on props. When reporters complained that it made them feel like they were delivering kindergarten "show and tell," Gail Bending, increasingly fearful of upsetting Newman, tried to placate everyone, explaining, "It's just another way to drive a point home."

Taken together, all of these elements—reenactments, stagings, props, the phony use of the word "investigates," the daily lifting of stories from newspapers and magazines to proclaim the station had "learned" information—were creating a new sense of deceit and tackiness.

In the newsroom, it also created a sense of dread. What might be coming next?

The station was still thin on actual reporters. The half dozen who actually left the building each day now had to fill both the five and six o'clock broadcasts, and some of them had suspect skills.

One was Dennis Edwards. He frequently claimed to have confidential "sources," none of whom were ever checked by newsroom management, who understood they rolled the dice whenever he went out on assignment. Remarkably, on socially sensitive stories, these "sources" invariably agreed with Edwards' point of view. On less sensitive stories, they tended merely to get him in trouble.

One night at a chemical plant explosion in Baltimore's Wagner's Point area, Edwards reported that "police sources" told him several people had died in the blast. No other reporters had the story. The reason soon became clear: There were no deaths. And no police source in a position to know had ever spoken of any deaths—all of which Edwards later had to admit.

Late one afternoon Edwards and Richard Sher went at each other in the newsroom over a phrase that most first-year journalism students could have settled. Glancing through the rundown of that evening's copy, Sher noticed a reference to police looking for the "alleged killer" of a young customer at an after-hours club.

I was sitting at my desk and talking to Pat Warren, and the two of us looked up and watched the argument transpire. Sher walked over to executive producer Mitch Friedmann with a sheet of paper in his hand.

"Hey, Mitch," he said, "we've got police looking for an 'alleged killer.' They're not looking for an alleged killer, they're looking for a killer."

The point was immediately clear, and Friedmann nodded his head. "I'll fix it," he said.

From across the room, Dennis Edwards looked up and shouted, "Hey, Sher. Come here." He pointed to the paper in Sher's hands. "What's that?"

"Just a piece of copy."

"Whose name is on it?"

"I don't know," said Sher.

"See that?" Edwards said. He pointed to his initials: "DE." Sher nodded.

"What's your problem?" Edwards said. The two men were now face to face.

"They're not looking for an 'alleged' killer," Sher said. "They're looking for a killer."

"It's only an allegation," Edwards said.

"No," Sher said, "you're wrong. It's not an allegation. The

kid was definitely killed. And now the police are looking for his killer."

"But the one who killed him has only been alleged to have killed him."

"So what?" Sher explained. "Whoever killed him, that's who the cops are looking for."

"But it's only alleged," Edwards said.

"Dennis, how long have you been a professional reporter?"

"Sher," said Edwards, voice rising sharply now, "go sit down and get out of my business. You're history around here."

"Dennis," Sher said, "you are the dumbest individual I've ever worked with. You can't even get the facts straight. You report people dead who are still living."

"You're nothing here," Edwards said.

"How about if we take it outside," Sher said, "and I blow your head off."

"Yeah," Pat Warren hollered across the room, "take it outside."

The argument seemed to symbolize the new atmosphere at WJZ. The place was constantly on edge. In some newsrooms, this is called "creative tension" and is considered a form of healthy journalistic competition. At WJZ, where actual journalism was a byproduct of packaging, it was simply a sign that Newman had been smart enough to alter the station but single-minded enough to alter it badly.

Local television news had gone through changes of life. The old, childish mannerisms—pay-attention-to-me-just-because-I'm-cute affectations—were outdated. The medium had been promoting itself as serious news for years, and Newman had sensed rightly that it was finally time to live up to the claims.

But with his tiny staff of anchors and reporters, some of whom didn't know a killer from an alleged killer, and thought it was fine to editorialize during objective news stories, he was going to have to fake it if he wanted to look serious.

In his mind, the best way to do this was to emphasize

the alleged talents of his anchors and bestow on them news-
gathering attributes that were utterly fictitious. Street reporters
were now afterthoughts. All of the station's promotional
spots were now devoted to the anchors and to reporting skills
that they had, in truth, never in their careers exhibited. The
airwaves were filled with these spots that had no basis in fact,
in which Vic Carter chased down a story from a helicopter, and
Sally Thorner and Denise Koch rushed breathlessly through
the streets to corner sources. Now when the hottest stories
broke (particularly in the post-September 11 world), it fell to
the anchors to report them as their own.

Sometimes they simply fronted for pieces that had been
put together by producers at the station. The producers did
whatever reporting was involved, and then all of the writing.
The anchors simply took credit. One night Sally Thorner,
still carrying her reputation for telephoning a department
store while a piece on Vietnam veterans aired, delivered a
package on ballistic fingerprinting. A producer had done all
the actual work, and the station promoted it as a Sally Thorner
investigation. Ballistics fingerprinting was, in fact, a subject
about which she knew nothing at all.

"Right," said Alex DeMetrick. "She's gonna take out her
Bergdorf-Goodman ballistics fingerprinting kit to illustrate
the piece."

Most often, the anchors would retrack stories put together
by network correspondents. The process was simple. Every
day, CBS sent packages to all of its affiliates, including WJZ.
The packages had one audio channel and one video channel,
and each station had the ability to separate the two.

A WJZ technician explained it to me one evening in the
control room, as several colleagues listened in. "We take out
the real reporters' voices and put in our own—our anchors'.
The pieces come in twenty-four hours a day, every hour on the
hour. They're fed to us on the web. We just download. And, to
make it easy, CBS sends the actual written script. All we have
to do is read the damned thing. They make it possible for us
to take credit.

"We do the whole thing in an editing booth," this technician said. "The anchors go back to an engineering booth and record tracks, and a tape editor lays the track over the reporter's original voice track."

"To the original reporter," I said, "it must feel like he's being plagiarized."

"Of course," everyone in the control room quickly agreed.

One evening, Newman waltzed into the control room where several of these same technical people prepared for the five o'clock broadcast. He seemed to be in an expansive mood.

"We're gonna be doing more national and international stories," he said.

"Great," one of the technicians said. "Not tracked?"

"We'll run the reporters' stories," Newman said, not quite answering the question.

So it was asked again. "Not tracked?" the same technician asked. "Because those retracked pieces are horrible."

Newman braced himself a little. He knew all the objections—ethical, aesthetic, and otherwise—and thought complainers were wrong.

"When I came here," he said, "our anchors had no credibility." Around the control room, people stiffened. "These retracks have helped restore their credibility."

"Don't talk to us like we're stupid," one of the technicians replied.

"They have," Newman said again. "They've restored their credibility."

It did not seem to dawn on him: He was claiming to have "restored" their credibility precisely by removing any basis for credibility—propping up the anchors to look more authoritative by using work they hadn't done.

"Tell me how plagiarizing makes them look better," a technician said now "And then tell me when our anchors didn't have credibility in this town."

Newman did not respond.

He was fixated on raising his anchors' profiles, using whatever it took—including music. He went to work on a song to accompany new promotional spots, and proudly took credit for some of the lyrics.

They went: "They're talking to me/ they feel like family/ With Denise, Vic, Sally and Kai/ I get all my news delivered personally./ They're Baltimore's favorite news team/ Is it any wonder why?/ More people make the choice/ to hear the friendly voices/ Of Denise, Vic, Sally and Kai/ They're talking right to me."

As Newman explained it, the song was WJZ's way of saying its anchors were just regular folks. As newsroom cynics took it, it was one more piece of trying to have it both ways, of reducing an important business to silliness but still claiming to be serious. In either case, the jingle didn't last long. Ratings kept tumbling, and WBAL was now drawing more viewers than WJZ. This meant one thing: Not a change in content, but another change in image.

For a while, as the ratings fell, Newman inserted a new slogan: "Baltimore's Favorite Station." It was an odd and misleading phrase, given that the ratings clearly said WBAL was now the town's favorite. In the newsroom, everybody saw it as one more pathetic little manipulation of the truth and felt embarrassed by it. But it was Gelfman who confronted Newman.

"How do we know we're Baltimore's favorite station?" he asked. "'Favorite' implies we're number one. The ratings don't say we're number one."

"It's a subjective word," Newman said. "They love our people; it's about having a better stable of people."

"Oh, come on," Gelfman said, "the fucking implication is that we're number one."

"I don't think it is," Newman said.

Gelfman turned and walked away, muttering, "Always a weasel argument."

But now Newman had changed course again. He bestowed upon WJZ a new title: "Baltimore's News Station," a phrase to be drummed across the airwaves at all opportunities.

He had an odd way of backing up the slogan: getting rid of

on-air people. He fired a young reporter, Kathy Fowler, who was widely regarded as one of the most aggressive television reporters in town. But she disagreed openly with Newman about some of the changes he was making. In her final day at the station, colleagues covered her desk with flowers, cards, bottles of liquor, and other presents. It was partly to sympathize with Fowler, and partly an ostentatious display to Newman that they were on Fowler's side.

Chris Ely was next to be fired. He was John Buren's backup sports anchor, a Baltimore native who had gotten the job by winning an on-air audition. Ely quickly became a viewer favorite. Then, after his wife died of cancer, Ely became a tireless public spokesman for breast cancer awareness.

"Chris has a whole history in Baltimore," Gail Bending explained to Newman, trying to save Ely's job and some of the station's image.

"It's an unnecessary expense," Newman said. Ely's position was cut from the budget, and Buren's backup became Stan Saunders, a reporter plucked from the newsroom, thereby diminishing the already-thin news staff.

Then he got rid of Art Donovan, the wildly popular Baltimore Colts Hall of Famer who had brightened the station's football coverage and reinforced its hometown image for years.

"In this town, Artie's a god," Bending said, urging Newman not to terminate Donovan.

"Doesn't matter," Newman said. He saw it strictly as another cost-cutting measure, and he followed this by cutting former Orioles slugger "Boog" Powell and Ravens footballer Kim Herring from their part-time sports analyst spots.

Having fired every other on-air sports person, Newman's next step was firing Buren. But, as with the others, Newman did not break the news himself. Buren learned of his termination by reading it in the morning newspaper. For sixteen years, he had delivered sports as part athletics, part schtick. But this didn't fit the new image as "Baltimore's News Station."

In the newsroom, everyone kept their heads down and

hoped to duck the angel of death. When the ratings continued to tank, many took heart: If the ratings dropped even farther, someone at corporate headquarters would surely notice and remove Newman.

It was one of the most remarkable things I ever saw in my time in television: reporters secretly rooting against their own station, hoping for short-term failure as a desperate means of gaining long-term relief.

By the fall of 1999, I was a sixteen-year veteran at WJZ. Newman was finishing his first year there. When he called me up to his office to talk about negotiating a new contract, I felt pretty confident. Clearly, he viewed me as one of the station's mainstays. When he saw me in the newsroom each afternoon, he headed straight for my desk. He wanted to talk about local issues. He wanted me to introduce him to the city's important people. On the city's mayoral election night, when no one else had results to put on the air, it was my connection to the right political people that put us far in front of the competition.

Newman seemed to appreciate all of this. And I could not bear to be around him.

I was offended by the things he was doing to WJZ, and I was ashamed that I had not confronted him more forcefully about it. I was suffering from a classic foxhole mentality. Yes, the war was bad. Yes, people were getting hurt. But, at least I wasn't one of them.

In the newsroom, reporters gathered in little groups and complained incessantly about Newman. When we got particularly frisky, we would complain to poor Gail Bending.

"Just remember," she told me once. "You have to respect someone before he can hurt you."

That autumn afternoon Newman called me to his office, he told me he loved my work and said I gave WJZ a local texture that no other station had. I nodded my head. He said it was time to give up my newspaper job and work full-time at WJZ.

"No," I said. "Thanks for the offer, but I've never thought

of myself as a TV guy. I'm a newspaper guy who's just gotten a little lucky."

But the offer wasn't intended strictly to flatter me. "I want to have access to you throughout the day," he said, "so I can put you on the air any given time." I had visions of him driving me nuts like everybody else, of being propped up to read breaking wire copy on the air and pretending the work was my own. I did not want to contribute to any such fraud.

"No," I said. "I'm not interested."

"Then," he said, "we have to cut your salary."

In negotiations that stretched over several weeks, I wound up taking a thirty-five percent cut in pay. Before I left his office that day, in an odd, inexplicable moment, Newman asked, "What do you think of me?"

The question threw me. It sounded uncomfortably like one schoolboy asking another if they could be pals. But it was my boss, and he was asking it at a time when we were negotiating my salary.

"You're okay," I said, hating myself for lying.

"No," Newman said, "I mean it. What do you think of me?"

"Really?" I said. "Really, I think you're a prick. And I don't like what you're doing to this television station."

He smiled defensively and immediately dropped the subject. I took the pay cut but felt a sense of liberation. I no longer felt obligated to shmooze with Newman when he saw me in the newsroom. I did my job as I had always done it. But I was fifty-five years old now, too old to fake it. When I saw Newman anywhere, I automatically turned away. It was my little act of rebellion against a man I now detested on grounds both professional and private: I would simply keep my distance.

Then came news from Bending: Newman had decided my commentaries seemed a little long. I was now being cut from seventy-five seconds a night to sixty seconds—including the time it took anchors to introduce me.

Goodbye

On May 11, 2003, the *New York Times* revealed that one of its reporters "committed frequent acts of journalistic fraud while covering significant news events," and that its own system of editorial checks and balances had failed to stop him.

In a remarkable self-examination that ran atop page one of its Sunday editions, the *Times* declared that the reporter, Jayson Blair, twenty-seven, "mislead readers and *Times* colleagues with dispatches that purported to be from Maryland, Texas and other states, when often he was far away, in New York... He stole material from other newspapers and wire services... He create(d) the impression he had been somewhere or seen someone, when he had not."

This was a terrible thing to imagine, for journalism is built on a foundation of trust. Take this away, and all else is gone. No longer do readers—or viewers—have any reason to pay attention. In the case of the *Times*, perhaps the world's most trusted newspaper, this fraud and deception happened over a period of months, involving "at least thirty-six articles Mr. Blair wrote."

As I read the story, I drew a direct line between the newspaper and my time in television news. It was made worse for these comparisons: At WJZ, the fraud and deception did not involve thirty-six stories but untold hundreds. It did not go on for months but for years. It involved not one reporter but many. And unlike the *Times's* young Mr. Blair, sneaking his efforts past trusting editors, this had transpired with the full understanding of WJZ's newsroom management, under explicit orders from the general manager Jay Newman.

Worse, as Dick Gelfman lamented, "They don't even see it as an issue."

In the extended aftermath of September 11, 2001, routine fraud became an ever more vital part of WJZ's hidden persona. The world had changed. After the terrorist attacks on the World Trade Center and the Pentagon, a new seriousness was called for. Like most stations around the country, WJZ met the immediate challenges of the attacks by switching directly to network coverage.

What else could any local operation do? We had no reporters in New York or Washington, but the networks did. We had no sources there, but the networks did. What we also had were modern technology, and Newman's incessant search for new ways to commit what had become an electronic shell game.

He sent Kai Jackson to cover the attack on the Pentagon. This sounds more impressive than the reality—precisely the station's intention. Jackson went as close as he could get to the Pentagon, which was, in fact, nowhere near the Pentagon or anyone connected with it. Security was too tight. No reporters were allowed within a few miles of the place, and neither Jackson nor anyone else at WJZ had sources there who might be telephoned for inside information.

But Newman wanted to promote a sense of the station's presence. The issue wasn't just the war, but WJZ's coverage of it. This wasn't just about America under attack—it was the *Eyewitness News* response to it—or what purported to be our direct response to it. So each night one of the anchors declared, "Kai Jackson is outside the Pentagon, and has this report..."

Then Jackson, live, stuck along the side of a highway

several miles from the Pentagon, would deliver a ten-second live introduction to some video package taped earlier in the day. These packages had been received back at the station, from network feeds, with the original reporter's voice removed and Jackson's voice then tracked over it. He might just as easily have stood by the side of a highway in Baltimore for all the independent information he was learning—or, more honestly, delivered an introduction from the newsroom and given credit to the network hands who had put it together.

Within days of the New York devastation, the station made even flimsier arrangements to boost its own profile. For five o'clock coverage, Sally Thorner at the studio anchor desk would say, "Denise Koch is tracking events in New York, and has this report." Then Koch, standing in the newsroom down the hall, a place from which she had not budged all day, would do her ten-second intro and then go to a network video package, retracked in the same manner as Jackson's.

For the six o'clock show, Koch and Thorner would switch roles. Koch, now anchoring, would say, "Sally Thorner has been tracking events in New York..." To discerning viewers this might have seemed odd, since the piece would invariably run just moments into the six o'clock broadcast. As everyone could plainly see, Thorner had not been tracking events in New York; she'd been anchoring the five o'clock news for the last hour.

But by placing his two lead anchors in front of network packages and tracking their voices over the video, the implication was: This is our work, this is WJZ bringing you the story as only we can, these are our anchors with sources everywhere. This implication reinforced repeatedly with the unceasing references to *Eyewitness News*, and with the ever-present promotional ads showing the anchors delivering their terrorism stories—including Kai Jackson on the side of some road "outside the Pentagon."

A couple of days after the attack, when security precautions were eased in New York, the *Baltimore Sun* sent me to Manhattan to write a few columns. At WJZ, management was delighted.

It meant I could phone in my commentary from the actual scene of the devastation—at last, a real Eyewitness!—while back in Baltimore they could run appropriate video footage from CBS.

What I saw in New York could have filled entire broadcasts, let alone the sixty-second commentaries to which Newman had reduced me. But we were past arguing now. For the only legitimate first-hand *Eyewitness News* look, I had sixty seconds a night to describe the greatest mass civilian murder and devastation in American history.

Night after night, in the extended aftermath of the terrorist attacks, WJZ continued the charade.

When the United Nations debated world reaction to the terrorism, we sent a series of reporters to Washington—simply to stand in front of the U.S. Capitol building and deliver their ten-second live introductions to network packages, with their own voices retracked over the network reporters' voices.

One day, after she'd gone through such motions for several days, Pat Warren trudged into the newsroom. Though she'd been standing in Washington, the network pieces were all about the UN debate and the reaction in the streets of Afghanistan and Iraq.

"Maybe Newman thinks our viewers are too dumb to notice the UN's not in Washington," I told Warren.

"Maybe Newman doesn't know the difference himself," somebody else replied.

"I'm spending entire days in Washington just so I can do a ten-second intro with the Capitol behind me," Warren said. "And even then he's angry."

"What do you mean?"

"One day the sun was too strong," she said. "At that time of day, it came in at an angle where it bleached out the Capitol. People couldn't even see it was there. So I spent the whole day there for a background that nobody could see, and he's screaming at people like we can control the weather."

To be sure, in the frantic scramble for viewers, WBAL

did some of the same kinds of business. They propped up their own people as voices of authority on the Middle East negotiations and the war that followed. But they seemed to make greater use of another technique, widely employed by local stations around the country.

WBAL was owned by Hearst-Argyle, which had twenty-four television stations with news operations. Often, one of WBAL's anchors would throw it to a Hearst-Argyle reporter in Washington—an "Eleven News reporter," in WBAL's shaky jargon—who would open the piece conversationally with the anchor, and then close the piece the same way.

But the pieces, while giving the appearance of being live—including the customized little conversations—were taped earlier in the day. The customized endings were known as "sig outs," and the taped segments were called "look-lives." They looked live, but they weren't. The look gave a sense of urgency.

Hearst-Argyle reporters would tape customized versions for several different stations—each with different call letters and microphone emblems yanked from a handy duffel bag.

Why use such deception? As TV analyst David Folkenflik suggested in the *Sun*, "Self-preservation. When their Nielsen ratings drop, station officials often turn to pricey consultants for advice. And some of these hired guns call for an infusion of flash and immediacy within newscasts to try to restore audience viewing levels. Live news reports—and 'look-lives'—can create that sense of immediacy in the minds of viewers."

But as Al Tompkins, who trains television news professionals at the Poynter Institute in St. Petersburg, Florida, told Folkenflik, "This has to do with deceiving the viewer...If a television station would lie to you about that, then why in the world should we believe their journalism?"

In the post-September 11 world, such issues arose nightly at WJZ.

One typical night, the station opened the five o'clock show with Kai Jackson reporting from Washington so he could front a network package about Secretary of State Colin Powell speaking to the United Nations about invading Iraq. But Jackson did no actual reporting of his own.

Then Christa Delcamp, standing next to Jackson, offered quick sound bites with three Maryland congressmen. She suggested it was reaction to Powell's speech. But she got the sound bites before the speech was delivered, and each congressmen wanted to hear Powell before commenting. The important thing, for the station, was simply the look of important people—even if they had nothing to say about a speech they had not yet heard.

Then came Katie Leahan, getting local person-on-the-street reaction—though most people she interviewed had not had time to hear, or digest, Powell's speech. Mike Schuh followed this with a report on Iraqi street reaction, which he somehow got while standing in the WJZ newsroom. Then came Richard Sher, for a report on "mixed reaction from China, Russia, and France." Also reported without leaving the newsroom.

When these reports concluded, Vic Carter offered a synopsis of the stories and then teased "an exclusive interview with Saddam Hussein." He did not mention that it was Dan Rather's exclusive interview, and not *Eyewitness News*'.

Does it matter? Newspapers carry wire service stories all the time. The *Baltimore Sun* carried stories from the *New York Times*, and other newspapers routinely carry stories reprinted from the *Baltimore Sun*, and the practice is common across the country.

The difference is one of credit—and of honesty. The newspaper does not attempt to take credit for entire stories they have not reported, or imply that its reporters are working in the heart of the action when they have not stepped out of the newsroom. It does not pretend to have sources, or important access, when it has none. If some other organization's reporter has done the heavy lifting, it is noted for all readers to see. In the newsroom at WJZ, most people considered the station's practices an embarrassment.

One November evening in 2002, after a succession of WJZ

reporters was hustled into place to front for late-breaking network pieces, Gail Bending called out to Richard Sher, "Richard, we need you right now to front for something."

"Okay," Sher called back, rising quickly from his desk, "what is it?"

"Al Quaida claiming response for the bombing in Kenya," Bending said.

"Can I see some copy?" Sher asked.

"It's being put in [to the TelePrompter] now," said a producer as Sher stepped quickly across the newsroom. He slipped on a microphone now and stood in front of a newsroom camera. A moment later, Sally Thorner, sitting in the studio down the hall, could be heard over a newsroom monitor, saying, "*Eyewitness News* has breaking news on the bombing in Kenya."

And Sher, looking at copy for the first time, peered into the TelePrompter and read, "This just in to the Eyewitness News Room..." Automatically, even under the toughest deadline pressure, there was still the Newman directive to call attention to ourselves above all else, still the reflexive response to make it look as if we had done some of the actual reporting, and that our own sources and quick reactions were vitally involved in breaking the story from the other side of the world.

When Sher got back to his desk, he muttered, "Look at this, it's like a bus station. They call out your name and say, 'Let's go, we need you to jump on this one.'"

And the problem wasn't only the false implication of expertise on international events. The station was using all its on-air people, and all of its hard-news time, for these stories— there was no one left for the station's primary mission: covering the news in its own community, where life went on in its myriad and often troubling ways.

For days on end, events in Baltimore and its surrounding counties went almost entirely unreported. At best, they were inconvenient afterthoughts, related in fifteen- or thirty-second stories boiled down from newspaper or wire stories while a succession of on-air people fronted for network pieces.

It wasn't that international events weren't important—but so was life at home. And it was the job of local television news operations to cover it.

When the station eventually got back to such reporting, the con game continued. In the fall of 2002, two snipers went on a killing rampage across the Maryland, Virginia, and Washington, D.C., areas. For days, local TV news operations delivered coverage throughout the day.

The problem was they had very little to report. The officer in charge of the investigation, Montgomery County Police Chief Charles Moose, gave daily press briefings in which he said almost nothing. Moose refused all one-on-one interviews.

This did not, however, keep WJZ's Dennis Edwards from saying otherwise. When a thirteen-year-old boy was shot, Edwards reported, "Chief Moose told *Eyewitness News* that the thirteen-year-old boy is an inspiration."

Had Edwards, in fact, gotten an exclusive interview with the close-mouthed chief? Absolutely not. Moose had made the remarks at a televised press conference just minutes earlier. But it was Edwards, and WJZ instinctively looking to promote themselves—even when there was no basis.

As the wall-to-wall coverage continued each day, so the charade was stretched and manipulated. Anchors with nothing to say tossed the coverage to reporters who had nothing to report. But words had to be spoken, or else viewers might change the channel.

One evening, I sat with Mike Schuh and Pat Warren. Each had spent time on sniper patrol—meaning, they were stationed near Chief Moose's headquarters or some other law enforcement operation across hours of extended coverage and had repeatedly been asked to deliver live reports as though they had new information to relate.

"The anchors throw it to you," Schuh said, "and they ask you questions. I'm rolling my eyes, thinking, 'I'm not comfortable with that question. I don't know how to answer it.' So words just come out of your mouth which don't mean a thing."

"And people at home are watching us," Warren said.

"Right," Schuh said, laughing ruefully, "and we're the voices of authority."

"The anchors ask us, 'What do you think?'" Warren laughed. "And I'm thinking, 'I'm gonna get sued, 'cause I'm saying stuff and I don't know anything.' I mean, at that point, we don't know anything. I'm just babbling. I'm thinking, 'Well, everybody says it might be a foreigner. Or somebody from the Middle East.' So you think, 'Do they want me to say something about that?' I don't know."

"It's just filling air time," Schuh said. "That's all it is. Because they want to stay on the air and look like they're on top of the story. But it's just pretending to be reporting."

When the two serial snipers were caught, WJZ quickly saturated the airways with promos. With its four anchors standing against a backdrop of the Baltimore skyline and martial music sounding, a voice declared, "The WJZ team is on the story as the snipers are brought to justice."

A viewer might have thought the station itself had captured them.

The cheap deceptiveness and fraud were general now. Late in 2002, health reporter Kellye Lynn, pregnant with her first child, told management she was taking four months of maternity leave. Newman thought this was too long for one of his high-profile people to be gone. The station had an investment in her. Plenty of viewers tuned in specifically for her "*Eyewitness News* Health Watch" reports.

"At first," Lynn said one night in the newsroom, "he told me that I should come in once a week after I give birth and record five spots at a time. But, legally, I'm entitled to maternity leave. So he backed off."

"He's actually giving you the time off?" I asked.

"Well, he called it a compromise," she said. In her eighth month of pregnancy, Newman had Lynn tape sixty health reports to be run over the coming months. They would be run during the news so that regular viewers would think she was still appearing live each night.

"Wait a minute," I said. "By definition, news is what's happening now. How do you come up with sixty health reports in advance and make them current?"

"Magazines," she said. "Health magazines, women's magazines, stuff like that."

"You take it right out of the magazines," I said numbly, "and then report it as *Eyewitness News?*"

"Well," she said, shrugging, "it's the way it's always been done here."

Lynn had no medical background. She had been hired when the station had an opening for a health reporter.

"The longer I do medical reporting," she said, "the more I realize how little I know about it."

"Can you take some basic courses?" I asked.

"Oh, I asked them when I got here," she said. "I asked if I could take some medical or nursing classes, just to understand some of the basics. They said it wasn't necessary."

Of course not. It wasn't the news that counted. It was just the look of news.

By the spring of 2002, I sensed things were coming to an end for my television career. I began to be like everybody else in the last months before contract negotiations: irritable, complaining, building up defense mechanisms in case the negotiations did not go well.

In fact, I had mixed emotions about staying.

When I looked at the nightly shows, I felt miserable. When I looked around the newsroom, I thought, "If viewers had any idea what goes on here, they would never watch again."

One day Newman stood talking to Katie Leahan, whose desk was across from mine. I had kept my distance from him now for about two years, either averting my eyes or pretending to have important work whenever he was nearby.

Now Newman looked down at Leahan and, in a voice loud

enough for me to hear, said, "You know, not everybody in this room hates me the way Olesker does."

He was offering an opportunity to make peace. I could say, "I don't hate you, Jay," and we could share a laugh and pretend to be buddies. I could pretend I liked him, and he could pretend he believed me, and maybe we could learn to get along. But everything else would remain: the phony "investigations," the lifting of other people's work, the false impressions of caring about the news in our own community.

I couldn't bring myself to respond. I kept my head down, as though I hadn't heard him, and continued looking into my computer screen.

I remember speaking to Newman only one more time before the beginning of the end. It was April of 2002. I interviewed Baltimore Colts Hall of Famer Lenny Moore about the death of his son Leslie, who had suffered for years from scleroderma, a disease that causes hardening of the skin.

On the night they held a fund raiser in Leslie's honor, I did a piece on the terrible effects of the disease. I wrote an intro and Vic Carter read it on the air—or tried to. With his usual indifference to such details as pronunciation, he hadn't bothered to learn how to say "scleroderma."

He tried once, and stopped halfway through: "...sclera..."

He started over: "Sclitero..."

Failed on a third attempt: "Scla..."

Paused, and simply said, "...derma."

As I waited for him to wrestle the poor word to the ground, I thought, how long is this going to take? I wondered, should I interrupt and pronounce it correctly for him? I was bemused at first—just another Bryant Stumble-ism—but then it turned to something else. It seemed symptomatic of so many other things: laziness, ineptitude, not caring.

When I finished delivering my commentary, I turned and walked into Gail Bending's office. Newman was there. I looked at the two of them and said, "Did you see what Vic did with that intro?"

Newman nodded his head but said nothing.

"This kid died of this fucking disease," I said, "and your idiot fucking anchor can't take three seconds before he goes on the air to learn how to pronounce it and give the thing a little dignity."

Newman nodded his head again but said nothing. And there the matter was dropped.

Here is how the end arrives.

One August evening after I'd finished my commentary, Gail Bending motioned me into her office.

"Jay's decided not to renew your contact," she said.

I sat down and thought, "So this is what it feels like." It felt like nothing. After all this time, I felt nothing for the station, or the work, or the nightly fraud. Except anger.

"You've sort of been expecting it, haven't you?" Bending said.

Actually, after nineteen years, yes and no.

A few months earlier, Newman announced he was expanding the news by another hour. The new show would start at four p.m., giving us three hours to fill each evening. But, astonishingly, the staff size would remain essentially the same. So I imagined they might want additional commentaries from me to help fill the time.

I remembered when they'd begun the five o'clock, and the general outrage that reporters' workloads were now being doubled. This time, the workload increased absurdly. Weeks after the four o'clock started, I stood outside Denise Koch's office with Ron Matz.

"I've never seen anything like it," Koch said. "It used to be reporters were doing a story every day. Then they were doing it two different ways. Now they're doing it three different ways."

"I'll do three different versions of the same story," Matz said. "Or, if they need to fill more space, they'll have me front for a piece I haven't done anything on. Like Winona Ryder's arrest. 'Here's Ron Matz with the absolute latest from California.'"

He shook his head at the absurdity. Though the four o'clock

show meant sixty more minutes of air-time to fill, Newman hired only two new reporters. They were nice young people, full of television skills, absent any knowledge of Baltimore, and just beginning to polish any sense of news gathering.

"The two new reporters," Bending said now, the night she broke the bad news to me. "Jay says he's got to let you go so he can pay for them."

"My salary," I said, "is not that big."

We both knew it. Newman added the four o'clock show because it was cheaper than paying for syndicated programming, and it kept the budget tight because it produced more corporate money. Never mind the quality of the new broadcast; he would find some way for the station to bluff its way through—running network promos as news stories, running clips from tabloid shows, retracking more network feeds, any cheap and tacky method he could find.

A few weeks after Bending broke the news, Newman finally called me upstairs to his office.

"You've done everything we've asked you to do, and more," he said. Then he mentioned hiring the two new reporters, and the need to keep the budget low, and how their stories would now replace my commentaries.

I said nothing. I was beyond debating with him, and beyond thinking anything I might say would change his mind. I let him talk for about ten minutes, and then I said, "Are you finished?" When he nodded his head, I stood up and walked out of the room.

And I said to myself, "Since my contract isn't up for six more months, I will spend the rest of my time here taking notes on everything I see and hear, and put it all on paper."

One night not long before I left, I watched a story from one of the new reporters on a newsroom monitor. The story was about the Maryland state's attorney's office. It was a nice, workable story, except for one remarkable fact, apparently unknown to the reporter: There exists in all the world no such thing as a Maryland state's attorney's office.

There is a Baltimore state's attorney's office. There is a Maryland attorney general's office. There are state's attorney's offices in all of the suburban counties. But there is no Maryland state's attorney's office—even though, at this moment, we were somehow airing a news story about one.

I turned to the little elevated office on my left, where the executive producer Mitch Friedmann and the assistant news director, Chris Coleman, were sitting. Friedmann was the volcanic one quick to scream at other people's mistakes. Coleman engaged in actual conversations with almost no one in the newsroom, perhaps because she had only been there for about three years.

"Hey," I called, hoping to get their attention before this piece ended and my live commentary was to begin. "There's no such thing as a Maryland state's attorney's office."

Friedmann and Coleman glanced at each other, and then at me.

"There isn't?" they each said.

And then it dawned on me. It was bad enough that the new reporter had botched it—but at least she had a slight excuse. She was new in town. But her story had been checked ahead of time by these two newsroom bosses. And they were just as clueless as she. The newsroom was run by people who knew plenty about television production and nothing at all about the things they allegedly were covering.

One evening Denise Koch turned to me and said, "I had a dream."

I raised my eyebrows but said nothing. Over years of working near her, I admired Koch for many things. She was smart and tough and conscientious. She took her job seriously. When Al Sanders died, she seemed to carry the entire station through extremely difficult emotional days.

But after all these years, I knew that I did not know her well. She was a private person. We were friendly with each other but not often personal. So, when she mentioned the dream, I was afraid to say anything at all, lest I scare away the mood.

"I dreamed I was on the air," she said, "and I lost control. And I looked off-camera and saw Jerry Turner standing over there, shaking his head at me very sadly. He told me he had never seen a worse, more amateurish performance."

"What do you think it means?"

"Look around," Koch said. "What do you think it means?"

Clearly, things had gotten out of control at WJZ. Koch said she wondered why she hadn't dreamed about Al Sanders instead of Turner.

"In the last months of Jerry's dying," she said, "he stopped talking to me."

"He did?" I said. "I never knew that. I thought you two were close."

She didn't talk for a moment. She scribbled a few wayward lines on a piece of paper.

"It bothered me for a long time," she said. "But I finally read in a book that he was probably jealous of me. I was not only replacing him, but I got to go on living while he didn't."

People die, and so do institutions when they don't change over time. Koch's dream had a nice romantic quality. Jerry's ghost would be the vision of all things good about television news, his dreamy, troubled presence roused now by the terrible state in which he now found his old station, and his old profession.

But the truth is a little less romantic.

In Turner's time the station had its problems, and now in Newman's time there was a new set of problems. The old ones were troubling, and so were the new ones. But Turner was there when the medium was growing up and was given to all the sins of immaturity. Television waved its arms about and cried, "Look at me," like a kid doing something reckless but charming. In the modern era, it was still waving its arms about. But it was playing recklessly with language, with the truth about its own work, and with ethics, all the while pretending to a new adult seriousness.

The old sins were out-front excesses: the preening and self

indulgence, typified by the five-part series on the secret fantasies of their anchors. The new sins were more about deviousness, about false claims, about pretending to be something we were not and hoping thousands of people watching were simply too dim to figure it out.

About the Author

Michael Olesker was a nightly news commentator for WJZ-TV's *Eyewitness News* for nineteen years. He is a columnist for the *Baltimore Examiner* and previously wrote a column for the *Baltimore Sun* for a quarter-century. He is the author of *Michael Olesker's Baltimore: If You Live Here, You're Home* and *Journeys to the Heart of Baltimore*. With Leo Bretholz, he co-wrote *Leap into Darkness: Seven Years on the Run in Wartime Europe*. A graduate of Baltimore City College and the University of Maryland, Olesker resides with his wife in Baltimore.

The future of publishing...today!

Apprentice House is the country's only campus-based, student-staffed book publishing company. Directed by professors and industry professionals, it is a nonprofit activity of the Communication Department at Loyola College in Maryland.

Using state-of-the-art technology and an experiential learning model of education, Apprentice House publishes books in untraditional ways. This dual responsibility as publishers and educators creates an unprecedented collaborative environment among faculty and students, while teaching tomorrow's editors, designers, and marketers.

Outside of class, progress on book projects is carried forth by the AH Book Publishing Club, a co-curricular campus organization supported by Loyola College's Office of Student Activities.

Student Project Team for *Tonight at Six*:

Stephanie Burger, '08
Gavie Heller, '08
Victor Van Valen, '08
Elizabeth Watson, '08

Eclectic and provocative, Apprentice House titles intend to entertain as well as spark dialogue on a variety of topics.

Financial contributions to sustain the press's work are welcomed. Contributions are tax deductible to the fullest extent allowed by the IRS.

To learn more about Apprentice House books or to obtain submission guidelines, please visit www.ApprenticeHouse.com.

Printed in the United States
131710LV00002B/3/P